Spain's Forgotten Novelist

Spain's Forgotten Novelist

Armando Palacio Valdés (1853–1938)

Brian J. Dendle

Lewisburg
Bucknell University Press
London: Associated University Presses

Associated University Presses
440 Forsgate Drive
Cranbury, NJ 08512

Associated University Presses
25 Sicilian Avenue
London WC1A 2QH, England

Associated University Presses
P.O. Box 338, Port Credit
Mississauga, Ontario
Canada L5G 4L8

The paper used in this publication meets the requirements of the American National Standard for Permanence of Paper for Printed Library Materials Z39.48-1984.

Library of Congress Cataloging-in-Publication Data

Dendle, Brian J., 1936–
  Spain's forgotten novelist : Armando Palacio Valdés, 1853–1938 / Brian J. Dendle.
    p.   cm.
  Includes bibliographical references and index.
  ISBN 0-8387-5294-2 (alk. paper)
  1. Palacio Valdés, Armando, 1853–1938—Criticism and interpretation.   I. Title.
PQ6629.A5Z665   1995
863'.62—dc20   94-28808
                                                               CIP

PRINTED IN THE UNITED STATES OF AMERICA

To Catherine, Mark, and Peter

Contents

Acknowledgments

I acknowlege with gratitude the assistance generously provided in the research for this work by: Dr. José Belmonte Serrano (Universidad de Murcia), Dr. Alvaro Félix Bolaños (Tulane University), José Luis Campal (Pola de Laviana, Spain), Lisa Cox (who diligently sought material accessible only in Argentina), Mme. Jacqueline Daniel (Département des Périodiques, Bibliothèque Nationale, Versailles), Mme. Catherine M. Dendle (Chambre de Commerce, Saint Nazaire), Peter J. Dendle (University of Toronto), Dr. Frederick de Rosset (Berea College), Dr. Salvador García Castañeda (The Ohio State University), Dr. Hazel Gold (Emory University), Dr. Stephen M. Hart (University of London), Dr. M. Gwen Kirkpatrick (University of California, Berkeley), Dr. Johanna Damgaard Liander (Harvard University), Dr. Martha L. Miller (University of North Carolina, Charlotte), Dr. José María Martínez Cachero (Universidad de Oviedo), Dr. Stephen J. Miller (Texas A & M University), José Payá Bernabé (Casa-Museo Azorín), Dr. Enrique Rubio Cremades (Universidad de Alicante), Dr. Mariano Ruiz-Funes (Murcia, Spain), Christopher Sheppard (Brotherton Collection, Leeds University Library), and Dr. Barry Taylor (Hispanic Section, British Library). A special debt of gratitude is owed to Dr. Noël M. Valis (The Johns Hopkins University), who generously shared her bibliography of Palacio Valdés. I wish also to thank the librarians of the Archivo Municipal of Murcia, the Biblioteca Nacional (Madrid), the Biblioteca Pérez de Ayala (Oviedo), the Bibliothèque Municipale of Dijon, the Bibliothèque Nationale (Paris), the British Library, the Brotherton Collection of Leeds University Library, Harvard University, the Hemeroteca Municipal of Madrid, Oxford University, Sheffield University, the University of Oviedo, and the University of Kentucky for their assistance. Research in Spain, France, and England was in part supported by grants from the National Endowment for the Humanities and the University of Kentucky Research Foundation.

I wish also to thank the heirs of Armando Palacio Valdés, who generously granted permission to quote from the novelist's works.

Preliminary versions of Chapters 2 and 3 were published in *Proceedings of the Pennsylvania Language Conference* (1988 and 1993).

Spain's Forgotten Novelist

1

Introduction

In the last half-century, the reputation of Armando Palacio Valdés (1853–1938) has suffered a remarkable eclipse. In his own day, Palacio Valdés enjoyed greater fame than any other Spanish contemporary novelist, with the exception of Benito Pérez Galdós; indeed, Palacio Valdés was better known outside of Spain than Galdós. In the late nineteenth century, Palacio Valdés was hailed by his American panegyrists William Dean Howells and Sylvester Baxter as one of the world's greatest novelists. Most of his works were translated into English and French; there were also translations into Czech, Danish, Dutch, German, Italian, Portuguese, Russian, and Swedish. Textbook editions of his works were used by generations of American students. Palacio Valdés's extravagant claim that his novel *Maximina* had sold two hundred thousand copies in its American edition found widespread credence.

In Spain, Palacio Valdés's success was obvious. The author of over twenty widely-read novels, he was one of the most popular writers in Spain in the period from 1880 to 1920. His novels were reprinted in inexpensive editions in such collections as "La novela rosa" (*Riverita*) and "Novelas y cuentos" (*Los majos de Cádiz*). His short stories and extracts from such works as *Papeles del doctor Angélico* were frequently reprinted in Spanish newspapers. *La hermana San Sulpicio*, initially a slow seller, became one of the most popular novels ever written in Spanish and, when filmed (both silent and sound versions), starred leading actors.

Palacio Valdés claimed friendship with the republican statesman Emilio Castelar, the actor Antonio Vico, and the novelists Leopoldo Alas, Benito Pérez Galdós, José María de Pereda, and Vicente Blasco Ibáñez. (But see pages 21 and 22, below, for his private disparagement of supposed friends.) At the age of twenty-two he became editor of the influential intellectual journal the *Revista Europea*. During his lifetime, his novels were praised by the republican statesman Melquíades Alvarez and by writers of such diverse political tendencies and literary tastes as Miguel de Unamuno, Ramón Pérez de Ayala, and Ramiro de Maeztu. Marks of his external success were his election to the Real Academia Española in 1906 and the award of the Cruz de Alfonso XII in 1920. In 1928, the Asociación de la Prensa of Madrid campaigned for Palacio Valdés to be awarded the Nobel Prize. Perhaps because he refused to take a public political stand (unlike Galdós and others of his literary contemporaries), he received a consistently reverential treatment from the Spanish press.

Apart from the sterile debate on the supposedly unwholesome influence of French naturalism on his early novels, Palacio Valdés inspired little critical controversy. His enthusiastic embrace of Catholic orthodoxy in the late 1890s guaranteed the acceptability of his later works in pious circles. Carlos María Abad, writing in the Jesuit journal *Razón y Fe* in 1924, emphasized that Palacio Valdés was a practicing and believing Catholic who frequently received the Sacrament. E. Fernández Almuzara, in *Razón y Fe* in 1938, celebrated Palacio Valdés's career in terms of the Catholic nationalism favored in the early years of the Franco regime.[1] Leading figures of the Franco cultural establishment participated in the ceremonies in October 1945 on the occasion of Palacio Valdés's reburial in the cemetery of Avilés.

Palacio Valdés also found favor in France in right-wing circles of the Third Republic. *La novela de un novelista* and *Años de juventud del doctor Angélico* were published as *feuilletons* (serial novels) in *L'Action Française;* the right-wing historian Louis Bertrand wrote the preface to the 1929 translation of *La hermana San Sulpicio;* the ardent Franco sympathizer Camille Pitollet prided himself on Palacio Valdés's friendship; four of Palacio Valdés's novels were published in Paris during the German occupation.

Furthermore, in the twentieth century Palacio Valdés carefully cultivated his image as the "patriarch of Spanish letters," a Spanish Tolstoi with a white, flowing beard, a vegetarian who rose above political and literary passions. His autobiographical writings and later essays reinforced the image of a worldly-wise and benign Christian, whose works were moral, entertaining, and without challenge to the existing social order. Literary manuals repeatedly employed such vapid adjectives as "charming," "delightful," "exquisite," "optimistic," "gentle," "serene," "rosy-colored," and "idealistic" to describe his works.

Such treatments served only to trivialize Palacio Valdés's effort and contributed in large measure to his later reputation for mediocrity and shallowness. Thus, the English scholar Gerald Brenan, despite his admiration for *La hermana San Sulpicio*, readily dismisses his work: "However, most of his books are too casually written and too unorientated to be classed as literature: all one can say is that they make pleasant books for a railway journey, easy to read, with some clever scenes and descriptions."[2] Furthermore, the left-wing orientation of literary criticism in the later years of the Franco era accorded scant sympathy to a novelist supposedly of orthodox religious and political sympathies. Only in his native Asturias did Palacio Valdés continue to command interest for his nostalgic evocations of the region of his youth.

In the last three decades, after many years of critical oblivion, two of Palacio Valdés's contemporaries, Benito Pérez Galdós (1843–1920) and Leopoldo Alas (*Clarín*) (1852–1901), have received recognition as Spain's most important novelists of the nineteenth century. There is also renewed interest in other late-nineteenth-century Spanish novelists: Emilia Pardo Bazán (1852–1921), who has been studied by Maurice Hemingway and others; Juan Valera (1827–1905) (studied notably by Cyrus C. DeCoster; a volume of significant studies has recently been assembled by Enrique Rubio Cremades); José María Pereda (1833–1906), whose complete works are being published in a critical edition by Editorial Tintín; and Jacinto Octavio Picón (1853–1924), the object of a recent study by Noël M. Valis.

Toward the close of the twentieth century, the works of Armando Palacio Valdés are also receiving scholarly reappraisal. In the last twenty years, pioneering studies by Daniel Henri Pageaux, Gilbert Paolini, D. J. O'Connor, Peter A. Bly, Noël M. Valis, and others have paved the way for Palacio Valdés's critical rehabilitation. Five of the fifteen papers presented at the Symposium on Spanish Literature, 1750–1915, held at the University of Kentucky in April 1990, treated Palacio Valdés. A recent volume of essays, *Estudios sobre Armando Palacio Valdés* (Dovehouse Editions Canada, 1993) contains studies by leading American, Canadian, British, and Spanish scholars.

PALACIO VALDÉS'S LIFE AND CHARACTER

The major events of Palacio Valdés's life are well-known and need only summary mention here. He was born in the Asturian village of Entralgo on 4 October 1853. His father, a lawyer, was of strong physical constitution; his mother, from a landowning family, was of delicate health and died in 1871. Six months after Palacio Valdés's birth, the family moved to the small Asturian town of Avilés where, according to Palacio Valdés's account, he spent a happy childhood. From the age of twelve to sixteen he attended the Instituto de Segunda Enseñanza in Oviedo where he formed friendships with the future journalist Tomás Tuero and the future critic, novelist, and university professor Leopoldo Alas.

From the fall of 1870 to 1874, Palacio Valdés studied Law and Administration in the University of Madrid, with the intention of a career teaching Political Economics. From 1873, he frequented the Ateneo of Madrid, where he became acquainted with many of Spain's leading intellectuals. For three months of 1874, he worked as a journalist for *El Cronista*.[3] In the winter of 1875 he became editor of the *Revista Europea*; in this journal he published lively portraits of leading contemporary orators, novelists, and poets. These *semblanzas* ("likenesses") were published in volume form in 1878 and 1879 as *Los oradores del Ateneo, Los novelistas españoles,* and *Nuevo viaje al Parnaso.* In 1882, in collaboration with Leopoldo Alas, he published a collection of biting critical reviews, *La literatura en 1881.*

From 1882 until his death, the principal events of Palacio Valdés's career are connected with his literary production and his family. At the age of twenty-eight he published his first novel, *El señorito Octavio* (The young gentleman Octavio) (1881), which was followed in 1883 by *Marta y María* (Martha and Mary) (1883). Both novels were highly successful with the reading public. On his thirtieth birthday (4 October 1883), Palacio Valdés married the sixteen-year-old Luisa Maximina Prendes Busto, from Gijón in Asturias. The couple had one son. Palacio Valdés's young bride died in the spring of 1885. Palacio Valdés would relate his enormous distress at this loss in *Maximina* (1887).

Throughout the 1880s, Palacio Valdés consolidated his success as a writer with what his biographer Angel Cruz Rueda terms the "the novels of fame": *El idilio de un enfermo* (The idyll of an invalid) (1883), the short-story collection *Aguas fuertes* (Acid waters) (1884), *José* (1885), the bildungsroman *Riverita* (1886) with its sequel *Maximina* (1887), *El cuarto poder* (The fourth estate) (1888), and, what was to be his most popular novel, *La hermana San Sulpicio* (Sister Saint Sulpice) (1889). In the following decade, Palacio Valdés published the "novels of maturity" (Cruz Rueda's term): *La espuma* (Scum) (1890), *La fe* (Faith) (1892), *El maestrante* (The grandee) (1893), *El origen del pensamiento* (The origin of thought) (1893), *Los majos de Cádiz* (The dandies of Cádiz) (1896), and *La alegría del capitán Ribot* (The joy of Captain Ribot) (1899).

On 8 November 1899 Palacio Valdés married for the second time. His bride, Manuela Vela y Gil, of working-class origins, came from Cádiz. She was sixteen years old when Palacio Valdés met her in 1891 and was his *compañera* (companion) throughout the decade. According to Pitollet, Manuela Vela y Gil's "tenacity" was responsible for the free-thinking Palacio's return to Catholicism.[4] After his "conversion," Palacio Valdés prefaced new editions of *Marta y María* (1906) and *La fe* (1909) with affirmations of his Catholic orthodoxy. (The texts of the novels, however, remained unchanged.)

Palacio Valdés's twentieth-century works were: *La aldea perdida* (The lost village) (1903) (an evocation of the Asturias of his youth), *Tristán o el pesimismo* (Tristan or Pessimism) (1906), *Papeles del doctor Angélico* (The papers of Dr. Angélico) (1911), *La guerra injusta* (The Unjust War) (Palacio Valdés's praise of France at war, published in book form in 1917), *Años de juventud del doctor Angélico* (The youthful years of Dr. Angélico) (1918), the autobiographical *La novela de un novelista* (The novel of a novelist) (1921), and *La hija de Natalia* (Natalia's daughter) (1924). Palacio Valdés continued writing in his seventies and eighties. His novels were: *Santa Rogelia* (Saint Rogelia) (1926), *Los cármenes de Granada* (The country villas of Granada) (1927), and *Sinfonía pastoral* (Pastoral symphony) (1931). He also wrote briefer fictional works—*Tiempos felices* (Happy times) (1933), *Los contrastes electivos* (Elective contrasts) (1936)—and collections of essays—*Testamento literario* (Literary testament) (1929), *El gobierno de las mujeres* (The government of women) (1931), *Album de un viejo* (The album of an old man) (1940).

Palacio Valdés's later years were marked by tragedy. His only child, Armando, was killed in a road accident in 1922. Since Armando had been a widower, Palacio Valdés and his second wife cared for his two granddaughters, Luisa and Julia. It is worth noting, as a sign of Palacio Valdés's cosmopolitan outlook, that his granddaughters were educated in schools in Bayonne (France), Gibraltar, and Brighton (England).

Palacio Valdés was seriously ill in the summer of 1924. His illness was followed by that of his wife in 1925 and 1926. Palacio Valdés fractured a femur in February 1928, with complications that obliged him to use crutches into the following year.[5] Illness prevented Palacio Valdés from traveling to France in the summers of 1934, 1935, and 1936. The last year and a half of his life were spent in the privations of a Madrid under siege. According to Cruz Rueda, in these final months Palacio Valdés suffered from cold and hunger. An infection of the prostate, followed by pneumonia, preceded his death on 29 January 1938. Palacio Valdés's widow died in November 1945.

What manner of man was Palacio Valdés? Apart from his combative years as the author of satirical portraits in the *Revista Europea* and his frequenting in the early 1880s of gatherings of young writers and journalists in Madrid,[6] Palacio Valdés lived a secluded life. Until the end of the nineteenth century, he spent his summers in Asturias.[7] In 1908, he bought a chalet (which he named "Marta y María") in Cape Breton in the Landes, where he spent five months every summer until 1934, when illness compelled him to remain in Spain. In Cap Breton he formed a close friendship with the French novelist Paul Margueritte (1860–1918). In his works he frequently expressed his admiration for England and for France.[8]

Pitollet has termed Palacio Valdés's manner of living as that of a "good bourgeois."[9] Palacio Valdés described his life in the last decade of the nineteenth century:

Since my wife died my life has been tranquil and melancholy, dedicated to work and to my son. During the summers I live in Asturias, and during the winters in Madrid. I like the company of men of the world better than that of literary folks, because the former teach me more. I am given up to the study of metaphysics. I have a passion for physical exercises, for gymnastics, for fencing, and I try to live in an evenly balanced temper, nothing being so repugnant to me as affectation and emphasis. I find a good deal of pleasure in going to bullfights.[10]

In 1928, relating her interview with Palacio Valdés's second wife, the journalist Matilde Muñoz emphasized the simplicity of Palacio Valdés's diet (milk, fruits, and stew), his habit of early rising, his daily gymnastic exercises, and his love of walking. Palacio Valdés's wife contrasted his present gentleness of character with an earlier ill-temper: "He is goodness itself, refinement personified. When he was younger, he had a somewhat violent temperament, but this disappeared with the years."[11]

Palacio Valdés read widely and had an especial interest in philosophy. Montaigne and Goethe were among his favorite authors. He was also fond of the romantics, highly praising Espronceda, Lamartine, and de Musset. Manuel Altolaguirre reported that he gave an enthusiastic reading of Spanish romantic poets to a banquet offered to him in wartime Paris.[12] When questioned in 1907 by Jules Laborde as to his literary preferences, Palacio Valdés expressed strong sympathies for the French romantics: "Men with warm and enthusiastic hearts, men stirred by an ideal. Jean-Jacques Rousseau above all others. In French literature, I also like Lamartine, a noble poet and a generous spirit, and Musset for his passionate sincerity."[13]

Palacio Valdés considered the *Quijote* and Longus's *Daphnis and Chloë* to be model novels. His later articles are filled with references to philosophers, novelists, poets, and religious thinkers.[14] He greatly admired Beethoven. His favorite saint was Saint François de Sales. He was interested in literary theory; however, his writings on aesthetics (the prologues to *La hermana San Sulpicio* and *Los majos de Cádiz*, his entry speech into the Real Academia Española) are ponderous and abstract, lacking the clarity and lightness of touch of his novels and essays. Palacio Valdés made no overt political statements; in private, he favored a republic and welcomed the dictatorship of Primo de Rivera in

1923. In extreme old age, in late 1935 and in 1936, he expressed in private correspondence his sympathies for the Italy of Mussolini and his feeling of disgust for the anarchical situation of the Spain of the Popular Front.[15]

Recently, Guadalupe Gómez-Ferrer Morant has published significant new biographical information. Gómez-Ferrer theorizes that Palacio Valdés underwent a progressive spiritual crisis in the 1890s, as did other contemporary European intellectuals. Gómez-Ferrer reproduces a letter of 11 November 1899 that Palacio Valdés wrote to his cousin Armando Miranda Palacio to announce his "conversion" to Christianity and his marriage to Manuela Gil. In the letter Palacio Valdés describes his conversion as "spontaneous and almost miraculous," the consequence of his revulsion at Nietzsche's teaching that the duty of the strong should be to crush the weak. On reading Nietzsche, Palacio Valdés had immediately rushed to a church, prostrated himself before a cross, and lovingly kissed Christ's feet.[16]

Regrettably, details of Palacio Valdés's relations with his "companion" in the 1890s are not available. Pitollet's claim that the "tenacious effort" of Manuela Vela y Gil had led to Palacio's conversion and marriage is intriguing, for it suggests an alternative to Gómez-Ferrer's thesis of a spiritual crisis: namely, a young mistress's badgering of a lover nearly two decades her senior.

Much of our knowledge of Palacio Valdés's life and character is suspect, for it derives from the author's own statements. Palacio Valdés provided autobiographical information in interviews with adulatory journalists, in the "Confidencia Preliminar" that precedes *Páginas escogidas* (1917), in *La novela de un novelista*, and in numerous essays. Scenes from his student days are evoked in *Años de juventud del doctor Angélico*. Critics have also often assumed—perhaps too readily—that a literary character, the altruistic and worldly-wise Angel Jiménez, is Palacio Valdés's alter ego and that the teachings of optimism, Christian charity, gentleness, and avoidance of excess propounded by Palacio Valdés in his later years should be accepted at face value.

Palacio Valdés was treated with respect, even adulation, in numerous homages during his lifetime. Studies of Palacio Valdés's life are adulatory. The first biography of Palacio Valdés, Luis Antón del Olmet's and José de Torres Bernal's *Palacio*

Valdés (1919), is an uncritical hagiography containing numerous factual errors. Palacio Valdés is presented as kindly, sentimental, gentle, and candid, "a smiling, happy apostle" unacquainted with "ambition, envy, anger, pride, sensuality, and vice."[17]

The principal biographical study of Palacio Valdés is that of Angel Cruz Rueda, *Armando Palacio Valdés, Su vida y su obra* (1925; rev. 2d. ed., 1969). Cruz Rueda provides some factual information not easily available elsewhere and places the early writings of Palacio Valdés in context. His study, written *con amore*, is reverential and makes no pretense to independent judgment.[18]

Constantino Cabal (1953) offers a highly sympathetic, informative, and somewhat novelized account of Palacio Valdés's career, drawing on local knowledge to conjecture a factual basis for certain characters and incidents in the novels.[19]

It would be unwise, however, to accept without question the image carefully cultivated by the mature Palacio Valdés, that of the "patriarch of Spanish letters," the Spanish Tolstoi who lived for his art, his family, and his studies of philosophy, literature, and history. Despite his claims to modesty, in his interviews with journalists Palacio Valdés stressed his international fame. Furthermore, the biting nature of Palacio Valdés's critical writings in his early years and the marked role of violence, melodrama, and madness in his novels should alert us against too-ready an acceptance of Palacio Valdés's pretensions to benevolence and candor.

Generosity is certainly lacking in Palacio Valdés's relations with those contemporary authors whom he so assiduously cultivated at the outset of his literary career. Peter A. Bly has suggested that Palacio Valdés distanced himself from Galdós when the senior novelist was no longer needed for his own professional advancement. José F. Montesinos, in his discussion of Palacio Valdés's grudging attitude toward Pereda, refers to the jealousy that Palacio Valdés ("egocentric and envious") felt toward other writers. María José Tintoré mentions Palacio Valdés's envious nature, evidenced in his off-hand treatment of Leopoldo Alas, the friend of his youth. Mariano Gómez-Santos also refers to Palacio Valdés's self-interested dealings with Alas and to his malevolence following the first performance of Alas's drama *Teresa* in 1895. Adolfo Alas draws attention to Palacio Valdés's public praise and private disparagement of Valera.[20]

Confirmation of Palacio Valdés's malevolence is found in the extraordinary interview that he granted to Alberto Guillén in 1920 or 1921.[21] Palacio Valdés dismissed Galdós ("who was as boring as a mastodon and who became a failure by writing too much"), Pereda (good at descriptions but incapable of understanding women), Valera (whose *Pepita Jiménez* was extremely boring), Pardo Bazán ("a sponge," a "fossil"), and Baroja (a writer of serial novels in the style of Ponson du Terrail or Montepin). Spain had in its history only three novelists of note: Cervantes, Blasco Ibáñez, and himself. He referred to all other Spanish novelists as "imbeciles." Palacio Valdés boasted that *La hermana San Sulpicio* had sold six hundred thousand copies in North America alone (a dubious assertion; I have never encountered a copy of the American translation in used-book stores). Guillén noted Palacio Valdés's "puerile joy" when praised.

Pío Baroja, ill-disposed toward his professional colleagues, found Palacio Valdés to be boastful, mendacious, spiteful, exceedingly vain, and jealous of other writers, "a man who put on an appearance of a goodness and cordiality that he did not possess." Baroja's hostility to Palacio Valdés was such that he visited Palacio Valdés's London publishers, William Heinemann, to establish that they had no recollection of having published his works.[22] (For Palacio Valdés's exaggeration of the American sales of *Maximina*, see "Palacio Valdés in Great Britain and America.")

The eccentric French scholar Camille Pitollet, when discussing his dramatic adaptation of *Los majos de Cádiz*, claimed that the Asturian novelist had lied.[23] (After their quarrel, Pitollet later developed a friendship with Palacio Valdés, whom he visited in Cap Breton.) The Guatemalan novelist and journalist Enrique Gómez Carrillo had a muted, if not negative, opinion of Palacio Valdés. He found that the salient characteristic of the middle-aged Palacio Valdés was a certain grayness: "he was a courteous, gray gentleman, gray in color, gray in character, gray in his voice, gray in his clothing."[24]

PRINCIPAL STUDIES OF PALACIO VALDÉS'S WORKS

Until the late 1980s, criticism of Palacio Valdés's works was for the most part uninspired. Criticism ranged from the moral (condemnation of naturalism, praise of Palacio Valdés's Catholic orthodoxy and benevolent optimism) to the superficial and belle-lettristic (praise of his psychological acuteness, Anglo-Saxon sense of humor, and nostalgic evocation of Asturias). The socio-logical and historical criticism of the 1970s and early 1980s (Gómez-Ferrer, Caudet) used Palacio Valdés as a whipping boy to attack bourgeois values.

The poet Ramón D. Perés y Perés offers insights into Palacio Valdés's work in his reviews for *La Vanguardia* (Barcelona) of the novels *El cuarto poder*, *La hermana San Sulpicio*, and *La espuma*. The reviews were republished in *A dos vientos* (Barce-lona: Librería "L'Avenç," 1892). Perés notes the modernity and originality of Palacio Valdés's novels and his tendency, with con-sequent loss of plausibility, to exaggeration and caricature. His novels, like those of Galdós, are too episodic; there is also a certain slowness in the development of his plots. His "realism" is closer to that of Dickens than to that of the French naturalists; his sense of humor is also Dickensian.

Augusto Martínez Olmedilla (1904) provides a judicious sum-mary of Palacio Valdés's work, emphasizing its theatricality. The Augustinian friar Graciano Martínez (circum 1906), defending Palacio Valdés against charges of irreligion, highly praises the "fervent Christian spirit" that informs Palacio Valdés's novels; *Tristán o el pesimismo* establishes Palacio Valdés's reputation as Spain's leading novelist, surpassing Galdós. Andrés González-Blanco (1909) offers urbane and sensible judgments of Palacio Valdés's works. He notes the savage humor of the essays in *La literatura en 1881* and of the novels *El cuarto poder* and *El origen del pensamiento*, the sentimentality of *Riverita* and *Maximina*, the lively portrayal of Gloria Bermúdez in *La hermana San Sul-picio*, and the ideological shift in *La alegría del capitán Ribot* to "a renewed and purified Christianity like that of Tolstoi."

In 1910, the Augustinian Francisco Blanco García attacks the naturalistic and Voltairian elements in Palacio Valdés but ad-mires his fine psychology and gift for observation. Alvaro Alcalá Galiano (1919), on the other hand, praises Palacio Valdés's healthy optimism, which is far from the crudeness and pessi-mism of the naturalists Zola and Maupassant; the French author whom Palacio Valdés most resembles is Alphonse Daudet.

The historian Rafael Altamira (1921), claiming Palacio Valdés to be a "bourgeois novelist," stresses his satirical vision. In 1924,

Andrés González Blanco praises Palacio Valdés's humor, modern sensibility, and knowledge of female psychology, while reproving the Zolaesque naturalism of *El idilio de un enfermo*. César Barja (1933) finds in Palacio Valdés an "optimism which represents the triumph of good over evil; of noble sentiments over brutal passions and selfish interests; the triumph of a smile in which shines a superior ideal to soften and gently comfort the heart."[25]

Rafael Narbona, in his brief, impressionistic *Palacio Valdés o La armonía* (1941), finds in Palacio Valdés "harmonic rhythm, moderation, eclecticism, balance, deep serenity," and a "healthy, subjective optimism."[26] Max Ríos Ríos, in the final chapter of his doctoral dissertation, published separately as *Armando Palacio Valdés Novela, Siglo XIX* (1947), indicates the cruelty in Palacio Valdés's humor and his tendency to exaggeration.

Edwin H. Cady, in his useful discussion of Palacio Valdés's correspondence with William Dean Howells (1948), notes the extent to which Palacio Valdés's work escapes conventional definitions of "realism."[27]

José María Roca Franquesa, in *Palacio Valdés, técnica novelística y credo estético* (1951), resumes Palacio Valdés's critical practice (impressionistic) and theories. The "novels of the first period"—those written before *La alegría del capitán Ribot* (1899)—reveal naturalistic features "in bad taste"[28] and portray priests and religion unfavorably. The later novels reflect healthier, more spiritual values.

The papers published in 1953 by the Ateneo Jovellanos of Buenos Aires to commemorate the centennial of Palacio Valdés's birth are of a generally high standard. María Martínez Sierra, recalling her youth, indicates the eagerness with which women awaited the latest novels by Palacio Valdés and the daring nature of Palacio Valdés's portrayal of Martha in *Marta y María* (Martha's taking of the initiative in love, the description of the onset of puberty, Martha's attempted suicide, the hint of incest). His portrayals of males (totally good or totally evil) are those normally created by female novelists; his heroines are angelic and, despite their lack of independence, bind men to their wishes. Arturo Berenguer Carisomo offers a sympathetic and intelligent overview of Palacio Valdés's work, emphasizing his humor, "Cervantine" realism, the balanced construction of such novels as

Los majos de Cádiz, La alegría del capitán Ribot, and *La hermana San Sulpicio,* and his simplicity of style.

In 1953 also, the *Boletín del Instituto de Estudios Asturianos* published fifteen articles on Palacio Valdés and his work. C. Cabal charmingly evokes Palacio Valdés's life and works. Emilio Martínez, M. Fontanillas, and Fernando Señas Encinas recreate the Asturias of Palacio Valdés's youth. Martín Andreu Valdés Solís recognizes the Catholic spirit and "Christian optimism" of the later works and laments the unsympathetic portrayal of Catholics in such novels as *La fe.* José María Martínez Cachero provides a useful bibliographical contribution to Palacio Valdés studies ("40 fichas").

In the slight *A. Palacio Valdés Romanziere* (1962), Maria Romano Colangeli admiringly glosses Palacio Valdés's lyrical descriptions of nature, superb characterization, portrayal of customs, and sly humor. She declares, but does not demonstrate, Palacio Valdés to be unequaled in "the coherence of his ideas, moral integrity, and inner equilibrium."[29]

In *Armando Palacio Valdés. Teoría y práctica novelística* (1976), Manuel Pascual Rodríguez glosses Palacio Valdés's theoretical writings. Palacio Valdés believed the novel should be "realistic" and didactic. The objectivity of his conventional, omniscient narrator is only apparent for the narrator-author frequently intervenes to comment on the action; the narrator's mastery over his text is absolute.[30] Palacio Valdés stressed the "argument" of his novels and, as realistic doctrine demanded, verisimilitude.[31] Palacio Valdés's dénouements restore a moral equilibrium.[32]

The absence of a comprehensive index in Pascual Rodríguez's densely-reasoned study renders it of limited utility to the scholar. Furthermore, Pascual Rodríguez's overriding concern with Palacio Valdés's theoretical writings is accompanied by a corresponding failure to appreciate the literary merits of the novelist's work. The limits of Pascual Rodríguez's theoretical approach become obvious in his bizarre, almost contemptuous, conclusion, in which he suggests that the modern scholar may find Palacio Valdés's novelistic theories more attractive than his novels.[33]

José María Roca Franquesa, in *Clases sociales y tipos representativos en la novelística de Armando Palacio Valdés* (1980), offers a succinct and highly useful overall view of Palacio Valdés's works. Roca Franquesa successfully defends the Asturian novelist against charges of marginality: Palacio Valdés treats such major themes of his day as false mysticism, religious doubt, the conflict between a false, literary view of the world and reality, political corruption, the role of women, and moral imperatives.[34]

The only lengthy study of Palacio Valdés's novels is Guadalupe Gómez-Ferrer's *Palacio Valdés y el mundo social de la Restauración* (1983). The historian Gómez-Ferrer treats a sampling of Palacio Valdés's novels as historical sources to document the society, customs, and attitudes of Restoration Spain. Gómez-Ferrer argues that the Asturian novelist is a Krausist in his "deep religiosity, respect for and love of mankind, liberty, and freedom of conscience."[35]

Gómez-Ferrer identifies a binomial polarization as Palacio Valdés's most common structuring device: city/countryside, good/evil, egotism/altruism, neo-Catholicism/liberalism, private life/public life, mediocrity/intelligence, science/faith, upper classes/middle classes. She discerns naturalistic elements in Palacio Valdés's distancing of the narrator from his subject (at times by humor), the portrayal of a "slice of life" (*Riverita*, *Maximina*), determinism of character by biology and environment (*La espuma*). *La fe*, however, goes beyond naturalism, for it opposes a mechanistic concept of the individual and portrays the triumph of faith.

The constants in Palacio Valdés's novels of the "third period" (works written after 1899) are "moral regeneration and exaltation of the countryside."[36] Palacio Valdés's praise of rural values, hesitancy with regard to industrial progress, and refusal to ally with the incipient workers' movements are typical of the indecisive and uncommitted petty bourgeoisie of the turn of the century who adopt "an apolitical, critical, and aesthetic attitude which will characterize a whole regenerationist and *modernista* literature."[37]

In the final part of her massive study, Gómez-Ferrer summarizes the major features of Palacio Valdés's ideology. In the 1880s, Palacio Valdés ("a Castelar republican") is sensitive to social questions; his petty-bourgeois refusal to accept the Restoration system has something in common with the later protest of the Regenerationists. In the early 1890s, Palacio Valdés is a progressive intellectual, conscious of the sufferings of workers. A personal crisis in the 1890s leads him to reject positivism and to adopt an ethical stance akin to that of the so-called Generation of 1898.[38] In religion, Palacio Valdés is a liberal Catholic, dismayed at the hypocrisy and lack of charity of many Spanish Catholics; his beliefs, based on love and charity, resemble those promulgated in the Second Vatican Council. Palacio Valdés sees three dangers for the middle classes: (1) romantic escapism (*El señorito Octavio*); (2) the degradation of involvement in Restoration politics; and (3) the moral contagion of association with the upper classes (*La espuma*). Finally, Gómez-Ferrer resumes Palacio Valdés's petty-bourgeois values: political scepticism; a concentration on the family and personal happiness; and an exaltation of the domestic role of women.

Gómez-Ferrer's work offers a deceptively coherent reconstruction of the society portrayed in Palacio Valdés's novels. However, her approach, even if we accept her debatable initial supposition that one can deduce a consistent ideological worldview from a novelist's portrayal of a limited number of individual characters, is overly schematic and fails to do justice to the complexity of individual novels. Other flaws in Gómez-Ferrer's study are: a determination to fit the early Palacio Valdés into a Krausist philosophical framework;[39] an ideological bias, common in progressive intellectual circles in the Spain of the late 1970s, in favor of political and social change; a consequent hostility to the values that Gómez-Ferrer attributes to Palacio Valdés; and a curious inability to appreciate the novelist's irony.[40]

Renewed interest in Palacio Valdés is evident in recent studies. Laura N. de Villavicencio (1977) notes imprecision, diffuseness, and abstraction in Palacio Valdés's descriptions.[41] Gilbert Paolini (1978) convincingly argues that in *La espuma*, *La fe*, and *El origen del pensamiento* Palacio Valdés rejects naturalistic determinism.[42] Guadalupe Gómez-Ferrer Morant (1982; rpt. 1986) analyzes the infantile role of woman favored in such novels as *Maximina*.[43] *El señorito Octavio* is studied by Noël M. Valis (1980) and myself (1987).[44] I have also studied *Marta y María* (1989).[45] Daniel Henri Pageaux (1982) treats *La hermana San Sulpicio*.[46] The novel that has aroused most modern interest is *La fe*, with studies by Jesús Fernández Alvarez (1969), Jennifer J. Wood (1985), Peter A. Bly (1988, 1993), and D. J. O'Connor

(1988, 1990).[47] D. J. O'Connor (1990) has also treated *El origen del pensamiento*.[48] Francisco Caudet (1984) and Jean-François Botrel (1985) examine *La aldea perdida*.[49] Gilbert Paolini (1990) studies *La alegría del capitán Ribot*.[50] Palacio Valdés's contributions to *ABC* between 1932 and 1936 have been reproduced and commented by myself (1990).[51] Essays on Palacio Valdés's early critical theories (Stephen Miller) and the novels *Marta y María* (Beth Wietelmann Bauer), *La hermana San Sulpicio* (Stephen M. Hart), *La espuma* (Maurice Hemingway), *La fe* (Peter Bly), *Los majos de Cádiz*, *Tristán o el pesimismo*, *Santa Rogelia* (myself), and *La aldea perdida* (Francisco Caudet, Ciriaco Morón Arroyo) appear in *Estudios sobre Armando Palacio Valdés* (1993).[52]

PALACIO VALDÉS IN GREAT BRITAIN AND AMERICA

In his conversations with journalists, Palacio Valdés frequently drew attention to his reputation outside of Spain. To advertise his international success, in the editions of his novels published on his behalf by the Librería de Victoriano Suárez, he listed foreign translations of his works.

Eleven of Palacio Valdés's novels were translated into English: *Marta y María* (*The Marquis of Peñalta*, 1886), *Maximina* (1888), *La hermana San Sulpicio* (*Sister Saint-Sulpice*, 1890), *La espuma* (*Scum*, New York edition, 1890; *Froth*, London edition, 1891), *La fe* (*Faith*, 1892), *El maestrante* (*The Grandee*, 1894), *El origen del pensamiento* (*The Origin of Thought*, 1894), *La alegría del capitán Ribot* (*The Joy of Captain Ribot*, 1900), *El cuarto poder* (*The Fourth Estate*, 1901), *José* (1901, 1961), *Tristán* (1925). His short stories ("¡Solo!," "Seducción," stories taken from *Aguas fuertes* and *Papeles del doctor Angélico*) were published in translation in 1993 (*"Alone" and Other Stories*).

In the final decade of the nineteenth century, Palacio Valdés was extravagantly praised by William Dean Howells in *Harper's New Monthly Magazine*. For Howells, Palacio Valdés was one of Spain's greatest novelists; *Maximina*, for example, was "a flawless praise of marriage and wifehood, and one of the most exquisitely touching and consoling books ever written."[53] Howells gently remonstrated with Palacio Valdés for his slight offenses against decorum, "the leprous taint of illicit intrigue which seems to infect all Latin work" (review of *Riverita*) and "a Latin frankness here and there" (review of *Maximina*).[54]

Similarly, in 1900, Sylvester Baxter in *Atlantic Monthly* lauded Palacio Valdés's novelistic skills; he declared the prologues to *La hermana San Sulpicio* and *Los majos de Cádiz* to be "two of the most valuable essays upon the art of fiction ever written." In 1914, Grant Showerman, who had visited Palacio Valdés in 1913, claimed in *The Sewanee Review*: "For keenness of observation, for the artist's instinct in selection, for truth to nature and freedom from the improbable, for measure in every one of its literary manifestations, it is not too much to say that no novelist in Spain or anywhere else has written a half dozen novels that surpass the half dozen best drawn from his pen."[55]

Spanish critics readily accepted Palacio Valdés's oft-trumpeted claims to success in England and America; they also held that Palacio Valdés was "Anglo-Saxon" or "Dickensian" in his humor. Nevertheless, Palacio Valdés grossly exaggerated the sales of the English translations of his novels. Baroja established that Heinemann (the English publishers of the translations of *La espuma* and *El maestrante*) had no recollection of his works. In his brief interview with J.-M. Carretero ("El Caballero Audaz") in 1914, Palacio Valdés stated that nearly two hundred thousand copies of *Maximina* had been sold in the United States, a claim which he repeated to Antón del Olmet and Torres Bernal in 1919, to Ramón Martínez de la Riva in the same year, and to Camille Pitollet.[56] In 1918 H. Peseux-Richard gave for American sales the astronomical figure of three hundred thousand copies of *Maximina* and two hundred thousand copies of *Tristán o el pesimismo*. José A. Balseiro, however, in the sixth edition of *Novelistas españoles modernos* (1948), more realistically deflates the sales figure of *Maximina* to four thousand copies.[57]

On the other hand, the textbook editions of Palacio Valdés's novels that—often abridged—were used in American schools and colleges in the first half of this century were highly successful and no doubt financially profitable. The most popular editions were of *José* and of *La hermana San Sulpicio*. (For a full listing of American textbook editions, see the Bibliography.)

PALACIO VALDÉS IN FRANCE

French studies of Palacio Valdés's works written in his lifetime were favorable, even panegyrical. L. Bordes (1899) emphasizes

Palacio Valdés's sincerity, simplicity, sympathetic treatment of characters, "gentle, pleasant humour," and benevolent irony. F. Vézinet (1907) declares Palacio Valdés to have two styles: (1) novels depicting Spanish characters in a Spanish milieu—*Marta y María, La hermana San Sulpicio*, and *Los majos de Cádiz*; (2) novels revealing a French (i. e., naturalistic) influence—*La espuma, La fe* (which is nonetheless "Spanish" in its dénouement), and *La alegría del capitán Ribot* ("French," since there is no religious intervention). Palacio Valdés ("the head of the Spanish naturalist school") avoids pornography and scatology and shows skill as a psychologist and as a "portrayer of landscapes."[58]

In a lengthy and comprehensive analysis of Palacio Valdés's novels, H. Peseux-Richard (1918) notes the predominant role of Christian charity in Palacio Valdés's ideology, his Dickensian sense of humor, his "exceedingly sharp critical sense," his realism that fails to shock the reader, his clarity of style, and skillful composition of plots. Peseux-Richard takes issue, however, with Palacio Valdés's scientific and philosophical pretensions that represent "an unfortunate ignorance of his true talents, a mere hobby."[59]

Jean Sarrailh (1927) notes Palacio Valdés's charm, serenity, and skill at depicting simple characters in their milieus. Like the French naturalists, Palacio Valdés paints strong amorous passions in such novels as *El maestrante*. He is Dickensian in his gentle humor and is also "the most French of Spanish writers" in his sense of order, balance, and simplicity and in the absence of Spanish violence and excess in his work.[60]

With greater insight, Camille Pitollet notes the element of *folletín* (newspaper serial novel) in Palacio Valdés's novels and the context of popular culture in which he wrote:

> It is the candid vision of an optimist which is, often, the vision of the *folletín*. He impresses neither by his style, which is that of familiar conversation, nor by the structuring of his novels, full as they are of irrelevant digressions, of *hors-d'oeuvres*, nor by the originality of his ideas, nor by the strength of his passions. But one should not forget that his period of greatest productivity was between 1881 and 1900, a period of social well-being, of abundant popular amusements, and of society entertainments which were far from being always ingenuous.[61]

Nineteen of Palacio Valdés's works were translated into French. These were *Marta y María, El idilio de un enfermo, Aguas fuertes, José, Riverita, El cuarto poder, La hermana San Sulpicio, La fe, El maestrante, El origen del pensamiento, Los majos de Cádiz, La alegría del capitán Ribot, Tristán o el pesimismo, La guerra injusta, La novela de un novelista, Años de juventud del Doctor Angélico, La hija de Natalia, Santa Rogelia,* and *Los cármenes de Granada.* However, seven major novels— *Marta y María, El idilio de un enfermo, José, Riverita, El cuarto poder, El origen del pensamiento,* and *Los majos de Cádiz*—were in Palacio Valdés's lifetime published only as newspaper serials. There was no French translation of *Maximina.* Only *La hermana San Sulpicio,* with three editions in the space of twenty-five years (1929, 1944, 1952), enjoyed a certain success.

Although Palacio Valdés never lost his admiration for England, he was a Francophile during the last thirty years of his life. He happily spent several months a year in his home in Cap Breton in the Landes. He defended the cause of France against Germany in *La guerra injusta,* as a reward for which he was made a member of the Légion d'Honneur. He offered flattering portrayals of French society in *La hija de Natalia* and *Santa Rogelia.* However, despite the praise of his work by French scholars, Palacio Valdés's novels found few French readers.[62] The contemporary Spanish novelist favored by the French public was Vicente Blasco Ibáñez.

BIBLIOGRAPICAL NOTES

There is no adequate bibliography of studies of Palacio Valdés. Joaquín de Entrambasaguas lists numerous bibliographical items in his introduction to *Tristán o el pesimismo* (Barcelona: Editorial Planeta, 1967). José María Martínez Cachero offers succinct comments on forty articles and books, many of them hard to locate.[63] Camille Pitollet's references to French studies of Palacio Valdés contain occasional inaccuracies.[64] Guadalupe Gómez-Ferrer's lengthy bibliography contains inaccurate references and phantom items *(Palacio Valdés y el mundo social de la Restauración.)*[65]

Individual works of Palacio Valdés have been edited by Joaquín de Entrambasaguas (*Tristán o el pesimismo*, 1958), Mariano Baquero Goyanes (*Tristán o el pesimismo*, 1971), Jorge Campos (*José*, 1980), María Dolores Alonso Cabeza (*La aldea perdida*, 1989), Guadalupe Gómez-Ferrer (*La espuma*, 1990), and José Luis Campal (*La fe* 1992; *La novela de un novelista*; *Album de un viejo* 1992; *El maestrante* 1993).

With the exception of certain French translations of Palacio Valdés's novels, published in magazines, and of listings of reprints of American textbook editions of Palacio Valdés's works, I have included in the bibliography that follows this study only items that I have personally consulted.

Unless otherwise noted, my references in the text are to first editions of Palacio Valdés's works. After being cheated by the publishers of *Marta y María*, Palacio Valdés published subsequent works and editions on his own account, using various printers and bookdealers. His *Obras completas* were published through the bookstore of his fellow Asturian Victoriano Suárez; the numbering of the volumes of the *Obras completas* varies. The "definitive edition" published by Editorial Fax in the 1940s and 1950s reproduces the Victoriano Suárez texts. The *Obras completas* published by M. Aguilar in 1945 contain occasional omissions.[66]

To avoid overburdening the text, I give in the present work only the English translations of quotes originally in Spanish and French. However, I have on occasions retained also the Spanish text where necessary to give the flavor of Palacio Valdés's writing. Palacio Valdés's style is often careless and his choice of words approximate rather than accurate. I have therefore preferred a free, rather than literal, rendering of his at times infelicitous prose. All translations are my own.

2

The Literary Apprenticeship, 1875–1881

P<small>ALACIO</small> Valdés collaborated in the *Revista Europea* between the spring of 1875 and March of 1880, when the journal ceased publication. He was its editor between 1877 and 1880. The *Revista Europea* was, with the *Revista de España*, the leading Spanish intellectual journal of its day. Devoted to introducing foreign ideas into Spain, it published articles on travel, scientific discovery, Darwin's theories, history, religion, and philosophy. As well as translations of articles by English, French, and German scholars, the *Revista Europea* included articles by such Spanish statesmen and philosophers as Emilio Castelar, Gumersindo de Azcárate, Francisco de Paula Canalejas, Julián Sanz del Río, and the young Marcelino Menéndez y Pelayo. The *Revista Europea* also published literary works by both Spanish and foreign authors. These works included Pedro Antonio de Alarcón's *El sombrero de tres picos*, J. Mélida's and I. López's abundantly annotated novel *El sortilegio de Karnak* (set in ancient Egypt), the Sanskrit drama *Sakuntala*, George Sand's *Marianne*, Tennyson's *Idylls of the King*, and Goethe's *Wilhelm Meister*.

In the *Revista Europea*, Palacio Valdés reviewed books, commented on events of intellectual interest, discussed economic theories, and published a macabre short story, *Crotalus horridus*. His major contribution was a series of studies of contemporary Spanish intellectuals and writers. The series consisted of fifteen articles entitled "Oradores del Ateneo" (1877–1878), ten articles on Spanish novelists (1878), and eight articles on Spanish poets (1879). The essays were published in book form in 1878 and 1879 (*Los oradores del Ateneo*, *Los novelistas españoles*, and *Nuevo viaje al Parnaso*). Thirty years later, Palacio Valdés published a selection of these articles under the title *Semblanzas literarias;* the Aguilar edition of the *Obras completas* reproduces this truncated version.

The "orators" of the Ateneo discussed by Palacio Valdés were: (articles appearing in *Semblanzas literarias)* Padre Miguel Sánchez, Segismundo Moret y Prendergast, Carlos María Périer, Juan Valera, José Moreno Nieto, Manuel de la Revilla, Gabriel Rodríguez, Francisco de Paula Canalejas, Francisco Javier Galvete, and Emilio Castelar (articles appearing only in the *Revista Europea)*; Laureano Figuerola, José Carvajal, Luis Vidart, Gumersindo de Azcárate, and Manuel Pedregal. Certain of these articles had been published previously in other journals.[1]

Curiously, in view of the political importance of certain of the "orators" (Segismundo Moret had served as Minister for the Colonies and Minister of the Treasury in Prim's cabinet of 1870; Emilio Castelar had in 1873 been one of the presidents of the First Spanish Republic), Palacio Valdés excluded political considerations from his discussions, confining himself to the oratorical skills of the *ateneístas* and to their ability to present arguments.

Palacio Valdés's treatment of the orators shows all the brashness of youth. (Later, in the prologue to the 1908 edition of *Semblanzas literarias,* he would acknowledge that the essays contained "personal allusions of doubtful taste.") With considerable sarcasm, Palacio Valdés attacks the superficiality, the vagueness, and the indiscipline of the philosophers of the Ateneo. At the same time Palacio Valdés parades his own erudition with references to the Greek and Latin classics and to the Germans Schiller and Goethe. At times, Palacio Valdés's remarks are perceptive, as in his recognition of the labyrinthine oratorical style of Juan Valera. Nevertheless, Palacio Valdés prefers the cutting epithet—his qualification, for example, of Gabriel Rodríguez as "el último abencerraje del progresismo" (the last Abencerraje of the Progressive political party)—to reasoned analysis of a speaker's ideology; his limitation of the discussion to rhetorical form undercuts the value of the philosophical content on which the Ateneo orators prided themselves. Palacio Valdés's sympathies are nevertheless readily apparent. He favors such progressives as Emilio Castelar and Gabriel Rodríguez; he heaps scorn on the Catholic apologists Miguel Sánchez ("a scabrous polemicist") and Luis Vidart; he characterizes *El Consultor de los Pár-rocos* as "Spain's finest satirical journal."

At times, a note of feeling replaces the adolescent sarcasm. Thus, the death from consumption of the young critic Francisco Javier Galvete leads Palacio Valdés to question, in a rhetoric over-loaded with romantic clichés, the meaning of life and death and to associate genius and suffering.

In 1878, Palacio Valdés treated nine contemporary Spanish novelists: Fernán Caballero, Benito Pérez Galdós,[2] Pedro Antonio de Alarcón, Juan Valera, Manuel Fernández y González, Francisco Navarro Villoslada, Enrique Pérez Escrich, José de Castro y Serrano, and José Selgas. The studies of novelists, presented in lively manner, are of much greater interest than those of the orators of the Ateneo. Palacio Valdés has firm, clearly expressed standards of judgment and an easy, confident style. He frequently discusses his critical task in a self-referential manner (*Los novel-istas españoles* [Madrid: Casa Editorial de Medina, n.d.], 91, 99); he often refers to non-Spanish novelists (Turgenev, Dickens, Manzoni, Balzac, et al.). Palacio Valdés seeks in the novelists warmth, spontaneity, energy, and a realistic portrayal of life (134–5); he dislikes superficiality; he objects to the absence of veri-similitude in Fernán Caballero, Alarcón, Fernández y González, Navarro Villoslada, and Pérez Escrich; he faults Juan Valera, one of his favorite novelists, for obscurity and lack of emotion. Like Flaubert, he objects to transcendental messages not inherent in the work of art; he thus criticizes the propagandizing of Fernán Caballero, Alarcón (*El escándalo*), and Selgas. "Any modern writer who does not offer a solution to a problem deserves a statue," he proclaims sarcastically (151).

The essays contain valuable information on Palacio Valdés's youthful enthusiasm for the popular novel. He writes of his schoolboy readings:

But this [punishment by his Latin teacher] did not end my fondness for all the misbegotten creations of Ponson du Terrail, Paul Féval, Sue, Fernández y González, Dumas and many others. My brain seemed to be the salon where the élite of Paris and the Sierra Morena [a bandit region] assembled. *Juan Palomo, Juan Valjean, Juan Lanas, The Lady of the Camelias, Los Siete Niños de Ecija, El Caballero del*

Aguila, Candelas, Manolito Caparrota and many others of a similar nature were all received in my salons with the most exquisite amiability, as *La Correspondencia* would put it. ("Fernán Caballero," in *Los novelistas españoles*, 1–2)

Palacio Valdés satirizes, in his discussion of Pérez Escrich, the procedures of the popular novel. Nevertheless, he had in his youth attempted to imitate the deeds of *Los siete niños de Ecija* ("Fernández y González," in *Los novelistas españoles*, 90). In his adolescence, he had reserved his Fridays for the reading of novels (those of Fernán Caballero; such foreign works as *Werther, Ivanhoe, Eugénie Grandet*, and *Wilhelm Meister*).[3] Even today he weaves fantastic novels in his head:

And in moments of respite from my busy tasks, instead of reading novels I spend my time writing them. But I write them inside my head, because nowadays I place my fantasy at the disposition of my heart and every few hours I weave, for my private use, tales so fantastic that all would consider them incredible. This is the custom of unlikely things ["cosas inverosímiles"]. ("Fernán Caballero," in *Los novelistas españoles*, 3)

Palacio Valdés's religious views are freely expressed in his essay on Pérez Galdós. Revealing a strong dislike of metaphysics, theology, dogmatism, and clericalism, he seeks a religion of the heart, a Christianity based on love (22–3). Furiously attacking all intolerance, he proclaims that the angry, vengeful Asian God is dying and that Christian sentiment ("the genius of the Divine Martyr") is today reborn in the spirit of liberty, equality, and fraternity, a spirit absent in those who usurp the name of Christians (24).

Finally, in 1879 Palacio Valdés published in the *Revista Europea* a series of eight studies of "contemporary poets." The poets and dramatists studied are José Echegaray, José Zorrilla, Ramón Campoamor, Antonio F. Grilo, Adelardo López de Ayala, Ventura Ruiz Aguilera, Gaspar Núñez de Arce, and Manuel de la Revilla. His approach, Palacio Valdés declares, is impressionistic: "I am always sure of my impressions, never of my opinions" ("Proemio," *Nuevo viaje al Parnaso. Poetas contemporáneos* [Madrid: Imprenta Plaza de la Armería, 1879], xi); both feeling and intelligence have a role in his criticism ("Echegaray," *Nuevo Viaje al Parnaso*, 5–8). Palacio Valdés abhors systems and favors the individual over the general ("López de Ayala," 88–9; "Núñez de Arce,", 147); he dislikes overt moral lessons and metaphysics in the drama (see the essays on Campoamor, López de Ayala, Ruiz Aguilera, Núñez de Arce, Revilla). As with the novelists, he prefers warmth, energy, simplicity, spontaneity, naturalness of expression, and freshness. He enthusiastically praises the romantic poet Zorrilla; in the same essay on Zorrilla, he acknowledges the beauties of the romantic verse of Byron, Chateaubriand, Heine, Hugo, and Espronceda. Palacio Valdés demands content, not merely form; thus, he recognizes the falseness of the theater of Echegaray ("an out-of-date romantic") and in scornful tones, which he later regretted, castigates Revilla's superficiality and lack of imagination.

In an important article published in September 1880, Palacio Valdés defined the critical process as consisting almost entirely of the operation of a sensitive imagination ("Cualidades de la crítica," *Revista de Asturias*, No. 17 [15 September 1880]: 266–8). In late 1880 and in 1881, Palacio Valdés published a series of drama reviews in *El Día*; sixteen of these essays were almost immediately reproduced in a collection of essays by Palacio Valdés and his friend Leopoldo Alas entitled *La literatura en 1881* (Madrid: Alfredo de Carlos Hierro, 1882). Palacio Valdés's criticism is frequently caustic; his style is pleasant, conversational, and direct. As in his earlier criticism, he seeks verisimilitude, spontaneity, energy, clarity, and precision of thought and sentiment; he sarcastically attacks all signs of "vagueness." Palacio Valdés advocates an art based on observation and thought (*La literatura en 1881*, 54). In the theater, he seeks a reflection of Spanish customs and sentiments, rather than slavish translations and wretched adaptations of foreign works (*La literatura en 1881*, 54, 74). The "realism" that he advocates for the theater will reflect the middle class and avoid a crude naturalistic reproduction of vice and low life (*La literatura en 1881*, 51). Nevertheless, in the polemic with Ricardo de la Vega that followed the publication of "Los teatros menudos" (*El Día*, 21 January 1881), Palacio Valdés strongly attacks the grotesque, exaggerated caricatures of the lower classes presented in the contemporary Spanish theater ("El sainete," *El Día*, 13 March 1881). Rather, Palacio Valdés observes in the lower classes tragic passions and sentiments of love, religion and patriotism ("El sainete," *El Día*, 6 April 1881).

Palacio Valdés's articles in the *Revista Europea* and *La literatura en 1881* reveal a critic who is perceptive, lively, widely-read, and totally self-confident. His defects are those of youth: a too-ready sarcasm and an intellectual brilliance that often dazzles the reader by pure tours de force. Palacio Valdés's criticism is impressionistic; he emphasizes the individual and dislikes general critical rules and didacticism in works of art. His values are "modern" in a nineteenth-century sense; he has a horror of superficiality, and an enthusiasm for spontaneity, energy, and realism. His attitude, in religion, art, and politics, is progressive. Interesting clues to Palacio Valdés's subsequent development as a novelist can be found in his admiration for the romantics, both Spanish and foreign, his strongly romantic imagination (evident in the cosmic despair and doubt present in his lament for the death of Francisco Javier Galvete), and in his recollections of his juvenile readings of romantic and popular novels.

CROTALUS HORRIDUS

The romantic note is strongly apparent in *Crotalus horridus* (1878), a bizarrely macabre tale dedicated to the novelist Benito Pérez Galdós. (The dedication is omitted from the Aguilar edition of the *Obras completas*.) The story relates, in the first person, a sailor's love for a wanton, beautiful, and mysterious creole, Anita, who is fascinated by rattlesnakes and who increasingly assumes the attributes of a poisonous reptile. Anita describes her snakelike power to kill with a kiss; she accompanies her account with a feverish, lascivious dance and the strange harmonies of a "rattlesnake song." Anita loves with the "love of a savage beast." Vengeful and insanely possessive, she decapitates a suitor and leaves false clues to implicate her innocent lover in the gruesome murder. Condemned to the gallows, the "diabolical" Anita blasphemes until the moment before her execution. The last three paragraphs raise the possibility of a final act of love on the part of Anita, inspired by the sight of her lover in the crowd witnessing the hanging.

The tale, with its themes of female treachery and outlandish, evil passions, with its relegation of the male to the role of helpless victim to a diabolical femme fatale, and with its evocations of the supernatural, the maleficent, and the bestial, is obviously related to romantic exoticism and to similar motifs in the literature of the fin de siècle.[4] The direct, fast-moving style and the considerable imaginative powers revealed in *Crotalus horridus* aptly inaugurate Palacio Valdés's career as a writer of fiction.

El señorito Octavio

Palacio Valdés's first novel was *El señorito Octavio* (1881). Palacio Valdés originally intended to publish the novel in the *Revista Europea*, with subsequent publication in book form by the Librería Fernando Fe. When the *Revista Europea* ceased publication in 1880, Palacio Valdés attempted to arrange publication by Miguel H. Cámara, the editor of *La Guirnalda* and publisher of the works of Benito Pérez Galdós. Galdós generously offered to pay for the printing of *El señorito Octavio*, although refused to accede to Palacio Valdés's request that he write a prologue to the novel.[5] The novel was finally published by Fernando Fe in 1881. Extracts from the novel were also published in *La Correspondencia de España*.

The novel was successful with the public, for there were three printings in the first year.[6] Later, in 1896, a considerably revised version of the novel was published by the Librería de Victoriano Suárez, as the third volume of the *Obras completas* of Palacio Valdés.

El señorito Octavio is set in Asturias in the 1870s, in the small town of Vegalora, located in a valley enclosed at one end by the brooding, cloud-covered Peña Mayor. Palacio Valdés ridicules contemporary figures and fads. The novel contains references to living writers, a satirical portrayal of clerical intervention in politics, and a caustic caricature of Krausist philosophy and jargon in the person of the ingenuous Homobono Pereda ("The Fetus").

The characters and plot of *El señorito Octavio* are heavily

melodramatic. The leading figure in the novel is Octavio
Rodríguez, an amorously-inclined youth who fancies himself in
love with Laura, the thirty-year-old wife of the Count of Trevia.
Octavio abandons his courtship of the down-to-earth eighteen-
year-old Carmen (who has already found consolation elsewhere)
to worship, in highly literary manner, the idealized Laura. Laura,
the daughter of a poor landowner, is miserably unhappy in the
clutches of her sadistic, pathological husband, who is himself
besotted with the cruel governess Florencia (the Baroness Zohiloff, in the first edition). Laura toys with Octavio's bookish passion; she finally gives herself to the brutal and ignorant farm
manager Pedro. Octavio, in a jealous rage, denounces the adulterous couple to the Count in an anonymous letter. The next morn-
ing, seeking to repair his fault, Octavio climbs the Peña Mayor
to warn the couple. Pedro flees. The Count, finding Octavio and
Laura together, murders them both and hurls their bodies into
the dark waters of the Lago Ausente. The novel ends on a burlesque note, with the Krausist electoral proclamation of Homobono Pereda.

For most of the novel, Octavio is treated ironically, even with
hostility, by the author. The foppish Octavio leads a secondhand
existence, basing his speech, clothing, possessions, fantasies, letters, diary entries, and convoluted courtship on literature. The
writers—for the most part of mediocre talent—who inspire his
extravagant behavior are listed: the French novelists Pierre-
Alexis Ponson du Terrail, Paul Féval, Emile Gaboriau, Alphonse
Karr, Jules Janin, Théophile Gautier, and Octave Feuillet, the
Spanish novelist Pérez Escrich, and the society columns of the
French press (170). Only toward the close of the novel does a
more "authentic" Octavio appear. A deeper, unconscious motivation is suggested by his two nightmares (230–2), his penning of
the anonymous denunciation, and his desperate attempt to save
the lives of the two lovers, when he adopts the role of leader in
place of superficial imitator of literature. The reader, however, is
insufficiently prepared for the abrupt change in Octavio's
behavior.

A similar inconsistency is apparent in Palacio Valdés's presentation of other characters. Laura merits our pity for her miserable
childhood and ill-treatment at her husband's hands. Her love of
Nature (her joyous hay-making with the villagers, the freedom

from societal constraint during her journey with Pedro to the *romería* ["pilgrimage"]) would seemingly justify her following her natural instincts. Nature itself leads woman to submit to the stronger male: "The relationship ordained by nature gradually developed between them: she, as a weak, delicate, needy being, submitting; he, strong and energetic, dominating and protecting" (190–1).

However, Laura's adulterous liaison is initially inspired by desire for vengeance, not by sexual passion. She reveals a measure of frivolity in the ease with which she recovers her spirits after the Count's brutality and in her failure to strongly discourage Octavio's courtship. Her attack of religious guilt when she is with Pedro on the Peña Mayor catches the reader unawares.

Pedro also is a contradictory figure. At once brutal and masterful, he is overcome with tearful sentimentality when jealous of Octavio; shortly afterwards, he proclaims his indifference to heaven and hell provided he can possess Laura (351). Declaring himself to be Laura's lover, he curses the Count in melodramatic vein (359–61).

The Count also shows marked inconsistencies. Brutal, cruel, totally selfish, insanely adopting the mannerisms and speech of a bygone age, he nevertheless at first refuses to consider killing his errant wife (311). He behaves above all as a villain of melodrama, degraded and enslaved by his passion for the merciless Florentina (Baroness Zohiloff), who demands that he slay his wife. Thus, in his encounter with Florentina in chapter 14, the Count expresses himself in such highly exaggerated terms that all verisimilitude is lost:

> —Estoy conforme con morir a tus manos, y quisiera más allá de la tumba seguir sintiéndolas eternamente en la garganta. . . . Oh, qué hermosa eres! . . . Te has apoderado de todo mi ser, como un veneno que va matando, sin sentirlo. . . . Mi alma es de otro temple que la de los demás hombres . . . por mis venas corre la sangre de los Médicis . . . y esta sangre pide un amor inquieto, palpitante, feroz. En ti sola pude hallarlo, porque eres aún más incomprensible y más loca que yo. (307)

> (I am willing to die at your hands, and even beyond the tomb would want to go on feeling them eternally on my throat. . . . Oh, how beautiful you are! . . . You've taken possession of my whole being, like a

poison which kills slowly and imperceptibly. . . . My soul is of a different temper to other men's . . . the blood of the Medici runs in my veins . . . and this blood demands a restless, vibrating, savage love. I found this love in you, because you are even more incomprehensible and insane than I.)

Despite the implausibilities and incoherences of plot and characterization, *El señorito Octavio* contains elements of interest. Scenes of rural and small town life, such as the evocations of Laura's sad childhood and of the joyful and malicious nightly gatherings in Don Marcelino's store, are vividly etched. Palacio Valdés's predilection for the miniature, rather than the grand scene, is evident in his careful descriptions (such as the opening account of the décor of Octavio's room) and in his lively vignettes of such characters as the sly socialist-republican Paco Ruiz, the pompous Krausist Homobono Pereda, Pereda's sententious conservative father, the commonsensical Carmen, and the clergyman devoted to politics and the pleasures of the table.

Humor, as well as Palacio Valdés's fondness for minor genres, is apparent in his pastiches: the letters that reveal character (penned by Octavio, Laura, a businessman, the diocesan lawyer, Homobono Pereda), the romantic effusions of Octavio's diary, and Homobono Pereda's election manifesto. There is a fine irony, as well as keen-sighted observation, in Palacio Valdés's rendering of Octavio's scorn of the girls of Vegalora (who represent reality rather than fantasy): "the young ladies of Vegalora, who without cause burst into loud laughter or became as serious as an alderman, those girls who notice one's tie and one's boots and who get angry if you don't greet them from a league away, and who melt into syrup as soon as a rich young man approaches and wishes them good afternoon" (181). Less effective are other, more heavy-handed attempts at humor: Homobono Pereda with his jargon; the boring, unifaceted characters who pay court to the Count; the clergyman who refuses to hear the impatient Octavio's confession.

Palacio Valdés's suggestions of a deeper world of the unconscious and of myth are of considerable interest. Noël M. Valis has convincingly described the instinctive and symbolical overtones of the scenes connected with the *romería* (with the accompanying background of the ballad of the *malmaridada* [unhappily married woman] and the journey through a Nature of palpably magical import) and of Pedro's following of unconscious urges as he plunges his overheated body into a cooling river.[7]

Also highly significant are scenes intended to shock the reader (Pablo's revelation of the hunger of his impoverished father, the roasting alive of a fox, the Count's atrocious cruelty to both animals and humans) and scenes that lead us into a realm of foreboding, of the supernatural, far distant from the superficiality of Octavio's conscious world. Thus, in chapter 9, Octavio's vivid nightmares express symbolically his fears of the Count's jealousy and violence. The themes of Paradise Lost, of a universe of God, angels, and demons who occasionally reveal their presence, pervade the novel. Laura longs for an angel to carry her to the summit of the Peña Mayor, where she would live "caressed by God and caressing her children" (79). Octavio is oppressed by a terror of mountain spirits as he contemplates the Peña Mayor from the lonely and sinister Lago Ausente (227). Finally, soon before Octavio and Laura are murdered, Octavio appears before the adulterous couple in the guise of a handsome and sinister angel guarding the gates of Paradise (353).

The first edition of El señorito Octavio bore the subheading "novel without transcendental thought." Noël M. Valis plausibly argues that the novel contains an unstated thesis of praise of what is natural and hostility toward what is artificial. Other implied assumptions of the author are a resentment of suffering caused by class differences (the desperate straits of the starving peasantry, the gratuitous cruelty of the aristocracy) and a strong current of misogyny. The examples of evil, or not fully responsible, women are many: Laura toys with Octavio; Florencia demands the death of Laura; the supposedly "innocent" Carmen flirts with Paco Ruiz;[8] Homobono Pereda discovers his proposed bride, the ignorant servant Adela, with a lover. The male characters, with the exception of the all-intrusive narrator, are no more favored than the females, being portrayed as foolish, sadistic, or brutal.

The characters, however, are too inconsistently portrayed and too lacking in self-knowledge for any coherent teaching to be evident. The contrast between those who base their lives on books (Octavio, Homobono Pereda) and those who follow instinct (Laura, Pedro) is insufficiently developed. When freed from the trammels of society, Laura adopts the "feminine" role of submission and Pedro that of the violent, protecting male. Laura, moreover, gives herself to Pedro not out of instinct but out of desire for vengeance and is tormented by guilt for her "sinful" behavior; she nevertheless finds in love woman's only source of happiness (254). Furthermore, the Cervantine criticism of those who confuse literature and life is rendered ambiguous: those who base their lives on books receive no better and no worse fate than those who follow their lusts; indeed, Octavio's bookishness disappears in time of crisis.

For the 1896 edition, Palacio Valdés considerably revised *El señorito Octavio*, reducing its length by a third. Many of the descriptions and speeches are eliminated or curtailed; the burlesque subplot of Homobono Pereda's courtship of Adela based on Krausist first principles disappears; one of Octavio's nightmares is suppressed, as also is Pedro's melodramatic denunciation of the Count in the penultimate chapter. Chapter 14, that of the Count's confrontation with the Baroness Zohiloff, is totally rewritten, with the suppression of references to Florencia's exotic, aristocratic background and of passages in which the Count demonstrates his abject enslavement to his degraded passion; the markedly melodramatic tone of the novel is correspondingly reduced. More curious is Palacio Valdés's suppression of references to contemporary figures (novelists, members of the Ateneo) and of the narratorial "I." In the first edition, the narrator introduces himself into the text on almost every page, obtrusively guides the reader through the plot, and jocosely converses with the reader about the nature of the novelist's task; he thus confesses his fondness for women and temptation to abandon his novelistic labors to marry the delectable Carmen (106–7).[9]

El señorito Octavio is seriously flawed as a novel. Palacio Valdés portrays without nuances characters who lack self-knowledge and who veer precariously between superficiality and the violent fulfillment of unconscious urges. The plot is melodramatic and contains disconcerting switches of mood; thus, scenes in which the Count appears, with his sadism and degraded passion, are strangely out of place in a novel that also offers delightful portrayals of everyday customs. Not only is the plot incoherent, but Palacio Valdés also reveals an inability plausibly to render conversation; the speech of the aristocrats and their dependents is stilted and unconvincing. At times, *El señorito Octavio* points the way to the mature Palacio Valdés, with its intimations of the strength of unconscious motivation and its awareness of rural grievances. Nevertheless, the novel contains too many disparate elements to be more than a literary tour de force.

3

The Novels of the 1880s:
From Asturias to Sevilla

In the novels that followed *El señorito Octavio* Palacio Valdés reaches his full maturity as a novelist. His mastery of the art is evident in the wide range of settings, subjects, and perspectives of the novels of the 1880s. The settings for the novels were for the most part the author's native Asturias, as in *El señorito Octavio*. *Marta y María* is set in "Nieva" (Avilés), *El idilio de un enfermo* in a region similar to the Valley of Laviana, *José* in the fishing village of "Rodillero" (Candás del Santísimo Cristo, where Palacio Valdés met his first bride), and *El cuarto poder* in "Sarrió" (a composite of Gijón and Avilés).[1] Three important novels are set outside Asturias. *Riverita* (apart from the courtship scenes, which take place in the coastal village of Pasajes near San Sebastián) and *Maximina* explore life in Madrid in the 1860s, 1870s, and early 1880s. *La hermana San Sulpicio* is the novel par excellence of Andalusia.

Palacio Valdés offers an impressive variety of themes and approaches. *Marta y María* (1883), with its detailed evocation of setting and of historical moment, its contrast between María's emotional coldness and pseudomysticism and Marta's healthy practicality, and its suggestion of unconscious motivation, is one of Palacio Valdés's better-constructed novels. A strong ideological commitment is evident in the attack on contemporary "religious" practices. Palacio Valdés's next novel, *El idilio de un enfermo* (1884), abandons overt ideology to combine considerable poetic power (the evocations of Nature, the elopement of two young lovers) and a naturalistic treatment of class barriers and of rural greed and cruelty.

The articles and stories of *Aguas fuertes* (1884) reveal Palacio Valdés's mastery of brief prose, a genre to which he would return in the twentieth century. The short novel *José* (1885) explores the harsh lives of fishermen and their wives in almost naturalistic vein.

The narrow milieus of the earlier works are abandoned in the sequel novels *Riverita* and *Maximina*, which rival Balzac's *Comédie humaine* in their densely-packed portrayal of an urban middle-class society. As well as the ironic depiction of a multitude of characters, *Riverita/Maximina*, reflecting the experience of Palacio Valdés's first marriage, describes the love of a sensitive Miguel Rivera and the ingenuous Maximina. The fundamental theme of the novels is that of the disappointment of aspirations. Despite excellent evocations of character and society, *Riverita/Maximina* is flawed by the melodramatic introduction of a villainous seducer and by the emotionalism of its tragic ending.

The tendency to melodrama is marked in *El cuarto poder* (1888), with its exaggerated treatment of devoted love, treachery, adultery, enslavement to passion, and suicide. *El cuarto poder* also offers an ironic portrayal of the pomposities, rivalries, and class resentments of a small Asturian town.

The scope of Palacio Valdés's novelistic skills is further evidenced in *La hermana San Sulpicio* (1889), Palacio Valdés's most successful novel with the reading public. *La hermana San Sulpicio* offers a lively portrayal of the customs of "exotic" Andalusia, related with considerable irony by a self-conscious first-person narrator who combines traits of romantic feeling and poetry with a strong practicality.

Marta y María

Marta y María, published in 1883, obtained an instant success.[2] The novel is set in the fictional town of Nieva, in northern Asturias. The action takes place in 1873, during the First Spanish Republic. The plot is of great simplicity. Two sisters of a well-to-do family follow very different courses. The elder, María, engaged to the young artillery officer Ricardo, the Marqués of Peñalta, is increasingly drawn to a religious life; María becomes involved in a Carlist conspiracy to seize a local arms factory and, finally, enters a convent. The disconsolate Ricardo marries María's younger sister Marta.

The impact of national events on the leading inhabitants of Nieva plays an important role in the novel. Nieva is located just outside the lines of Somosierra (the boundary between governmental forces and Carlist rebels at the time of the siege of Bilbao during the Third Carlist War, 1872–1876). Carlist newspapers are smuggled into Nieva; Carlists and clerics call on loyal Catholics to join in the struggle to "exterminate" the government; local Carlists attempt to seize the armaments factory in order to obtain arms with which to fight governmental troops. Although Palacio Valdés's scorn for Carlist rhetoric and ideology is obvious, the supporters of the "vacillating" Spanish republic of 1873 are not left unscathed. The military governor who receives the captive Carlists is a brute; the "sovereign people"—the mob that insults and attacks the helpless Carlist prisoners—are the dregs of the populace. Contemporary economic concerns are also noted: Don Mariano de Elorza demands adequate railroad connections between Nieva and the rest of Spain, lest the commerce of the town pass to the neighboring city of Sarrió; the source of the Elorza family fortune is explained in detail.

In the first edition, *Marta y María* (Barcelona: Biblioteca "Arte y Letras," 1883) bears the subheading "novel of customs," an appellation that suggests the French *roman de moeurs* rather than a Spanish *costumbrista* origin. Although secondary to the moral purpose of the novel, the depiction of the life and customs of the inhabitants of Nieva provides, when coupled with the evocation of the historical moment, a realistic background against which the ideological conflict takes place. There is no idealization of Nieva, a dreary town of unending drizzle, chill, and ramshackle streets. Customs are related in passing: the soirée held in the Elorza mansion, the pseudocourtships of adolescents, the bullying undergone by military cadets. Vignettes of minor characters—the pompous dowry-hunting young lawyer, the hysterical and neurotic mother of the two sisters, María's superstitious, fawning servant, the philandering factory-owner, the spiteful, envious young ladies, the politically progressive Don Mariano—create a density of setting. Realistic details—the nervousness of young men at a dance, the sweat and body odors of the dancers, the selfishness of the party-goers—contribute to the plausibility of the tale.

Despite its apparent "realism," *Marta y María* is based on a series of dualities. The most obvious and significant contrast is that between the two sisters: María is highly intelligent, self-absorbed, and "spiritually" inclined; her sister Marta, on the other hand, is down-to-earth, practical, and unselfish. Further conflicts exist between Carlists and liberals, between religious enthusiasts and those lacking dogmatic fervor, and between the emotionally cold (María) and those whose responses to life are grounded in feeling (Marta, Ricardo, Don Mariano). Crucial also to Palacio Valdés's vision is the opposition of "romantic" and "realistic" approaches to life. Thus, the Verdi opera sung by María is answered by the howling of dogs; María's exalted readings of romantic novelists and the lives of saints are paralleled by Marta's practicality and indifference to books; the romantic prose with which the journalists of the 1840s saluted Doña Gertrudis's charms contrasts strongly with the subsequent humdrum fates of worshipers and idol.

The leading character in the novel is María, who from the beginning is scathingly treated. Cold by nature, she flees intimacy with her fiancé and places a barrier of religious pieties between herself and her family. Indifferent to the feelings of others, she disdains Ricardo's passion, offers no comfort to her dying mother, and abandons her father and Ricardo to loneliness. María is manipulative to excess: she convinces Ricardo to attend mass and attempts to persuade him to betray his military duty; her pious justifications for taking the veil are couched in bookish terms. María's actions are inspired not by experience but by literary models:[3] her early readings were of the Spanish equivalent of Gothic novels, "bloodthirsty narratives of terrible and monstrous crimes"; romantic readings lead her to dream of an all-encompassing love; her religious life is in part inspired by an attempt to imitate the pious example of Saint Elizabeth of Hungary. Pride, excess, and self-exaltation dominate her behavior. Thus, she contemplates the manner, rather than the content, of her confession (69). Her practice of humility is ostentatious: she kneels before her father in penitence for an imagined fault; she washes the feet of beggars (but nevertheless cannot bring herself to kiss the sores of a sick woman); she experiences an "intimate joy" (156) in impressing superstitious villagers with her rumored miracles. The conscious imitation of a saint's life, rather than a genuine response to situation, inspires her confes-

sion to the military tribunal. However, in the prosaic Spain of
the nineteenth century, she receives not martyrdom but release
on bail to her father.[4]

Although cold to her family, María sobs with an excess of
emotion before the image of Jesus (48). There is, however, a
strong desire for self-abasement connected with María's adoration of Christ. She calls on Jesus to punish her (48); her self-
mortification leads to fainting, convulsions, vomiting, and finally
a vision of Christ, whose body she embraces (171–2). Her "humility" nevertheless reflects sexual perversion rather than mysticism. As a child, María had become so enslaved by passion for
another girl, so willing to be dominated and humiliated, that she
deliberately burned herself with an iron (160–1). Similarly, as
she enters the convent, she espies a nun before whom she wishes
to prostrate herself: "There arose in her breast a certain extravagant inclination toward the nun and an intense, burning desire
to prostrate herself before her and plead: 'Teach me, direct me!'
Oh, if only she were allowed to give her a kiss, however tiny!'"
(335). Furthermore, María's reaction toward the nuns—she experiences "a sweet, voluptuous tremor" whenever she sees them—
contains obvious sexual elements.

María's distorted sexuality not only suggests lesbian passion
but also masochism. In the name of religion, María persuades
her servant to flagellate her. Palacio Valdés relates her excitement
("a delicious trembling") as she undresses herself (124–5) and
lingeringly evokes her physical reaction—a voluptuous mixture
of pleasure and pain—as her naked body is lashed:

Respirábase en el cuarto una atmósfera de misterio y recogimiento
que enajenaba a María y la penetraba de un placer embriagador. Su
hermoso cuerpo, desnudo, se estremecía cada vez que cruzaban por
él las correas de las disciplinas con un dolor no exento de voluptuo-
sidad. Apretaba la frente contra los pies del Redentor, respirando
ansiosamente y con cierta opresión, y sentía latir en sus sienes la
sangre con singular violencia, mientras el dorado y sutil vello de su
nuca se levantaba de un modo imperceptible a impulso de la emo-
ción que la embargaba. De vez en cuando sus labios, pálidos y trém-
ulos, decían en voz baja:—¡Sigue, sigue! (128–9)

(An atmosphere of mystery and concentration pervaded the room,
transporting María and inundating her with an intoxicating pleasure.

Her beautiful, naked body shuddered under the lashes of the whips with a pain not entirely lacking in voluptuous delight. She pressed her forehead against the feet of the Redeemer, breathing heavily with a certain feeling of oppression, and she felt the blood pulsating in her temples with extraordinary violence, whilst the emotion which possessed her caused the fine, golden down of the nape of her neck imperceptibly to stand on end. From time to time her pale, trembling lips gasped: "Go on, go on!")

The first edition of the novel contains a full-page illustration, by J. Luis Pellicer, of the flagellation of the naked, fleshy María.

The two other major characters, although not developed to the same extent as María, are Ricardo and Marta. Ricardo is spontaneous, voluble, likable, honorable, good humored, imaginative (and thus prone to nightmares), and highly emotional. A simple man, he is putty in the hands of the manipulative María. He is also deeply sensitive, reacting strongly to his fiancée María's coldness, suffering loneliness and depression on the death of his mother and on his abandonment by María, who, he sadly realizes, is incapable of "the tenderness of feeling, the constancy, and the modest, humble self-denial which good wives and mothers should possess" (355).

Marta, who at the beginning of the novel is thirteen years old, is on the surface a much simpler creature than María. In contrast to María's perverted sexuality, Marta's sensuality—her plump arms that engage Ricardo's attention as she kneads dough, her odor of fresh linen—suggests health and is not divorced from everyday, practical pursuits. Marta cares for the immediate needs of her family (food, emotional support), has little interest in books, easily laughs, and is as easily upset. Unlike the "pious" María, Marta consoles her dying mother and her grieving father; she has the strength and self-confidence to react angrily to the platitudes of the attending priest. Marta has the manifest approval of Palacio Valdés.[5] With her practicality, her serenity, her affection for others, "her healthy, balanced temperament," she is a worthy spouse for Ricardo.

Despite Palacio Valdés's claim in the introduction to the 1906 edition of the novel that he attacks only false mysticism, *Marta y María* represents an obvious criticism of certain contemporary religious practices and beliefs.[6] The church of Nieva is frequented only by women. The sermon preached during the *novena del Sagrado Corazón* is fatuous (72);[7] religion is trivialized by the invitation to the congregation to obtain spiritual pleasure by "spending fifteen minutes each day in a friendly chat with the Sacred Heart of Jesus" (77). Superstition abounds among the working-class women of Nieva. Catholics, encouraged by priests and clerical literature, are deeply involved in the Carlist rebellion. The "saintly" María is self-centered; her spiritual models, when described in Palacio Valdés's mocking prose, are porcelain figures, devoid of reality. "Religion" is moreover easily perverted for individual ends. María uses the words of religion to justify her coldness to her family and to attempt to persuade Ricardo to dishonor his military oath. The "Christ" worshipped by María is a figment of her sickly imagination. The nuns whom María assumes to be "angelic" are ill-tempered, vengeful, and hypocritical.

Characters less obsessed with "religion" are portrayed with greater sympathy. Marta, concerned with the "reality" of a household and healthily involved with others, possesses an emotional authenticity that the pretentious María, with her bookishness and sermonizing, lacks. Her Voltairian father, Mariano, accepts the moral precepts of religion but has little affection for church services, prayers, and the clergy; he nonetheless genuinely cares for his neurotic and hysterical wife and achieves the true marriage ordained by God and rarely attained on earth (324). Similarly, Ricardo, a "sincere Christian" (354), is drawn to church worship and pious observances only by María's manipulations.

María, with her perverted sexuality, is not the only example in the novel of the influence of the unconscious. In two remarkable chapters (9 and 10), suggestive of Jungian rather than Freudian import, Marta experiences powerful urges toward union with Nature (or an equivalent annihilation in death), as she undergoes a physical and symbolic passage to puberty. On an excursion to a nearby island, Marta abandons her friends (the society she has hitherto known) and leads Ricardo through a secret, dark, and narrow tunnel (a vaginal journey to another universe) to emerge onto an isolated, sunlit beach. In this miniature Eden, Marta becomes deeply distressed, as she fears being swept away by the uncanny music of the waves and of the breeze and hears a lament issuing from the rocks. Despite her fear of death, Marta wishes to die, accompanied by Ricardo, in the embrace of the ocean. A powerful sexuality pervades the scene, as Marta demands that Ricardo breathe on her, kiss her hands, her face, her hair, her lips (an obvious parallel with María's previous imagining of the embrace of Jesus).[8] On the return journey in the boat, Marta, pale and motionless, stares at the waves. (Palacio Valdés. comments that it is easier to decipher the mystery of the sounds of the ocean and of the secrets of the wind than to penetrate a young girl's thoughts [232].) Remorsefully remembering the beach, desiring a final peace, Marta seeks death by plunging into the sea; she is saved from suicide by Ricardo.

In *Marta y María*, Palacio Valdés continues the satire of attitudes based on literature that was initiated in *El señorito Octavio*. *Marta y María* is much more tautly constructed than the confused earlier work. The varied elements of the novel are well-combined: a realistic evocation of the milieu and historical background, an element of adventure and suspense (the Carlist conspiracy), a sly humor as Palacio Valdés mocks the foibles of his characters, and a strong visual sense that, on occasion, provides a certain erotic titillation.[9] The author's control of his narrative is impressive. Completely sure of his ideological stance, Palacio Valdés intervenes directly to mock the "virtuous" María's search for martyrdom and to approve the emotionally healthy, "human" attitudes of Marta. Although simplistic and formulaic, the contrast between the two sisters leads to a straightforward narrative presentation. Furthermore, the reader's emotions are involved in the closing chapters, when Palacio Valdés touchingly and solemnly evokes the loneliness that awaits Don Mariano[10] and Ricardo and the final happiness achieved by Marta, Don Mariano, and Ricardo. The obvious didacticism of the novel has led critics to overlook original elements in *Marta y María*: the overt association between religion and sexual perversion,[11] the advocacy of a practical Christianity based on concern for others rather than devotion to clerical rites, and, above all, the powerful role assigned to the unconscious.

EL IDILIO DE UN ENFERMO

Marta y María was followed by *El idilio de un enfermo* (1884). The opening two chapters, set in Madrid, reveal the influence of a scientific naturalism. The protagonist of the novel, whom we first meet in a doctor's consulting office, is the sickly Andrés Heredia, an anemic poet who fears that he has consumption; however, his ill health derives, as the doctor indicates, from the unnatural life of the cities. Heredia's background is given in naturalistic detail: his parentage (a *mésalliance* between an aged judge and his young niece), his economic circumstances, his loss of health through sexual excess and the strains of urban living. The satire of romantic, bookish attitudes present in *El señorito Octavio* and *Marta y María* continues in *El idilio de un enfermo*: Heredia's juvenile lachrymose verse is mockingly described; there is no relation between Heredia's youthful poems on death and his terror when confronted with the possibility of illness.

The rest of the novel, with the exception of the closing chapter, is set in the fictitious Asturian village of Riofrío, where Heredia seeks to restore his health. Numerous local characters are sketched in brief but lively manner: the garrulous easygoing peasants whom Heredia meets on the train; his uncle, the outgoing Carlist priest Don Fermín; the picaresque, womanizing seminarian Celesto. There are also powerfully-etched evocations of the beauties of the countryside. Indeed, in chapter 6 the bookish Heredia is moved to tears when he realizes that true poetry is to be found in Nature.

The plot of the novel centers around Heredia's initially tentative, and then more serious, courtship of a seventeen-year-old peasant girl, Rosa. The difference in social class between Heredia and Rosa provides the mainspring of the tale. Rosa at first refuses to have anything to do with a *señorito*, rightly fearing the loss of her reputation with the young men of the region; uncle Fermín justly reprimands Heredia's frivolity and inability to appreciate the consequences of his thoughtless behavior. Half-unconsciously, Heredia adopts the methods of an accomplished seducer to gain the attention of the inexperienced Rosa.

What is merely a summer flirtation for Heredia nevertheless takes place against a chilling background of peasant lust and cruelty. Rosa's father, the miller Tomás, is a sordid, calculating animal, sycophantic to Heredia, brutal to those within his power. Tomás's fifty-year-old brother, the unsavory and ignorant *indiano* (returned emigrant) Jaime, attempts to rape Rosa. Thwarted in his lust, he finally decides to marry Rosa, who is subjected to

repeated beatings, at times to the point of her losing consciousness, by her father who tries to compel her to accept the sordid
match. When Rosa continues to refuse, the vengeful Jaime places
his brother's family in financial ruin.

After an attempt to say farewell is frustrated by the emergence
of an enraged Tomás, Heredia accompanies Rosa (who is barefoot
and clad only in a shift) in a flight across a moonlit countryside,
evoked in terms of remarkable poetic power, to deliver her to the
protective custody of an aunt. Nevertheless, despite its lyrical
elements, El idilio de un enfermo is a realistic, not idealistic,
novel. (The title, of course, is ironic.) Thus, when the two are
hiding in a hayloft, Heredia attempts to possess the trusting Rosa
by force; when this fails, he finally achieves his purpose with
honeyed words. The next day, the two feast while surrounded by
servile villagers, until Heredia, heedless of warnings to flee, is
arrested by the guardia civil. The scene of rustic celebration is
pervaded by a sense of a relentlessly impending doom; we are,
indeed, plunged for a while into a universe of classical tragedy,
far removed from the everyday world of rural Asturias.

The novel ends rapidly, if realistically. Heredia, with his family
connections and social category, is released from prison the next
day, to return to his idle and unhygienic life in Madrid. He later
learns that Rosa has fled her wretched home to become a servant.
Within a year, Heredia dies of consumption.

El idilio de un enfermo, despite the harsh criticism with which
it was received by Leopoldo Alas and Andrés González Blanco,[12]
is a masterpiece in miniature. Classical in its simplicity, the tale
is fast-moving and full of suspense. To the end of the novel, the
reader hopes for the impossible, a marriage between Rosa and
Andrés Heredia. Class barriers, however, cannot be breached. El
idilio de un enfermo reveals a decided increase in Palacio Valdés's novelistic range when compared with Marta y María. No
longer attempting a "transcendental" thesis, Palacio Valdés now
readily passes, with virtuoso skill, from describing the everyday—the evocation of Heredia's life in Madrid, the character
sketches of the inhabitants of Riofrío—to the creation of an archetypal universe of Nature (for example, the elopement by
moonlight that assumes a magical quality reminiscent of Alain-
Fournier's Le Grand Meaulnes) and of classical tragedy (the
doom-ridden feast of the two lovers, in which Heredia ignores

the choruslike invocations to flee). Indeed, the power of the novel derives in large measure from the juxtaposition of two quite different realms: a universe akin to that of Greek tragedy, in which men and women are the pawns of gods, and a more humdrum world of contingency.

Many of the characters behave with little signs of rationality. The peasants are for the most part sordid animals whose lusts and petty greed would not be out of place in a novel of Zola. Heredia, furthermore, has a quality of heedlessness, of unawareness both of his own motivation and of the consequences of his actions. His punishment for meddling in what he does not understand is severe: the failure to realize his potential, the loss of a Rosa whom he has been unable to appreciate, the banal death foretold in the opening chapter of the novel.

El idilio de un enfermo is a veritable tour de force. The mood of the novel (expressed throughout with an understatement perhaps more characteristic of contemporary English fiction, rather than of Spanish) constantly changes, as Palacio Valdés, always in control, switches from scenes of a humorous banality (the Heredia of Madrid), to powerful evocations of the beauty of Nature, to a playful "idyllic" courtship, to the cruelty and materialism of the peasants, to a magical elopement, and finally to a "realistic," commonsensical ending. The refusal to sentimentalize character or situation is a further measure of Palacio Valdés's skill. Thus, the spirited Rosa, returning to the world of humans after her temporary sojourn in the realm of the gods, suffers no condign punishment for her escapade; far from feeling sorry for herself, she seeks a practical solution for her situation.

AGUAS FUERTES

In the same year (1884), Palacio Valdés published a volume of short pieces entitled *Aguas fuertes*; the articles and stories had previously been published in the Barcelona journal *Arte y Letras* in late 1882 and early 1883.[13] Some of the articles relate, in a light tone, Palacio Valdés's observations of the life of Madrid: the customs of the city ("El Retiro de Madrid," "El Paseo de Recoletos," "La Castellana"), the debates of future lawyers ("La Academia de Jurisprudencia"), the rudeness and inefficiency of the librarians of the National Library ("La Biblioteca Nacional"). The misplaced aspirations of young poets are satirically but accurately treated in "Los mosquitos líricos." In the important essay "El último bohemio," Palacio Valdés, keenly aware of the economic situation of writers, attacks the plague of the Spanish literary world, the "romantic bohemianism" that has led so often to poverty and degradation; the romantic theory of inspiration is false and ridiculous, for literature is born of constant effort, not chance.

Most of the articles are anecdotes or short stories. "El pájaro en la nieve" is a moving tale, related with considerable compassion, of a blind man's death of starvation, exposure, and abandonment. A romantic influence is often evident: "Lloviendo" at the same time recalls Larra (the humorous overgeneralization) and anticipates Ramón Gómez de la Serna (the playful and imaginative association of disparate elements); "El drama de las bambalinas" relates the murder of an adulterer; a nightmare is described in "El sueño de un reo de muerte." "El hombre de los patíbulos"—a tale described by Julio Cejador as "terrorífico-humorista"—is a gruesome account of a man who assiduously attends public executions and who relates with pride, in a matter-of-fact tone, the first execution that he witnessed, that of his father. Many of the articles and stories serve to reveal character ("Los amores de Clotilde," "El profesor León," "La Abeja," "Los Puritanos").

Three stories that appear in current editions of Aguas fuertes were absent from the first edition (1884). They are "El crimen de la calle de la Perseguida" (an anecdote with a surprise ending), "El potro del señor cura" (a tale in the vein of the stories of Alphonse Daudet), and "Polifemo" (a somewhat sentimental revelation of character).

Later, in 1890, Palacio Valdés published "Seducción," an "agua fuerte" that has never been included in the collection Aguas fuertes. In this article (his contribution to his friend José Lázaro's journal España Moderna), the author narrates in the first person his attempts to find a topic for the article; he finally eavesdrops on the conversation of a married couple and reproduces the husband's account of a frustrated love of his youth. The narrative holds the reader's interest to the end; with its theme of a tale within a tale within a tale, it recalls the structure of the *Arabian Nights*.

A further excursion by Palacio Valdés into the short story is the "novela" ¡*Solo!* (1899). In this brief tale, Palacio Valdés evokes the happiness of a middle-aged merchant, married to a young and frivolous *madrileña* (woman of Madrid), and his three-year-old son as they vacation together on a farm. The affectionate presentation of the loving adoration that father and child feel for each other turns to tragedy when the father drowns.

The articles and stories of *Aguas fuertes* reveal Palacio Valdés's mastery of the brief genre. The narrator's control of his material is manifest in his concision, in his rapid development of plot and sudden revelation of character, in his eye for the bizarre, in his light and often ironic tone, in the ease with which he chats with the reader, and in his skill with dialogue, so strikingly lacking a few years previously in *El señorito Octavio*.

JOSÉ

Palacio Valdés's next novel was *José* (Madrid: Imprenta de Manuel G. Hernández, 1885). Set in the fishing village of Rodillero, on the coast of the Bay of Biscay, *José* ("a novel of maritime customs") relates the harsh lives of villagers dependent on the sea. Palacio Valdés's narratorial stance is one of omniscience, as he narrates the deeds and thoughts of the various characters; the author also at times interjects himself into the narrative to declare himself a witness to the events described.[14]

The narrator frames his tale in the traditional manner of a storyteller, with an explanatory introduction that precedes the novelistic action. The narrator, representing a culture superior to that of his characters, declares the simplicity of the customs and the lack of complexity of the "comedias y dramas" of Rodillero; he compares the physical attributes of the women of Rodillero to those of the Greeks and Romans; he refers to Dante, to the Italian Renaissance, and to Spanish history. However, the contrast between the narrator's perspective and that of the ignorant villagers is never developed in the body of the novel.

José shows traces of the ruling literary mode of naturalism. The vulgar language of fishwives is reproduced; technical terms are used (for example, the listing of names of sails, 242), albeit sparingly; as in Zola's *L'Assommoir* (1877) and Galdós's *La desheredada* (1881), women use physical violence on each other; Fernando de Meira commits suicide. From the outset, the reader is introduced to an environment both physically and morally harsh. Rodillero stinks of the remains of rotting fish; its stream is polluted. The men of Rodillero, in their constant struggle for survival, soon lose their natural vivacity as they move from home to sea to tavern; unlike Spanish peasants ("misers, intriguers and deceivers," 10), they are generous to others. The women of Rodillero, on the other hand, are enterprising and rule their families; the women tend to be greedy, foul-mouthed, and quarrelsome (10).

The tale is simplicity itself. The fisherman José is thwarted in his plans to marry Elisa by the hostility of her mother, the duplicitous Isabel, who arranges for José's boat to be destroyed. Finally, the ruined nobleman Fernando de Meira provides José with money for a new boat and takes legal steps for Elisa to be removed from her mother's house prior to obtaining authorization for her marriage to José.

Character portrayal is rudimentary. José is timid and honest. Isabel is hypocritical and greedy. Elisa is timid. Fernando de Meira prefers starvation to betrayal of family reputation. Rufo, the sacristan's son who sabotages José's boat, is imbecilic. While individuals are depicted in simplistic manner, the portrayal of village life is of greater interest. The villagers face death at sea and suffer starvation if fish cannot be located. They are capable of compassion, feeding the starving Fernando de Meira, and at times play childlike jokes on each other. The villagers flamboyantly manifest their deeply-felt religious beliefs: Elisa is bloodied as she completes a vow to climb on her knees to the chamber of the Christ of Rodillero; in the final chapter, the sailors who survive the storm hear mass barefoot.

Palacio Valdés does not idealize the villagers. The women of Rodillero are crude-tongued, violent, and emotional. José's mother and the sacristan's wife, in their hatred, hurl invective at each other and come to blows. The timid and innocent Elisa is slapped and insulted by José's mother. The women are superstitious, believing in witchcraft and evil omens. The women also lack compassion. As a child, José is neglected and foully abused by his mother; as an adult, he is cheated by Isabel and exploited by his sister. Children also have their cruelty, bullying the idiot Rufo. Fishermen are envious and at sea deceive those in other boats to obtain a temporary advantage; the sailor Bernardo remarks: "everyone in this village would give an eye to blind his neighbor" (246).

José was well received by critics.[15] It was translated into French, Dutch, Swedish, German, Czech, Portuguese, and Danish. In the United States, there were two English translations (1901 and 1961) and four textbook editions for high-school and college students. Nevertheless, *José* is an overrated work, lacking the transcendental vision of *El idilio de un enfermo*. The narrator is given to generalization and explains characters' motives in a pedestrian manner. Characterization is oversimplistic. Despite the vivacity of the disputes of the women of Rodillero, the dialogue is often stilted. *José* is, indeed, little more than an extended short story. Its strengths lie in Palacio Valdés's colorful rendering of visual scenes and in his forceful presentation of the greed and rivalries of the fishwives.

RIVERITA AND *MAXIMINA*

Riverita (Madrid: Tipografía de Manuel G. Hernández, 1886. 2 vols.) and its continuation *Maximina* (Madrid: Tipografía de Manuel G. Hernández, 1887. 2 vols.)—the two novels form a single work—are a curiously flawed attempt at a bildungsroman.[16] While tracing the growth of the protagonist Miguel Rivera ("Riverita") from a fairly happy childhood to bereavement and a despair of nihilistic proportions, Palacio Valdés offers a pessimistic vision not only of middle-class Madrid society but also of human existence.

The novels contain some autobiographical elements. Rivera, like Palacio Valdés, frequents the Ateneo while studying law in Madrid. Palacio Valdés endows Rivera with qualities of intelligence, sensitivity, and generosity. Rivera also shares with Palacio Valdés the less attractive trait of irritability.[17]Maximina's character is based on that of Palacio Valdés's young bride, Luisa Maximina Prendes Busto; like Palacio Valdés's wife, Maximina gives birth to a son. The conclusion to *Maximina* reflects the author's personal anguish at his wife's death in the spring of 1885.[18] Rivera's determination not to remarry should Maximina die no doubt echoes Palacio Valdés's feelings at the time of composition of the novel (*Maximina*, 1: 153–4).

Riverita begins comically, with the mischievous pranks of the eight-year-old Miguel Rivera and his cousin Enrique. The second marriage of Rivera's adored father to the despotic *sevillana* (woman from Sevilla) Angela Guevara promptly leads to Rivera's expulsion from home and from contact with his beloved baby half-sister Julia. The novel then follows Rivera's not unhappy years in boarding school, his wastrel life (which includes "nights of love and debauchery" [1: 222]) in the company of his Uncle Manolo, his reencounter with Julia and consequent return to the household of his cold stepmother, his love affair with a romantically-inclined married woman (Lucía Población), and his involvement as the editor of a newspaper. At the age of twenty-seven, Rivera passes a summer in the fishing village of Pasajes on the Basque coast, toys with the affections of and falls in love with the impoverished fifteen-year-old orphan Maximina, is wounded in a duel, and finally, at the coaxing of his half-sister Julia, weds Maximina.

One of the strengths of *Riverita* is its wealth of clearly-delineated characters, drawn from a variety of social backgrounds. In *Riverita*, Palacio Valdés portrays, with fine irony, as densely-populated a society as that of Balzac's *Comédie humaine*. The characters include numerous members of Rivera's family: his ne'er-do-well uncle Manolo, his other uncle (the cold and pompous Bernardo), and Rivera's cousins (the taurophile Enrique, the pedantic Carlos, the dandy Vicente, the bad-tempered Eulalia). Among his relatives' friends and acquaintances, Rivera meets the shy pharmacist (and secret philanthropist) Facundo Hojeda, the gigantic Colonel Bembo, the dandy Juan Romillo, and the ambitious young politician, the Cuban Arturo del Valle. Uncle Manolo introduces Riverita to his lodging-house companions and to the suitors of the hypochondriacal, ill-tempered widow Anita whom Manolo ultimately marries. Boarding school offers the occasion for vignettes of eccentric teachers (the sexually-repressed and bullying priest Don Juan Vigil, the easygoing headmaster Colonel Jaime, the atheistic republican Marroquín). Miguel in school befriends the asinine Pedro Mendoza (who will later become the editor of the newspaper *La Independencia*). The adolescent Miguel also becomes enamored of the school washerwoman, the plump and tyrannical Petra (whom the revolutionary Marroquín later weds "before the altar of his conscience" [1: 135]).

The multiplicity of characters and Rivera's observations as he wanders through diverse sectors of Madrid society afford the opportunity for much social criticism. Bernardo's "proper" household, with its rigid etiquette (which barely conceals the envies and hostilities of the children), is, in Rivera's eyes, a "farce," a "familia de sainete" (family from a light comedy) (1: 195). Arturo del Valle's sentimental defense of the causes of neglected children and of the emancipation of slaves is merely a stepping-stone to a conservative political career. Rivera is repulsed by the "philosophical jargon" of the University, the self-seeking intriguers of the Ateneo, and the sycophants of the Conde de Ríos's *tertulia* (salon).

In the second volume of *Riverita*, through his cousin Enrique, Rivera enters another social milieu, that of the aged bullfighter El Cigarrero and his cronies. Pursuing his relationship with Julia, Miguel meets the eccentric military cadet Utrilla. In Madrid society, he renews his acquaintance with Lucía Población, and attends the salon of the stupid General Conde de Ríos (the founder of *La Independencia*). In the coastal village of Pasajes, Rivera becomes familiar with the family of the lodging-house keeper and his niece Maximina and takes part in the games and dances of the villagers.

As a true bildungsroman, *Riverita* traces the moral and intellectual growth of the protagonist. Rivera is imaginative and highly sensitive, both as a child and as an adolescent. Intelligent—his wit costs him dearly in society—and generous, he is also lonely. Indeed, loneliness makes him return to live with his stepfamily. An intellectual, he attempts to draw conclusions from his experiences. Although capable of decisiveness (his "seduction" of Lucía Población) and courage (his duel), Rivera is for the most part an observer of society, rather than one to control events. Significantly, it is his far-sighted half-sister Julia who arranges for Maximina to come to Madrid, whereas the more passive Rivera, prey to "tedium and vanity, vile passions which big-city life had awakened anew in his brain" (2: 214), is inclined to abandon the relationship with the girl he loves. The passage to adulthood contains much suffering (rejection by his family) and false starts (the frivolous, unquestioning years spent with Uncle Manolo; his exploitation by Mendoza and others; his entanglement with the bizarre Lucía Población). Although Rivera is capable of malice (he guffaws at Enrique's misfortunes; he leads Mendoza into trouble; he dreams of torturing his stepmother), good nature and sensitivity to others' sufferings are Rivera's dominating traits.

The young orphan Maximina is portrayed as modest, hardworking, timid, and ingenuous; her happiness depends on Rivera's treatment of her. Maximina is deeply religious; indeed, she plans to take religious vows if Rivera will not wed her. Rivera, however, continuing the teaching of *Marta y María*, attacks convent life:

> I am not in favor of convents. One can only practice the finest of Christian virtues—charity and sacrifice of self for others—in society. Of what use are all the virtues that a young woman can acquire if they remain hidden within four walls and if the world never obtains any benefit from them? The only nuns whom I full-heartedly respect and admire are the sisters of charity. (2: 174)

The leading characters in the novel can be divided into two classes: those who need power, which they use to bully others (the snobbish Uncle Bernardo, the rancorous Angela Guevara, the priest Don Juan Vigil, the laundress Petra, the despotic Anita, Maximina's aunt Rosalía), and their highly sensitive victims (Rivera, Rivera's father, the vivacious Julia, the innocent Maximina, Maximina's father, whose conscientiousness drove him to suicide). The drive for power in the first group can be stronger than affection; thus, Angela Guevara, like the Teresa of *José*, mistreats the child she loves. A warped sexuality is present in certain characters: Don Juan Vigil affects to despise the women ("porcuzas" [sows]) he lusts after; Petra despises the enslaved Miguel who in turn responds to her mixture of blows and caresses with obsessed devotion, taking pleasure in the humiliations she imposes on him;[19] Lucía Población wraps her sexual desires in the rhetoric of George Sand and seeks the stimulus of danger.

Palacio Valdés mocks all forms of inauthenticity. He parodies falsity of language: the romantic amorous rhetoric of Lucía Población, the literary commonplaces used by Rivera to woo the willing Lucía, the vacuous speeches of the Ateneo, the hollow prose of newspaper editorials, the clichés of the letter in which Uncle Manolo announces his marriage. Palacio Valdés also attacks a sterile emphasis on appearance, such as Manolo's obsession with clothing.

Selfishness and lack of generosity are marked targets of Palacio Valdés's ire. Rivera scorns the self-seeking and emotional hardness of the middle and upper classes of Madrid. He also indignantly protests the fickle and unjust behavior of bullfight *aficionados* who insult and physically mistreat the aging El Cigarrero on his attempt to return to the bullring.

However, Rivera does not meet only with disillusionment. He finds two freezing, starving children late at night on a Madrid street. His generosity in feeding them is echoed by the restaurant waiters who rush to feed the waifs and by the restaurant owner who refuses to accept payment for an act of charity. Rivera's disgust at the mother's treatment of her children is reproved by Facundo Hojeda, who indicates the miserable circumstances in which single mothers live; Hojeda himself devotes his time to helping the destitute. Valentín's protection of his niece Maximina is another example of disinterested sacrifice. Further insight is provided by contact with bullfighters who, to Rivera's surprise and unlike practitioners of the liberal professions, respect each other's labors and refrain from backbiting (2: 84). El Cigarrero's sober dignity in the face of a hostile crowd is exemplary, all the more so when his brother is killed in the same *corrida*. Rivera himself is not emotionally incapacitated by his childhood deprivation; he loves his half-sister Julia; he instinctively recognizes the innocence and true affection of Maximina.

Riverita is also a comic novel. Frequently, Palacio Valdés uses an aptly-chosen ironic phrase to undercut the pretensions of pompous characters. Often, amusing incidents are described (Enrique's attempt at being a *banderillero*; Rivera's hiding from Lucía's servants; Rivera's arrest by *carabineros* [revenue agents] who suspect him of smuggling). Rivera's ill-intentioned satirical tale of the Chinese city of pigs ("Cerdópolis," 2: 193–6) would merit inclusion in any anthology of Palacio Valdés's short stories. On two occasions, Palacio Valdés narrates scenes of grotesque visual farce: the formal dinner ruined by the outrageous dispute between Enrique and Eulalia and by Rivera's uncontrolled laughter (vol. 1, chapter 3); Rivera's further laughter during an examination of conscience that provokes the priest Don Juan to chase the crucifix-bearing Miguel around the schoolroom.

With its emotional honesty, urbane presentation, balanced unfolding of plot, wealth of characters, insight into the behavior of society and individuals, and combination of comic episodes and scenes of potentially tragic import, *Riverita* is a minor masterpiece. *Riverita* recalls at times the works of other novelists: Balzac's *Comédie humaine* in its creation of a society in miniature; Flaubert's *L'Education sentimentale* (1869) in the reticence of its portrayal of the emotional development of Rivera; and Clarín's *La regenta* (1884–1885) in the scathing reproduction of imbecilic conversation, such as that of the lodging-house companions of Uncle Manolo.

But above all *Riverita* looks forward to the twentieth-century novels of Pío Baroja. Palacio Valdés's characters, like Baroja's, have an emotional directness, as they react with antipathy or sympathy toward each other. The random nature of Baroja's works—the multiplicity of characters who are introduced and then disappear, the sudden revelations of character, the wandering from social milieu to social milieu—is already present in Palacio Valdés's novel.[20] Like so many of Baroja's characters, Rivera reacts to people and situations in both emotional and intellectual manner. His search for authenticity and spontaneity of feeling, his characterization of established institutions as farcical, his alienation and sensitivity, the recognition of the psychologically perverse nature of much "love" (Petra's sadism, Rivera's masochism, the priest Don Juan's repressions, Lucía Población's romantic distortion of feeling), and the focusing on absurdity of character (Utrilla) strikingly anticipate Baroja.

Perhaps because of its sentimental portrayal of Rivera's child bride, *Maximina* found great favor with many nineteenth-century critics.[21] *Maximina* traces Rivera's marriage to the sixteen-year-old Maximina, the establishment of their household in Madrid, their marital happiness, the birth of their son, Rivera's financial ruin after imprudently guaranteeing the newspaper *La Independencia*, his abortive attempt to be elected as a liberal deputy to the Chamber of Deputies, Maximina's illness and death, and Rivera's final despair and search for meaning in the universe.

Maximina contains vivid sketches of social life: the jokes and quarrels of journalists, the Chamber of Deputies with its boring speeches, the revolutionary *tertulia* of Marquina, the festive celebration of the Revolution of 1868 in Madrid, a boring drama reading by a failed playwright. Political life is scathingly portrayed. At the governmental level, corruption and treachery are hidden under a mantle of affability; in the provinces, the quarrels of the two grotesque *caciques* of Serín anticipate the similarly savage portrayal in Baroja's *César o nada*.

One of the liveliest episodes of the novel relates the meeting of Enrique, now a *banderillero*, and the *chula* (woman of low social class) Manolita. Their salty repartee, her vigorous rejection of his advances, her father's initial brutality and hostility (which turns into friendship when he learns that Enrique is a devotee of the bullring), are convincingly and feelingly evoked. Despite his family's opposition, Enrique crosses class lines to wed the ignorant and innocent Manolita and, we must assume, to find happiness. Enrique enthusiastically describes the simple and inexpensive life that he and the practical and undemanding Manola share (2: 148–9). In other passages also, Palacio Valdés reveals his sympathies for the laboring classes. Rivera compares to their detriment members of the Chamber of Deputies with poor workers; Rivera, abandoned by his middle-class friends, is rescued from destitution by a printer who gives him employment as a proofreader.

Related to the respect for the values of the working classes is Rivera's increasing disillusionment with the hypocrisies and egotism of the middle classes. Rivera admires Maximina's "naturalness and modesty" (2: 12). Rivera's taste for the natural is further reflected in his insistence that his child receive as much fresh air as possible (2: 126).

The central theme of *Maximina*, like that of Flaubert's *L'Education sentimentale*, is that of the disappointment of aspirations. Uncle Bernardo, the pompous champion of propriety in *Riverita*, becomes the prey of a pathological jealousy and has to be committed to an insane asylum. The confident Uncle Manolo is now enslaved by a possessive wife. The cadet Utrilla, disappointed in love and with a grotesque sense of personal honor, shoots himself, dying in atrocious agony and regretting too late his deed. The amiable Rivera, through an act of generosity, is reduced to financial ruin and is abandoned by his self-seeking friends. The warm, high-spirited Julia is ruined by the vile machinations of an upper-class wastrel.

The religious theme of *Maximina* is developed in the closing chapters. Maximina is portrayed from the outset of the novel as deeply religious; Rivera, on the other hand, has little faith (1: 136). However, in the antepenultimate chapter of the novel Rivera explains, after contemplating the immensity of the celestial system, that love is the law of the universe and that man, separated from God, seeks the Eternal (2: 283–4). After a moment of silence, Rivera and Maximina, at Maximina's suggestion, recite the Lord's Prayer.

After Maximina's death, Rivera's religious feeling increases (2: 303). He learns "the negation of self" (2: 304). He is also, "like the Son of God in the garden of Gethsemane," shaken by doubt (2: 305–9). He contemplates the universe with horror:

Acudió a su memoria el recuerdo de algunos amigos muertos en la flor de la edad después de crueles sufrimientos; el de otros que, cansados de luchar contra la suerte, habían caído al fin rendidos en la miseria; vio los más nobles e inteligentes de ellos desempeñando humildes puestos, y encumbrados los necios y los perversos; se acordó de su buen padre, cuyos últimos años fueron amargados por una mujer soberbia y caprichosa; se acordó de su hermana, una criatura toda luz y alegría, engañada vilmente y sumida para siempre en la desgracia; recordó, en fin, a aquel ser angelical mitad de su propio ser, arrebatado al mundo cuando acababa de poner los labios en la copa de la dicha. . . .

La Creación se le presentó de pronto con un aspecto terrible; los seres devorándose los unos a los otros sin piedad; el más fuerte martirizando al más débil constantemente; unos y otros, engañados por la ilusión de la felicidad que no ha de llegar jamás para ninguno, trabajan, padecen en provecho de cada especie, éstas en provecho de otras, y así sucesivamente, hasta el infinito. El mundo, en suma, se le ofreció como una estafa inmensa, un lugar de tormento para todos los seres vivos, más cruel aún para los conscientes; la felicidad absoluta para el Todo, porque es y será eternamente; la absoluta desdicha para los individuos, porque eternamente se renovarán para padecer y morir. (2: 310–1)

(He remembered some of his friends who had died in the flower of youth after cruel suffering; others who, tired of struggling against fate, had finally fallen exhausted into poverty; he saw the most noble and intelligent of them in humble positions, and obtuse, evil people in high places; he remembered his good father, whose final years were embittered by a proud, capricious woman; he remembered his sister, a girl full of light and joy, vilely deceived and disgraced forever; he remembered, indeed, that angelical being, his other half, snatched from the world at the moment when her lips had just touched the cup of happiness. . . .

He suddenly perceived Creation in a monstrous form; beings pitilessly devouring each other; the strongest constantly torturing the weakest; all, deceived by the illusion of a happiness that none would ever know, striving and suffering for the benefit of their own species, with each species exploiting other species, and so on to infinity. The world, in short, seemed to him an immense swindle, a place of torment for all living beings, cruelest of all for those who are conscious; absolute happiness reserved for the All, which is and will be for all eternity; absolute unhappiness for individuals, condemned to eternal rebirth to suffer and to die.)

Shuddering with horror, Rivera sobs: "My God, my God! Why hast thou forsaken me?" (2: 311).

The most obvious flaws in *Maximina* are to be found in the implausibility of the portrayals of Alfonso Saavedra and Maximina herself. The "diabolical" Saavedra is a villain of melodrama, as he schemes to force his attentions on Maximina and deliberately ruins Julia. Maximina herself has her melodramatic gesture, as she threatens to stab herself to ward off the advances of Saavedra. The child-bride Maximina, deeply religious, lachrymose, timid, submissive, and utterly devoted to her paternalistic husband (who refuses to let her read such works as Balzac's *Physiologie du mariage* and who protects her from knowledge of "certain social vices") is a figure reminiscent of certain of Dickens's child heroines. Although a late-twentieth-century reader can attach little credibility to, and feel little sympathy for, such a character, Maximina was, as Palacio Valdés proclaimed in the introduction to *Páginas escogidas*, drawn from life.

Maximina is a puzzling novel in its unevenness. The sparseness of the vignette portrayals of characters and scenes, the lively dialogue that accompanies the courtship of Enrique and Manolita, the intensity of feeling with which Palacio Valdés conveys the sense that all things must pass, the tragic fates of Julia and Utrilla, and the fine irony with which Palacio Valdés compares the deeds of his characters to those of classical mythology[22] would, in themselves, make *Maximina* one of Palacio Valdés's finest works. However, there are too many pedestrian elements in the novel for it to be considered a masterpiece. The author sermonizes at length on the vulgarity of seducers; motives are explained in leaden manner; the portrayal of Saavedra is melodramatic, unconvincing, and unnecessary, as if Palacio Valdés were seeking a means to prolong the novel. The heavy emotionalism of the ending of *Maximina*, as Riverita experiences a Buddhistic revulsion against life, is conveyed in an overcharged manner repellent to the modern reader.

EL CUARTO PODER

El cuarto poder (a "novel of customs") (Madrid: Tipografía de Manuel Ginés Hernández, 1888. 2 vols.) is on the surface a comic novel, offering an affectionately ironic portrayal of the foibles of the inhabitants of a small Asturian coastal town (Sarrió) in the 1860s. At a deeper level, *El cuarto poder* is a novel of good and evil, detailing the corruption wrought in the apparently naive by selfishness, sensuality, pride, greed, and foolishness.

In part, *El cuarto poder* laments the passing of an earlier, happier way of life, that of the Asturias of Palacio Valdés's youth. At the beginning of the novel, the inhabitants of Sarrió, despite their constant and imbecilic altercations, cooperate for their mutual benefit: the theater is always filled; there are no political intrigues, since, in a commercial town, there is no interest in obtaining governmental employment; artisans preserve the customs of their ancestors in dances and *romerías*.

At times, the innocent traditions of the working classes take on a magical quality. For the ironically nostalgic narrator, the joys of the *romería* of San Antonio[23] recall a lost Arcadia or the Garden of Eden: "Man must have been created for this, and not to be accompanied in the brief days of his existence by overwhelming labors, angry vengeance, pale envy, and gnawing sadness. The tradition of Paradise is the most logical and venerable of all human traditions" (2: 166–7). In this idyllic setting, the simple songs of the girls of Sarrió have a mysterious, sacred quality: "holy maxims, mysterious, benevolent formulae which no one could touch without committing sacrilege" (2: 169).

Nevertheless, despite the occasional glimpse of a lost Paradise, life is hard for the working class of Sarrió. The good-natured seamstress Nieves must support a paralyzed mother and a wastrel brother. Another seamstress, Teresa, justifies her interest in *señoritos* (young men of the upper class): workers are drunkards and wife-beaters incapable of supporting their families; sailors are absent most of the year. The courtship by *señoritos* of working-class girls can occasionally end in marriage, as in the case of Don Rosendo's liaison with the *cigarrera* (cigar seller) Paula, of which Pablo was the subsequently-legitimized offspring. Only after many years of matrimony, however, is Doña Paula slowly admitted to middle-class society. Class competition at the weekly dance often leads to blows. The resentment of working-class males is strong; Pablo fears for his life at the hands of the jilted barber Cosmé. Contacts between the classes are not only sexual or hostile; a relationship of easy familiarity exists between the seamstresses preparing Cecilia's wedding gown and Don Rosendo's family. As in earlier novels, Palacio Valdés's sympathy for the laboring classes is manifest: he captures the sly humor of sailors; he, as narrator, extols the beauty of the girls of Sarrió; with her coarse vitality, the seamstress Valentina can terrify her seducer Pablo Belinchón.

The eccentricities of the middle classes of Sarrió are ironically noted. The cod merchant Don Rosendo Belinchón has a mania for making toothpicks; a poet has a platonic passion for obese married women; the lady-killer Pablo Belinchón can talk only of horses. Comic episodes abound: altercations interrupt the musical performance in the opening chapter; Pablo skulks in hiding for over a year from the threatened vengeance of the abandoned Valentina; a drunken, bullying mayor has the inmates of a brothel escorted to prison in their underwear; in his fear of criminals, the mayor pursues and shoots an innocent citizen.

The pompous and foolish Don Rosendo Belinchón ("our hero,"

"this great thinker)" is presented in mock-heroic terms. Like Octavio in *El señorito Octavio* and María in *Marta y María*, the pretentious Belinchón has been corrupted by literature.[24] Aping foreign ways, he introduces into his country estate trees, plants, and animals expensively imported from abroad. When the coldly condescending Duque de Tornos is received by Don Rosendo, the narrator bitterly notes that the healthy, patriarchal family dinners of the Belinchón household are replaced by foreign menus and cutlery (2: 173).

Belinchón's ingenuous and self-centered belief in progress ("those romantic sentiments of progress, that love for the moral and material improvement of his birth place" [2: 190]) leads him to found a newspaper, *El Faro de Sarrió*. Although the narrator satirizes the cliché-ridden prose of the newspaper and the simplistic policies of its editorial columns, the vicious personal attacks leveled in *El Faro de Sarrió* and its rival *El Joven Sarriense* destroy the social fabric of Sarrió.[25] Private life no longer exists and the town is soon divided into two warring bands. Street brawling, political turmoil, vendettas, jealousy, and spite become the order of the day.

The destruction of civic harmony occasioned by the founding of *El Faro de Sarrió* is paralleled by a struggle between the forces of good and those of evil in Belinchón's own family. Belinchón has two daughters, Cecilia and Venturita. The young engineer, Gonzalo de las Cuevas, trapped by his own sensuality, breaks his engagement to Cecilia to marry the pert young Venturita. Gonzalo's uncle solemnly warns that God himself cannot help the man who is false to his word (1: 237).[26]

For Gonzalo, Cecilia represents, emotionally and intellectually, "the angel" (1: 220). Gonzalo's uncle extols her virtues: "the poetry of woman, which consists of exquisite sensitivity, resignation, sweetness, self-sacrifice, and not the ephemeral disposition of form, as impetuous youth believes" (1: 234). Even after Gonzalo marries her sister Venturita, Cecilia, reserved, long-suffering, devoted to serving others, silently continues to love her former fiancé, for whom she becomes "a sister and a mother always watchful to spare him any annoyance, to clear the thorns from his path" (2: 180).

Cecilia's inner suffering receives dramatic visual expression. She sheds a solitary tear on learning that Gonzalo is to wed her sister, a tear that an angel carries to God (1: 250). She weeps two tears when the insensitive Gonzalo urges her to marry another (2: 95). Only at the end of the novel can Cecilia give vent to her suppressed love, as she cuts locks from the hair of Gonzalo's corpse, places tresses of her own hair in the dead Gonzalo's hands, and bathes his face with the kisses she could never tender during his life. In the closing lines of *El cuarto poder*, Cecilia, Gonzalo's "true spouse," faints from excessive grief: "The spouse, his one and only true spouse, could not in the end bear such pain and fell unconscious to the ground" (2: 338).

Venturita represents "the demon" (1: 221). Mendacious, capricious, superficial, and sensual ("a true odalisque" [2: 9]; "a capricious sultaness" [2: 90]), a neglectful mother, she is totally indifferent to the feelings of others. There is an almost vampirelike quality about her as, on her honeymoon, she bites Gonzalo and sucks his blood. A reader of French novels, obsessed with court life, she seduces (or is seduced by) the Duque de Tornos. (The Duque de Tornos, a cold, rancorous, spiteful, cowardly cuckold, personifies evil and falsity.)

The closing chapters of the novel are increasingly melodramatic as the extent of the triumph of evil becomes apparent. Cecilia sacrifices her reputation in the eyes of Gonzalo to prevent his discovery of Venturita's adultery.[27] Doña Paula discovers her daughter Venturita's guilt, becomes paralyzed, and dies. In a nightmare scene, the madly jealous Gonzalo furiously rides through the darkened countryside to discover confirmation of his wife's adultery and his own dishonor.

The final chapter of *El cuarto poder* is one of the most powerful ever penned by Palacio Valdés. It begins on a note of exceeding violence, as Gonzalo, rejecting the opportunity to kill the offending aristocrat in a duel, pummels the duke almost to the point of death. Then, with considerable psychological acuity, Palacio Valdés portrays Gonzalo's continued enslavement to his erring wife. Clinging to her memory, preserving around him her clothes, and imagining her presence everywhere, the obsessed Gonzalo hopes still to have the chance to pardon her. Cecilia, fearful of Gonzalo's intentions, hides the ammunition for his rifles and revolver. The news of Venturita's flight from the convent in which she is incarcerated to join the duke leads in Gonzalo first to feverish excitement and then depression. Finally, after three days, beset by hallucinations that his wife is calling him, Gonzalo goes out in the rainy night to the pier. After temporarily forgetting his project while watching a ship enter port, he recalls his purpose, attaches a weight to his body, and drowns himself.

The importance of *El cuarto poder* lies not so much in its satirical portrayal of the squabbles of a small town but above all in its dramatic and powerful depiction of stupidity, obsession, and moral depravity. Although occasionally anticlerical,[28] *El cuarto poder* is nonetheless a profoundly moral work, in the sense that the *romans-feuilletons* of Eugène Sue, with their titanic battles between good and evil, are moral novels. Biblical parallels are established: the simple joys of the *romería* recall the innocence of Eden Lost; Gonzalo and Venturita represent the roles of Samson and Delilah (2: 10). Good characters (the gently-loving and ever-constant Cecilia, Doña Paula who, despite her humble origins, has a sense of self-worth, Don Melchor with his ethical sense) exist but fail to prevail over the forces of evil (represented in the Duque de Tornos and Venturita). Gonzalo, enslaved by his sensual passion for his indifferent and vicious wife,[29] rejects all that is noble in his life freely to choose evil. The corruption of evil rapidly spreads: Gonzalo's enslavement leads to the unhappiness of Cecilia, the death of Doña Paula, Gonzalo's suicide, and the painful bereavement of Don Melchor. Similarly, Rosendo's failure, in the conduct of his journal, to exercise restraint and to respect others, leads to family suffering, the plunging of Sarrió into spiteful vendettas, and the death of the benign mayor Don Roque.

LA HERMANA SAN SULPICIO

The first edition of *La hermana San Sulpicio* (Madrid: Tipografía de Manuel G. Hernández, 1889. 2 vols.) is preceded by a "Prólogo," over seventy pages in length, in which Palacio Valdés resumes his aesthetic theories. Artistic skill, Palacio Valdés believes, is the fruit of "reflection and experience." A work of art conveys, through feeling, the Absolute. Art, based on a divine principle (the idea of the beautiful), can only be moral. Artistic sincerity is an absolute condition for any literary work. The principal cause of "decadence" in modern literature is *efectismo*, which Palacio Valdés defines as the awakening at any cost in the reader of strong, violent emotions. French naturalism offers too limited a definition of realism. In the novel, characterization takes precedence over plot (rather than the reverse situation, as in the *folletín*). Palacio Valdés, regretting past sins, now seeks to avoid violent effects in his novels. To psychological analysis (the procedure of the Goncourt brothers), Palacio Valdés prefers portraying a character's effect on the external world, that is, his deeds and words. Endings to novels, whether happy or unhappy, should restore a moral equilibrium. Palacio Valdés favors a *humorismo* that, while stemming from the artist's imagination, respects noble sentiments. He takes issue with the French naturalists for stressing the bestial components of human nature, rather than progress "toward what is rational, conscious, and freely-chosen" (1: lxxi).

Palacio Valdés's exposition of his aesthetic principles and his observations on the modern novel are urbanely presented, well-reasoned, and the result of careful thought. Worthy of note are his emphasis on the Idea (the debt to Hegel is obvious), his condemnation of *efectismo* and of the narrowness of French naturalism, and his stress on the moral nature of literature.

The "Prólogo" has never been reprinted.

La hermana San Sulpicio, despite initial slow sales, was to prove Palacio Valdés's most popular work. The novel, of "Andalusian customs," is set in Andalusia, the first four chapters in the spa town of Marmolejo and the remaining chapters in Sevilla. Palacio Valdés, suffering from intestinal troubles, had first visited Marmolejo in 1884; he spent a month visiting Sevilla in 1886; the novel itself was written in Asturias.[30] Gloria Bermúdez ("Sister San Sulpicio") had already been introduced to the reader in *Riverita* as the favorite teacher of Maximina (*Riverita*, 2: 199).

The first-person narrator of *La hermana San Sulpicio* is Ceferino Sanjurjo, a young *gallego* (Galician) who has trained as a doctor but who fancies himself above all as a lyrical and descriptive poet. In Marmolejo, Sanjurjo meets two young nuns, who are persuaded to dance *seguidillas*. Sanjurjo follows Sister San

Sulpicio (Gloria Bermúdez) to her native Sevilla, ascertains that she has not taken permanent vows, uses political influence to have her returned to her home, courts her despite the opposition of her mother and the administrator of the family fortune (Don Oscar), and, vigorously overcoming obstacles, after a very short delay weds her. Sanjurjo presents his story as one of total success. An "outsider," he penetrates the society of Sevilla, plucks a highly attractive bride (one whose virginity is guaranteed[31]) from the clutches of an order of teaching nuns and a hostile family, obtains a magnificent dowry, vanquishes his enemies, establishes himself with his bride in Madrid, and can regard with disdain his poverty-stricken dramatist friends.

La hermana San Sulpicio offers an outsider's vision of Andalusia. Sanjurjo's evocation of Córdoba and of his approach to Sevilla is self-consciously poetic and literary (1: 104–11). "Oh, qué árabe, qué árabe es todo esto!" ("Oh, how very Arabic all this is!"), Sanjurjo excitedly exclaims on his arrival in Sevilla (1: 114). The exotic—for a *gallego*—attractions of Sevilla are numerous: the blinding sun, the crowded, narrow streets, the friendliness of the people, the Andalusian accent (which Sanjurjo endeavors to reproduce in the text), the ready wit and repartee of the Andalusians, and the charms of a river excursion. The greatest attraction, of course, is Gloria Bermúdez, with her dark eyes and hair, her vehement, passionate soul, her imperious energy, her childlike sensibilities and jealousies, and her ardent devotion to Sanjurjo. The prospect of courting Gloria through the *reja* (window grating) sends Sanjurjo, a poet and a Northerner, into imaginative (and self-consciously ironical) transports:

Gloria me quería, me daba una cita, y esta cita tenía el singular atractivo para un poeta y un hombre del Norte de ser a la reja. ¡La reja! ¿Verdad que este nombre ejerce cierta fascinación, despierta en la fantasía un enjambre de pensamientos dulces y vagos, como si fuese el símbolo o el centro del amor y la poesía? ¿Quién es el que, por poca imaginación que tenga, no ha soñado con un coloquio amoroso al pie de la reja en una noche de luna? Estos coloquios y estas noches tienen además la incalculable ventaja de que pueden describirse sin haberlos visto. No hay mosquito lírico de los que zumban en las provincias meridionales o septentrionales de España que no haya expuesto sus impresiones acerca de ellos y armado un tinglado más o menos armonioso con los dulces acordes de la guitarra, el aroma de los nardos, la luz de la luna esparciendo sus hebras finísimas de plata sobre la ventana, el cielo salpicado de estrellas, el azahar, los ojos fascinadores de la doncella, su aliento cálido, perfumado, etc., etc. Yo mismo, en calidad de poeta descriptivo y colorista, había barajado en más de una ocasión estos lugares comunes de la estética andaluza, con el aplauso de mis convecinos. (2: 17)

(Gloria loved me, she had arranged to meet me, and this meeting had the singular attraction for a man from the North of being at the *reja*. The *reja*! Isn't it true that the word itself fascinates and awakens in one's fantasy a swarm of sweet and vague thoughts, as if it were the symbol of love and poetry? Who, however little imagination he may possess, has not dreamed of an amorous colloquy beneath the *reja* on a moon-lit night? Furthermore, these colloquies and nights have the incalculable advantage that they can be described without ever having been seen. There is no lyrical insect buzzing in the southern or northern provinces of Spain who has not poured forth his impressions and cobbled together something more or less harmonious out of the sweet chords of the guitar, the aroma of spikenards, the light of the moon scattering its delicate silver threads on the window, the star-strewn sky, the scent of orange blossom, the maiden's fascinating eyes, her warm and perfumed breath, etc., etc. I myself, as a descriptive, colorist poet, had on more than one occasion shuffled together these commonplaces of Andalusian aesthetics, to the applause of my neighbors.)

The "timid," almost fastidious Sanjurjo is struck by other aspects of Andalusian life. He notes the cleanliness of workers' houses in Marmolejo, which he compares with the "dirty, stinking hovels inhabited by farm workers in my native Galicia" (1: 21). A visit to the tobacco factory brings Sanjurjo into contact with the uninhibited, brazen female workers. In the working-class district of Triana, he witnesses poverty, drunkenness, and violence. Chapter 13 describes the customs of barbarians and exemplifies the *efectismo* that Palacio Valdés had claimed to abhor in the prologue to the novel. The Conde de Padul takes the horrified Sanjurjo to a tavern filled with whores and drunken ruffians; with atrocious bravado, the Count uses his dagger to nail his own hand and that of an Englishman to a table.

As narrator of the novel, Ceferino Sanjurjo is self-consciously composing literature. He refers to the act of narration (1: 7), converses with the reader (1: 113), and—as in a "novel"—draws attention to the "veracity" of his tale (2: 160, 283). At times, Sanjurjo imitates Cervantes by confusing the boundaries between "novel" and "life." Thus, Sanjurjo informs Sister Saint Sulpicio that she is described in the recently published "novel" of Maximina (1: 47, 49). Later, he declares, with ironic truth: "What's happening to us, Gloria, seems like a novel" (2: 19).

Ceferino Sanjurjo presents himself as possessing a dual nature: he is a poet and he is a *gallego*. As a poet, he offers conventional "cultural" evocations of Andalusia. (See, for example, his effusive evocation of the meaning of the *reja*, quoted above.) His poetic fatuity is self-evident: his experiences provide the material for publications; the titles of the poems he reads to the Casino exemplify mediocrity. As a "poet," he imitates Zorrilla's Don Juan Tenorio in believing that his love of a nun "was precisely what brought me nearer to God and offered a sure path to salvation" (1: 152).

Sanjurjo's "poetic" personality is superficial and serves in the novel to provide the occasion for self-mockery. Sanjurjo's *gallego* stubbornness and closeness with money, on the other hand, are much more deeply rooted in his character. Sanjurjo's stinginess with tips is merely comical. Much more important are Sanjurjo's positive traits: his practicality and prudence in matters that affect his vital interests, his astuteness in dealing with devious people, and his readiness to take decisive action. Thus, Sanjurjo energetically prevents the kidnapping of Gloria by appealing to an anticlerical mob and to the force of the law; skill in negotiation and firmness of character win Sanjurjo his bride and her substantial dowry. Sanjurjo's intelligence is manifest both in his ability as a writer and in his verbal wit that parallels that of the *sevillanos*.

Sanjurjo is more than a shallow poet and a calculating *gallego*. Despite the irony implicit in the first-person narrative, Sanjurjo convincingly portrays his anxiety-ridden sensitivities as a lover. He suffers alternately elation, jealousy, loneliness, and despair. Under nervous strain, he maliciously strikes at his friend Villa's sensitivities. When thwarted, he desires vengeance. At times, he throws caution to the winds. Believing Gloria to have jilted him, he denounces her as a "whore" (2: 100). Imprudently, he strikes both the bandit El Naranjero and his malevolent rival Daniel Suárez. He is emotionally shaken when Gloria sings: "Yo sentí un vivo escalofrío, un fuerte estremecimiento, como si hubiera tocado en el botón de una máquina eléctrica" (I felt a sudden chill, a sharp jolt, as if she had pressed the switch of an electrical machine) (2: 190). After her song, Sanjurjo weeps, as his love becomes mixed with a desire for death (2: 191).

There are further complexities in Sanjurjo's character. Befitting his role as narrator, he enjoys power; thus, he finds the motion of a train to be intoxicating, communicating "the sensation of power and triumph" (1: 103). He recognizes the sensual attraction of the outline of Sister San Sulpicio's thigh as she dances in her nun's costume (1: 99). Although enamored, Sanjurjo is no fool. He questions whether Gloria Bermúdez is too frivolous to make a good wife; the army officer Villa explains that *sevillanas* do indeed make excellent spouses; for Villa, the women of Galicia, despite their surface timidity, are less trustworthy (2: 264).[32]

Gloria Bermúdez possesses depths that are barely explored in the novel. Despite her wit and outgoing good humor, there are suggestions of a darker side to her soul. As an unhappy pupil of the nuns, she had suffered nervous attacks, had physically assaulted a teaching sister, and had attempted suicide (2: 75). Her jealousy when she suspects Sanjurjo of infidelity is excessive (2: 79–80). There is also considerable strength in Gloria. She is determined to achieve happiness in love; she therefore refuses to feign sadness when expelled from her mother's house (2: 261–2). In the final chapter, Gloria, in an act of vengeance, deliberately scandalizes the nuns.

Other characters in the novel are unifaceted. Curiously, in a novel that supposedly extols Andalusian customs, the Andalusians portrayed in *La hermana San Sulpicio* are for the most part evil or eccentric. The *malagueño* (man from Málaga) Daniel Suárez is an ill-spoken, cynical dowry hunter. The Anguita sisters are spendthrifts who behave without decorum as they anxiously seek spouses. Their father is a maniacal collector of art. The Count of Padul is a cynical and ignorant wastrel; his daughter Isabel is superficial. The priest Don Sabino has rotting teeth and is coarse and venal. Doña Tula, Gloria's mother, is hypocritical and false.

Among the eccentrics portrayed in the novel are the inventor who keeps the hotel in Marmolejo and the arrogant and complaining Catalan Llagostera.[33] Some characters are physically deformed. The energetic lodging-house keeper, Matilde, is tiny; her brother Eduardito is gigantic. Don Oscar ("cíclope-enano") is a dwarf with a massively developed upper body.

As in *El cuarto poder*, humiliation and slavery to passion are major themes. Gloria suffers extravagant humiliations in the convent. Isabel, the Condesa de Padul, scorns and toys with her suitor Villa. Eduardito is obsessed with his love for an ugly, older woman. The thirty-year-old Raquel Torres mistreats and insults her kindly octogenarian husband. (Sanjurjo interprets her premature death as "a true sarcasm of destiny, if not a tremendous lesson of Providence" [2: 199].) Elenita takes pleasure in the amorous sufferings of her teacher, the priest Don Alejandro. The more Paca's parents beat her, the more determined she is to marry the wastrel Joaquín Fierabrás (2: 129–30). In her turn, Paca cruelly beats her husband, who in his drunkenness crawls about the floor meowing like a cat (2: 135–7). In chapter 13, excessive consumption of alcohol contributes to the degraded behavior of the rogues and prostitutes and to Sanjurjo's loss of self-control and resort to violence.

La hermana San Sulpicio has been intelligently studied by Daniel Henri Pageaux. Pageaux emphasizes the ironic and literary nature of the novel and its conscious recourse to the phrases and stereotypes of the "popular novel" or *feuilleton*. Thus, characters are presented in terms of good and evil or are caricatured. In place of a "romantic" or "costumbrista" Sevilla, Palacio Valdés presents "a postromantic Andalusia, seen through a temperament which is both poetic and realist"; rather than treating social problems, Palacio Valdés substitutes "a land of carefree joy in life and of 'popular' good humor."[34]

With its fast-moving plot, deftly-sketched characters, facility of expression, scenes of exotic Andalusia, and tale of successful young love, *La hermana San Sulpicio* achieved a well-deserved popularity. Despite its lightness of tone, *La hermana San Sulpicio* continues the criticism of values based on literature that Palacio Valdés had begun in *El señorito Octavio*. The ironic self-conscious narrator, the narrator's deliberate pretense to ingenuousness, the tongue-in-cheek recourse, as Pageaux has so well demonstrated, to the stereotypes of the popular novel, undercut ostensible "romantic" and "realistic" elements in the novel.[35] The themes of sexual manipulation and enslavement, prominent in *El señorito Octavio*, *Marta y María*, *Riverita*, *Maximina*, and *El cuarto poder*, appear in *La hermana San Sulpicio* in minor characters as an ironic counterbalance to the "healthy" love of Sanjurjo and Gloria.

4

The Novels of the 1890s

P<small>ALACIO</small> Valdés's first two novels of the 1890s, *La espuma* (1890) and *La fe* (1892), were attacked by critics as showing the marked influence of French naturalism. In *La espuma*, Palacio Valdés vigorously satirizes the vulgarity and immorality of the upper classes; the novel is anticlerical in its hostility to the religious practices of Madrid society and reveals considerable class feeling in its rendering of the sufferings of miners. *La fe* is equally anticlerical in its portrayal of a hypocritical, ignorant, and violent clergy and the sexually-frustrated, neurotic spinsters who vie for their attention. The spiritual progress of the protagonist of the novel, the naive and idealistic Padre Gil, from religious doubt to mystical certainty is unconvincingly drawn.

El maestrante (1893), with its stark portrayal of jealousy, madness, sexual perversion, torture, rape, and murder, is the most melodramatic of Palacio Valdés's novels. *El origen del pensamiento* (1893) treats affectionately the eccentricities and mores of middle-class Madrid. The novel teaches balance and the avoidance of excess, whether in behavior or in speech.

Los majos de Cádiz (1896), in its exquisite balance and control, is probably Palacio Valdés's finest work. The novel relates, with considerable psychological acuity, the jealousies and emotional degradation of working-class couples in nineteenth-century Cádiz. An air of transcendental magic pervades the work, which ends happily as selfless love conquers neurotic passion. *La alegría del capitán Ribot* (1899) also portrays the triumph of conscience, although in much more exaggerated fashion than in *Los majos de Cádiz*. As in *La hermana San Sulpicio*, the idealism of the novel is undercut by the ironic, first-person narrator. The demonstration of impeccable moral behavior would lend credence, at least in so far as *La alegría del capitán Ribot* is concerned, to Guadalupe Gómez-Ferrer's thesis that Palacio Valdés underwent a progressive spiritual crisis in the 1890s, culminating in his "conversion" to Catholicism in 1899 and his marriage to Manuela Vela y Gil.

La espuma

La espuma (1890), like José María de Pereda's La Montálvez (1888) and the Jesuit Luis Coloma's best-selling Pequeñeces (1890), offers a satirical and hostile vision of contemporary upper-class life in Madrid. The novel is centered around the family of the wealthy banker Antonio Salabert, the Duque de Requena. Salabert is a low-born, boorish bully. Grotesquely avaricious and ill-mannered—he habitually expectorates on the carpets of others' houses—Salabert is treated with obsequious sycophancy by a swarm of "well-bred" hangers-on. His illegitimate daughter Clementina is cold and capricious; the tortures she endured as a child at the hands of her cruel mother explain in part her savage temper and overweening pride.

Madrid society is scathingly portrayed. The young wastrels of the "Club of the Savages" are self-centered and ignorant; they affect, following their British models, an ironic disdain for all feeling; they live on credit or on the manipulation of gullible women; they compete for the dowries of the daughters of the nouveaux riches.

A strong vein of social criticism pervades La espuma. (The title was appropriately translated into English for the New York edition as "Scum.") The "aristocracy" squander money to maintain appearances or for sensual gratification. In obviously nationalistic vein, Palacio Valdés emphasizes that flowers and food for banquets are expressly brought from France for the pleasures of a greedy and vulgar society. Salabert's wealth is derived from swindling and from the exploitation of workers. Contrasted with the porcine appetites of Salabert's dependents are the workers in the mines of Riosa, prematurely aged, malnourished, paid starvation wages, and suffering from mercury poisoning. Remedies—better pay and food, healthier living quarters, elimination of child labor, reduced working hours—are proposed by a socialist doctor, to the embarrassment of Salabert's guests who visit the mines.

The anticlericalism of *Marta y María* is equally evident in *La espuma*. A pious lady reacts to the hideous sufferings of the miners by paying for a new costume for the baby Jesus in the local church. The doctor who denounces the greed of the rich and the sufferings of the poor is a socialist, not a Catholic. The Lenten observances of the upper classes are treated satirically. The society priest Ortega preaches to the assembled aristocrats the connection of religion, property, and tradition. Palacio Valdés comments with scathing sarcasm on the spiritual practices of the pious gathering:

Al cabo, la piadosa reunión se dispersó. Todas aquellas almas biena-venturadas y temerosas de Dios salieron del palacio de Alcudia y se dirigieron a sus moradas, donde les aguardaba la copa de tortuga humeante, el salmón con salsa mayonesa, las ricas ensaladas de col de Bruselas y las apetitosas *bouchées de crevettes*. La oración de quietud, aquellas horas de unión contemplativa con la Divinidad, les había abierto de par en par el apetito. No hay nada que vigorice el estómago como la convicción de tener de su parte al Omnipotente y la esperanza fundada de que más allá de esta vida, si hay fuego y tormentos eternos para los pelagatos y descamisados que se atreven a discutirle, para las familias cristianas, esto es, para las que tienen religión y propiedad y antepasados, no puede haber más que bienan-danza, una eternidad de salmón con mayonesa y de *crevettes à la parisienne*. (*La espuma* [Barcelona: Imprenta de Heinrich y Com-pañia, 1890], 162–3)

(Finally, the pious gathering dispersed. All those saintly, God-fearing souls left the Alcudia Palace and journeyed home, where a bowl of steaming turtle soup, salmon with mayonnaise, rich salads of brus-sels sprouts, and appetizing *bouchées de crevettes* awaited them. The prayer for quietude and the hours of contemplative union with the Divinity had given them an enormous appetite. Nothing invigorates the stomach so much as the conviction that the Almighty is on one's side and the well-founded hope that in the next life, even if there is eternal fire and torment for the ragamuffins and riffraff who have the audacity to doubt, for Christian families, that is, for those who have religion and property and ancestors, there can only be bliss, an eter-nity of salmon with mayonnaise and *crevettes à la parisienne*.)

Like Pereda and Coloma, Palacio Valdés offers a strongly moralistic vision. Sexual disorder degrades. The scheming widow Pepa Frías seduces her daughter's husband. Clementina leads the ingenuous and neurasthenic Raimundo Alcázar into debt and the abandonment of his studies, before casting him aside for a lover with political connections. Above all, the sensual enslavement of Salabert by the lower-class tart Amparo ("la malagueña") offers a grim cautionary tale. By the end of the novel, Amparo has looted Salabert's fortune and the banker—the victim, it is hinted, of syphilis (2: 262)—has been reduced to imbecility.

Despite the force of Palacio Valdés's feeling—his hatred of the moral indifference of the rich, his awareness of the sufferings of the workers[1]—*La espuma* is a flawed novel. Its strength lies in Palacio Valdés's power to evoke the grotesque, such as his evocation of the gross appetites and vulgarity of Salabert and his portrayal of the grand society ball in which the whore Amparo makes an unwelcome entry. The novel lacks the classical concision of Palacio Valdés's major works (*Marta y María*, *El idilio de un enfermo*, and *Los majos de Cádiz*). There are too many characters, insufficiently differentiated; the presentation is too episodic and casual. The fundamental failure, however, derives from Palacio Valdés's lack of sympathy for the society he portrays. Palacio Valdés is alienated from his subject; the reader likewise finds the crassness and superficiality of the characters of *La espuma* of less than riveting interest.[2]

LA FE

Palacio Valdés's next novel, *La fe* (1892), is also a literary failure. The novel is set in the same coastal region of Asturias as *José* and *El cuarto poder*, in the fishing village of Peñascosa, near the port of Sarrió. *La fe*, however, unlike *José*, offers little treatment of local customs. The only specifically Asturian element is the cold and rainy winter climate. The petty jealousies and local pride of the inhabitants of Peñascosa, who consider themselves far superior to the townsfolk of Sarrió, are those of any small Spanish town.

La fe resembles *La espuma* in its satirical portrayal of contemporary society—the clergy of Peñascosa and their female followers—and in its heavy anticlericalism.[3] With the exceptions of the protagonist of the novel, Padre Gil, and the self-sacrificing and joyful Padre Norberto who labors to redeem the prostitutes of Peñascosa, the clergymen of Peñascosa are backbiting, envious, hypocritical, ignorant, manipulative, and violent. The pious ladies of Peñascosa ("nervous virgins and mystic widows" [La Fe (Madrid: Manuel Ginés Hernández, 1892), 214]) vie to pamper their favored confessors. The narrator refers with heavy sarcasm to the gatherings of self-satisfied priests and obedient flock, which offer "an approximate vision of what must surely be the kingdom of God on earth" (101).

The pettiness of the clergy of Peñascosa forms the background for the vicissitudes of the young and idealistic Padre Gil. From his arrival in Peñascosa, Gil attracts women to the confessional, thereby incurring the jealousy of his fellow-priests. The ardent Gil had been instructed in the ways of the mystics by his teacher, the rector of the seminary of Lancia. In his desire to imitate Christ, he faces two spiritual challenges: the conversion of the misanthropic atheist Alvaro Montesinos and the guidance of a possible "saint," Obdulia, the spinster daughter of the lascivious hunchback Osuna.

Alvaro, crushed by the cruel and joyless upbringing he had received from his pious father and devastated when his beautiful young bride had eloped with his money and a lover, avoids the company of humankind. Accepting the doctrine of Schopenhauer, Alvaro holds the world to be composed of suffering and egotism, with the individual the powerless instrument of the blind needs of the species: "Inside the universe there lies concealed a cunning, perverse force, driving and directing us towards a goal unknown to us and which has nothing to do with us" (131). Since we are the creatures of instinct, moral judgment is irrelevant (290–1). Man has no choice over his fate: "My wife was born with claws to tear. I was born with a soft heart made to be torn apart. It would be a contradiction were she not to claw and I not to be clawed" (292). Love is an illusion, serving Nature's need to procreate (294).

Attempting to counter Alvaro's arguments, Gil, who obtains his bishop's reluctant permission to consult forbidden books, reads a Life of Jesus based on modern criticism and studies science and theological justifications of faith. The result is doubt, loss of religious belief, and—following his reading of Kant—the realization of the impossibility of philosophical certitude. Unable to convert Alvaro, who dies a dignified unbeliever, Gil is tormented by a scepticism that he abandons only at the end of the novel when he achieves the mystic's blissful serenity and indifference to worldly affairs.[4]

Gil not only fails to change Alvaro's beliefs: in his Christian Quixotry and ignorance of the world, he causes Alvaro great spiritual pain when he ingenuously abets Alvaro's wife in her evil scheme to pass the night under her husband's roof in order to legitimize her unborn child. Gil is equally naive in his failure to recognize the hysterical sexual frustration of the false "saint" Obdulia, who manipulates him to accompany her on a journey to a convent where she will take religious vows. Instead, she attempts the seduction (or rather, in her violence, the violation) of the shocked and embarrassed Gil. Later, abetted by the hypocritical Padre Narciso, she accuses Gil of rape. The unfortunate priest, by now indifferent to worldly concerns, is condemned to a lengthy prison term.

Padre Gil's encounter with Alvaro is presented seriously. The narrator treats Gil's relationship with Obdulia, on the other hand, with irony. Gil at first shows toward her "that rancorous scorn characteristic of all the mystics" (63). Soon he realizes that she is a possible saint, "a Christian with a zealous heart like his, touched by divine love and thirsting after perfection" (63), "one of those souls he had only seen described in the works of the mystics" (68). He takes the "virtuous maiden" as a spiritual model, as a second Saint Teresa (70–1). Her numerous mortifications are compared, in their variety, with those of the sexually jaded who search new sensations: "Many and diverse were those [mortifications] that the valorous maiden imposed on her flesh in the space of a few months. Just as debauched men exhaust their imagination in the search for new pleasures, so also did she excel in inventing varied torments for her delicate body" (71–2).

La fe contains too many disparate elements to convey any sense of coherence. The satire of clerical hypocrisies is effective, if superficial. The tale is naturalistic in its dwelling on Obdulia's sexual hysteria and fantasies and in its hints of pathological abnormality in the cases of Gil (whose mother, holding the baby Gil in her arms, had committed suicide) and Obdulia (who suffers from nose bleeds and fainting fits, who had spent two years paralyzed as a teenager, and who had a craving to eat chalk, and who, like María in *Marta y María*, burns her own arm by way of mortification). Furthermore, the novel lacks verisimilitude. Gil's failures—his attempt to reconcile Alvaro with his wife, his absurd elopement with Obdulia—are caused by his ignorance and lack of common sense. The consequences—the ruin of Alvaro's life, Gil's condemnation to a lengthy prison term—are disproportionate. The summaries of Gil's studies are tedious and out of place in a novel. The ending—Gil's redemption by grace that restores his faith—is stated rather than demonstrated and has little connection with the rest of the novel.[5]

Although *La fe* lacks coherence as a novel, it offers a curious link to other literary works. Jesús Fernández Alvarez has convincingly established Palacio Valdés's debt to Henry Fielding; Don Restituto, the priest who devotes himself to agriculture, is based on Parson Trulliber of *Joseph Andrews*.[6] Obdulia, with her false piety and hysteria, resembles María of *Marta y María*. The "science" of the criminologists who measure Padre Gil's cranium in prison is as irrelevant as that of the criminologists in chapter 6 of Galdós's *La desheredada*; their science anticipates also that of the crazed Don Pantaleón Sánchez of *El origen del pensamiento* (1893). Many years later, Palacio Valdés would also return to an ironic account of a Quixotic saintly figure in *Santa Rogelia* (1926).

The universe portrayed in *La fe* resembles that of certain novels of Leopoldo Alas, Benito Pérez Galdós, and Pío Baroja. The hypocrisies of the priests, the dangerous relations between priest and penitent in the confessional, and the hints of a Manichean universe in which evil may well triumph refer the reader immediately to *La regenta*, published in 1884 and 1885 by Palacio Valdés's childhood friend Leopoldo Alas. The portrayal, ironic and ambiguous, of the Quixotic Padre Gil obviously suggested, as Peter A. Bly has convincingly demonstrated, to Galdós the character of Nazarín (*Nazarín*, 1895).[7] The Schopenhauerian views of Alvaro will be reproduced, again in the context of a debate, in the views of Iturrioz in Baroja's *El árbol de la ciencia* (1911). Furthermore, both *La fe* and *El árbol de la ciencia* exemplify—in Obdulia's sexual hysteria, in the death of Baroja's

Lulu—the workings of the unconscious to satisfy Nature's imperative to reproduce the species.

El maestrante

El maestrante (1893) is the most melodramatic of Palacio Valdés's novels. Set in Lancia in the 1850s, the novel offers excellent *costumbrista* sketches of middle-class life in a small Asturian town, with portrayals of balls, of *tertulias* (social gatherings) in which young ladies entice future husbands, of a wedding feast, and of a cruel *cencerrada* (burlesque serenade) to protest an ill-assorted marriage. Palacio Valdés presents minor characters by stressing one or two eccentric facets: the effeminacy and malice of the aging hermaphrodite Manuel Antonio ("el marica de Sierra" [the queer from Sierra]); the coarseness of the *indiano* Don Santos who wishes to marry the wealthy young beauty Fernanda Estrada-Rosa; the grotesque ignorance of the servant and reputed bear-slayer Manín; the obsession with cards of Jaime Moro; the fierce insanity of the Carlist Barón de los Oscos and his drinking companion Fray Diego; the childishness of the ancient sisters Meré; the phobia against the military of the retired bureaucrat Cristóbal Mateo. Two comic characters are obviously derived from *costumbrista* literature, although with their roles confused: the *gallego* Saleta, whose exaggerated tales are worthy of Estévanez Calderón's Manolito Vázquez; and the *malagueño* Valero, who champions common sense in a heavy Andalusian accent.

The boredom of provincial life is relieved by malicious gossip and cruel practical jokes. With its portrayal of monomaniacs, with its appreciation of the crucial role of money in matrimonial arrangements, and with its sinister opening scene, which plunges us into the world of the *folletín*,[8] *El maestrante* recalls the universe of the Balzacian novel. Although Palacio Valdés's descriptions lack the biting sarcasm of those of his friend of adolescence Leopoldo Alas, the portrayal of the monotonous, "vegetative" life of Lancia reminds us of the Vetusta evoked in Alas's *La regenta:*

> Always the same ill-defined, vegetative, dreaming life; the same gatherings in back rooms sipping with delight the honey of backbiting.

The coarse nicknames forever weighing like leaden slabs on the happiness of respectable families. In the Bombé, on sunny evenings, the same groups of clergymen and army officers parading up and down. The enormous bells of the basilica invariably tolling at fixed times. The pious old women scurrying to the rosary or the novena. The monotonous chant of the prebendaries loudly resounding in the solitary high vaults. In Altavilla, at dusk, the eternal groups of light-hearted youths, laughing a lot, talking loudly, and frequently making room to let pass some abundantly-endowed pert seamstress or maidservant to whom they rendered allegiance with their eyes, with their words, and, not infrequently, with their hands. And there, in the heavens, similar groups of dark, sad clouds piling up in silence over the ancient cathedral, listening in the melancholy autumn nights to the lamentations of the wind as it passed by the lofty metaled spire of the tower. (*El maestrante* [Madrid: Los Hijos de M. G. Hernández, 1893], 286–7)

Behind the everyday social world of the middle-class inhabitants of Lancia lie the manias and violent passions of the leading characters. The "maestrante," Count Pedro Quiñones, is an arrogant eccentric semiparalyzed by apoplexy; in a jealous rage he strikes the vicious blow that finally kills Josefina, the foundling deposited on the steps of his house in the initial scene of the novel. Two other characters, the young Count Luis de Onís and the young heiress Fernanda Estrada-Rosa, provoke the reader's pity. Luis, the former *novio* (fiancé) of Fernanda, is the timid offspring of a father who had died of melancholia, and of a domineering, insane mother obsessed with chastity. Luis fears damnation and suffers from black rages and despair, from which he is cured by the healthy life on his model farm (102). Fernanda, furious at being supplanted in Luis's affections by the scheming Countess Amalia, gets drunk and provokes the monstrous Don Santos who rapes her. After an unsuccessful attempt at suicide, Fernanda is obliged to marry her violator, who demands a dowry. When widowed, she, as a "scorned woman" (292), is delighted to observe the sufferings of Luis, tormented by remorse for his sin.

The plot revolves around the "love affair" of Amalia, reluctantly wedded to the much older Count Pedro, and the ingenuous Luis, as dominated by his scheming mistress as he had been by his crazed mother. Amalia is demonic in her self-assured toying with the powerless Luis. She is motivated by a malignant sensuality: "What emanated from her being was a delight in sensuality, a sensuality which included also the malignant joy of satisfied caprice, of vengeance and of treachery" (147); her eyes have "the cruel glare of a domesticated wild animal" (147).

However, when the lonely Luis renews his interest in the widowed Fernanda, Amalia, obsessed by jealousy and fears of aging, turns into a nineteenth-century Spanish Medea.[9] Allied with a spiteful dwarfish servant, Amalia hits back at the helpless Luis by devising fiendish tortures for their illegitimate daughter Josefina. Palacio Valdés, from the vantage point of a superior morality, strongly condemns her frenzied sensuality:

> Tenderness had never entered that ardent, despotic, tormented spirit; she was totally ignorant of the poetic delights that ennoble and excuse passion. She had spent her life in insane agitation, tormented by the desire for happiness at any cost. For the last seven years she had lived under the sway of insatiable lust. Never had a melancholy feeling of remorse indicated the presence of a moral sense in that depraved nature. Her increasingly exacerbated desire for pleasure had lately dragged her into numerous dangerous excesses. (366–7)

Amalia's torture of her daughter (a substitute for the hapless Luis) contains an element of perverted sensual pleasure:

> At these moments Amalia experienced a diabolical sensation, a mixture of pleasure and pain, somewhat akin to what we feel when an abscess is lanced. Her abscess was that soulless passion, a mixture of love, lust, pride, and raging jealousy. Unable to wound her former lover with the same cruelty that tore her breast, she satiated her appetite for vengeance on the fruit of their love. When she had the child bloodied and trembling at her feet, she believed that she could perceive in the girl's anguished eyes, gestures, and tone of voice her lover humiliated and supplicant; the savage joy she felt made her eyes shine and her nostrils dilate. Josefina was a portrait in miniature of Luis. . . . When those beautiful blue eyes, gentle and resigned, turned towards her and when those red lips twisted as they implored pardon, the Valencian woman felt her withered body tremble with sensual delight, with something that recalled the joys of her adulterous love. (375–6)

El maestrante contains a fast-moving plot, good character portrayal, and lively scenes of provincial life. The power of the novel, however, lies in elements that it shares with the popular novel: the violent passions of the protagonists, the awakening of the reader's anguish as an innocent child is tortured to death, the reliance on perversion and insanity to motivate characters, and the outraged moralistic perspective of the narrator as he condemns the "diabolical" evil of the wicked Countess.

EL ORIGEN DEL PENSAMIENTO

El origen del pensamiento was published in the same year as El maestrante (1893). By way of contrast to the heightened emotions of El maestrante, the novel offers a portrayal, half affectionate and half sardonic, of the petty bourgeoisie of Madrid. Social setting, rather than individual passion, is the dominant element in El origen del pensamiento. The novel begins with a social scene, an evocation of the lively banter and concerns of the students and lower-middle-class government employees who frequent the Café del Siglo. The account of middle-class mores continues with the descriptions of the courtship of the protagonist Mario de la Costa and Carlota, of their wedding, and of the literary salon of Doña Fredesvinda.

Certain of the characters meet with the obvious approval of the narrator. Mario, a truant civil servant who, with the support and encouragement of Miguel Rivera is enabled to achieve fame and fortune as a sculptor, is ingenuous in his dealings with others. He represents values of decency, despising the seducer Don Laureano Romadonga, risking his life to save a poor worker from suicide by drowning, and behaving as a model of an affectionate husband and father. His journalist friend Miguel Rivera, the protagonist of Riverita and Maximina and obvious alter ego of Palacio Valdés, is compassionate, intelligent, and courageous, his only defect being a tendency (like that of the youthful Palacio Valdés) to mockery. Mario's bride, Carlota, is devoted to her husband and child, possesses feminine intuition,[10] and is of a sane and balanced temperament. Her serenity, her physical beauty, and her noble moral qualities, as Rivera explains, make her the ideal wife for an artist; to choose as spouse a nervous, imaginative woman, on the other hand, would lead to an unhappy marriage (*El origen del pensamiento* [Madrid: Los Hijos de M. G. Hernández, 1893], 314–5).

El origen del pensamiento is a comic novel in its portrayal of foolish pride and eccentricity. The narrator presents without malice minor idiosyncrasies, as in the case of the café violinist Timoteo, who sprays his auditors with saliva, has the look of "a surprised fish" ("besugo atónito") (367), and uses extravagant romantic clichés to protest his love, which is nonetheless genuine, for Carlota's sister Presentación. The artistic Doña Fredesvinda is bizarre in her excessive pretensions. The "languid" Juanito Corneta, the son of the president of the *Liga de Productores*, dazzles Presentación who, in her turn, snubs the besotted Timoteo. The civil servant Dionisio Oliveros, the prolific writer of novels, dramas, comedies, and poems, is self-centered in his offer to the grieving parents Mario and Carlota to write a play on the theme of their kidnapped child.

Other characters are selfish, manipulative, and hypocritical. The mother of Carlota and Presentación, Doña Carolina, controls and exploits her daughters' suitors. The aging Don Laureano Romadonga is a cynical seducer of women. The priest Don Jeremías Laguardia is calculating and violent. The cherubic Godefredo Llot, the "favorite son of the Church," is a confidence trickster. Adolfo Moreno, the son of Doña Fredesvinda, is, despite his scientific pretensions, idle and mendacious.

El origen del pensamiento approvingly portrays qualities of balance and common sense, virtues exemplified in Mario, Carlota, and Rivera. Compassion for others—Mario's disgust at a greedy shop assistant's hounding of an indebted worker, Sánchez's generosity in feeding a starving man, Mario's concern for the welfare of his insane father-in-law—is a further lesson exemplified in the novel. Exploitation of others receives condign punishment. The seducer Romadonga, who admires "energetic women," is terrorized into matrimony by the dagger-wielding, foul-tongued Concha, a teenaged *chula* (working-class woman) from Lavapiés. The greedy priest Laguardia is cheated of his savings. Godofredo Llot is thrown into jail.

Balance is also required in art. Despite the envy of other sculptors, Mario's work excels with its Hellenic sense of measure, calm, and refusal of dramatic effect (316). Another form of excess, that of an overluxuriant literary style, is also condemned.

Thus, Palacio Valdés satirizes the prose of Catholic apologists by quoting samples of Llot's ecclesiastical journalism:

> The Middle Ages were the constant theme of his dithyrambs. Gothic cathedrals. Gothic cathedrals! Godofredo could never sufficiently describe the light "filtering through the stained glass, the voice of the organ resounding in the lofty vaults, the prayers of the faithful ascending amidst clouds of incense, the metaled spire of the tower pointing like a finger toward heaven." (242)

Romantic exaggeration and cliché, degraded into late-nineteenth-century sentimentality, are mocked in Timoteo's avowals of love:

> —Pero la adoro a usted con toda mi alma. Es usted desde hace mucho tiempo la estrella confidente de mis amores, y adonde quiera que el destino me arrastre bien puede estar segura que eternamente será mi bandera, bajo la cual pelearé hasta derramar la última gota de mi sangre. . . . (370)

> ("I adore you with all my soul. For a long time you have been the true star of my love, and wherever destiny may take me, you can be sure that you will eternally be my banner, under which I shall fight until I have spilt the last drop of my blood. . . .")

> —Presentacioncita—aulló de nuevo Timoteo,—¡quisiera morir por usted! Quisiera morir cuando el sol traspone los montes lejanos del horizonte, cuando muere la luz entre celajes de ópalo y grana. Quisiera morir, y sería feliz si supiese que en mi tumba solitaria vendría usted a depositar algunas margaritas silvestres. . . . (371)

> ("Presentacioncita," Timoteo howled again, "I would like to die for you! I would like to die when the sun sinks behind the distant hills on the horizon, when the light dies amid clouds of opal and scarlet. I would like to die, and I would be happy if I knew that you would come and place a few wild daisies on my lonely tomb. . . .")

The most obvious satire in *El origen del pensamiento* is that of the jargon and tenets of scientific materialism. The simpleminded retired merchant, Don Pantaleón Sánchez (a name suggesting his modest origins and the pantaloons he once sold), learns from the cynical wastrel Adolfo Moreno that the perfume of flowers is, in scientific terminology, "the smell of its excrement." As he becomes versed in anthropological and physiological science, Pantaleón reduces all behavior to simplistic terms. The novel should be an experimental study of pathology (319); poetry is "a congestive and frequently morbid state of the brain" (331); and genius is "a sickness of the cerebral lobules" (333).

Pantaleón's mania at times takes a Quixotic, comic form. During his "famous anthropological sally" (305), Pantaleón is frightened to discover that a veterinarian's anthropological measurements reveal criminality. During the same sally, he preaches to an assembly of outraged priests that "there is not one God but four, namely, oxygen, hydrogen, carbon, and nitrogen. . . ." (299)

His constant use of jargon, his ideological belief in the struggle for life, lead Pantaleón to suppress natural feelings of affection and compassion. As eccentricity turns into obsession and then into madness, Pantaleón loses emotional contact with those around him. He dismisses his hideous scarring, in a failed experiment, of his daughter Presentación as "Transformations of matter. One more martyr to science!" (272). His crazed search for the "origin of thought" leads to the kidnapping and proposed penetration of the skull of his grandchild.

The final chapters of the novel, as the reader anxiously fears for the child's fate in the hands of the scientific fanatic, recall the suspense and horror of the ending of El maestrante. The overall tone of El origen del pensamiento is, however, very different from that of the preceding novel. El origen del pensamiento is a comic novel, with its evocation of the delusions of the lower middle classes, its ironic vision of their foibles, and its teaching of social virtues of altruism and kindness. In the last two pages of the novel, in words that border on rhetorical exaggeration almost to the point of parody, Mario, intensely moved by his suffering and the contemplation of the sunset, wishes, like Rivera in the closing pages of Maximina, to take refuge from the egotism of this world in some painless nirvana:

¡Glorioso sol, llévame contigo, llévame por encima de las montañas y las olas, sobre las verdes llanuras y las espumas del Océano; llévame lejos del triste sueño de la existencia a reposar bajo tu pabellón tejido de estrellas! He visto a mi hijo inocente padecer horribles martirios. He visto a ese desgraciado que ahí queda infligírselos por un impulso fatal. Mi espíritu sangra y no comprende nada. Glorioso

sol, arrástrame contigo; condúceme al templo de la verdad y la Bon-
dad infinitas, a la morada de ese Poder en cuyo seno divino todas
las contradicciones se resuelven, todos los dolores se apagan! Quiero
ver desde esas puras estrellas que ocultas con tu presencia a esa
mísera tierra encadenada a su feroz egoísmo, a su tristeza y oscuri-
dad. (476)

(Glorious sun, carry me away with you, carry me over the mountains and the waves, over the green plains and the Ocean's foam;
carry me far from the sad sleep of existence to rest beneath your tent
woven of stars! I have seen my innocent child suffer horrible torments. I have seen the unhappy wretch who still lives torture him
following some fatal impulse. My spirit bleeds and understands
nothing. Glorious sun, bear me with you; lead me to the temple of
infinite truth and Goodness, to the dwelling of that Power in whose
divine bosom all contradictions are resolved, all sorrows are
quenched! I wish to contemplate from those pure stars that you con-
ceal with your presence this miserable earth chained to its ferocious
egotism, its sadness, and its darkness.)

Rivera, who had equally suffered with the loss of his bride,
understands Mario's suffering. The final line of the novel, however, is an affirmation of life on earth, as the loving and practical
Carlota indignantly rejects Rivera's support for Mario's pessimistic mysticism.

LOS MAJOS DE CÁDIZ

In May 1917, Palacio Valdés declared *Los majos de Cádiz* to
be technically his finest work, superior to the others in the intensity of its story ("fábula"), its harmonious proportions, and its
original setting. The fact that its characters were not members of
the middle class explained its lack of success with the public.[11]
Los majos de Cádiz (1896) is probably the most carefully constructed novel of Palacio Valdés. The first edition is preceded
by a prologue ("Observaciones acerca de la composición en la
novela") in which Palacio Valdés presents his concept of "the
harmonious novel": the absence of all excess (a Hellenic concept), a carefully planned structure, an essential balance or
harmony, a good "theme," no exaggeration or falsity, and verisimilitude. Longus's *Daphnis and Chloë* is a perfect novel: "A

simple, interesting tale; finely observed characters presented without artifice; exquisite portrayals of nature; lively descriptions of customs; a noble and transparent style. All things in this admirable work form an irresistibly enchanting, harmonious whole" ("Prólogo," *Los majos de Cádiz* [Madrid: Tipografía de los Hijos de M. G. Hernández, 1896], v–xxxvi).[12]

These characteristics of simplicity, of authorial control, harmony, and morality are evident in *Los majos de Cádiz*. The action is presented in masterful fashion; the ever changing combinations of courting couples and lovers are as exquisitely choreographed as a ballet. The omniscient narrator confidently enters his characters' thoughts; his observations, which are only impartial in appearance, are nonetheless presented in ironic manner. The narrator plays with the reader, offering, as is frequent in Palacio Valdés's novels, a double dénouement—Velázquez's decision to emigrate, followed by his decision to remain in Cádiz— and a skillful resolution of the frustrated and paradoxical loves of the leading characters.

The tone of the novel constantly changes. There are scenes of suspense, such as the appearance of a mysterious character at the end of the first chapter and the latent violence that pervades chapters 14 and 15; of joyful Andalusian *costumbrismo* (witty *piropos* [flattering compliments], jokes, dances, songs, local customs); of tragedy (the painful loneliness of Velázquez); of comedy (chapter 14, "La Boda de Pepa," in which the drunken groom tries to fight his father-in-law who has failed to deliver the promised dowry); of wisdom (the cultivated speech of Paca la de la Parra); of ill omen (dark popular superstitions); and of sheer poetry.

The city of Cádiz is evoked realistically, with mentions of specific streets, shops, and buildings. The establishment of setting in the first paragraph, which I quote in its entirety, is a model of concision: "Sucedía esto allá en Cádiz, en una taberna del Campo del Sur, no lejos de Capuchinos, frente del mar Océano." ("It happened in Cádiz, in a tavern of the Campo del Sur, not far from Capuchinos, facing the Ocean.") The next two paragraphs are also descriptive, of the store and of Soledad's opulent flesh.

But the initial physical description provides only a certain verisimilitude; the exterior world plays a reduced role. *Los majos de Cádiz* takes place at an undetermined time in the nineteenth century.[13] The action takes place outside of time, in a transcendental, magical world, a world that reflects characters' spiritual torments rather than an exact historical moment. By way of contrast to episodes of orgy and *juerga* ("nights on the town"), other scenes, such as that of Soledad's wandering through the streets of Cádiz in chapter 6 and the marvelous "Noche Gaditana" (chapter 15) that precedes the dénouement, transport us to a time that exists outside of history.[14] The impression of atemporality is increased when various classical references are combined with the exaggerations of Andalusian speech to plunge us into a universe formed of Greek mythology and of the popular culture of Cádiz.[15]

Secondary characters are portrayed with convincing simplicity and realism. This "realism," however, is far from the naturalism of Zola, in spite of the depiction of the violence, alcoholism, and relaxed morals of the proletarians of Cádiz. The major characters (Manuel Uceda, Velázquez) are presented sympathetically in psychological terms; they are victims who consciously suffer the consequences of their passions and errors.

The principal theme of *Los majos de Cádiz* is love. The form of love most respected by Palacio Valdés is that of the "señorito" Manuel Uceda, who offers an unselfish, platonic devotion to the ignorant proletarian Soledad, whom he had saved from rape. Manuel Uceda's courage, generosity of spirit, and constant devotion are not automatically corresponded. His excessive admiration and upper-class ways cause only boredom and disdain in Soledad and bitter disappointment for Uceda. His love is not a blind passion; rather, it is conscious and self-sacrificing. Thus, when Soledad insults him, he defends his concept of love with intelligence and dignity:

El cariño que te he tenido no te autoriza para insultarme. No te pongas tantos moños. Si eres hermosa, otras lo son también, y si te quiero, no es por tu mérito, sino por ser la primera mujer con que he tropezado. . . . Después de todo, quizá no esté enamorado de ti, sino de la imagen que de ti se ha formado en mi corazón. . . . Porque, a la verdad .. . , voy viendo que interiormente vales bien poquito. (212)

(The love I have had for you does not authorize you to insult me. Don't be so vain. If you are beautiful, so are others, and if I love you,

it's not because of your merit, but because you're the first woman I
met. . . . After all, perhaps I am not in love with you but with the
image I've formed of you in my heart. . . . Because, in truth, I see that
you're not worth much inside.)

Manuel's reasoning is based on an inner concept of morality and
constancy, not on her merits, as Soledad recognizes, excusing
herself.

In any case, moral harmony is established at the end of the
novel when Soledad confesses that Manuel is "el único hombre
decente con que he tropezao en la vida" (the only decent man
I've met in my life) (269) and when she acknowledges the nobility of his behavior (277). At this moment Uceda, the theoretician
of love and master of himself, openly recognizes Soledad's childishness and her need for the protection that he will provide.
Passion leads to boredom; true love, unselfish and conscious,
brings its own reward:

> Porque en este mundo el amor engendra el amor, pero el capricho
> sólo engendra el hastío. A pesar de tus locuras te he seguido quer-
> iendo porque adivinaba en ti un espíritu infantil a quien no se puede
> exigir la responsabilidad de sus actos y también porque respetaba
> en mí el primer amor que tú habías logrado inspirar. (284)

> (Because in this world love engenders love, but caprice only pro-
> duces boredom. In spite of your craziness, I went on loving you
> because I saw in you a childish spirit that cannot be held responsible
> for its acts and also because I respected in myself my first love that
> you had inspired.)

Soledad, in spite of her ignorance and stupidity, acknowledges
the perverse and neurotic nature of her passion for Velázquez:

> —No se puede llamar amor lo que he sentido por ese hombre. . . .
> Era una locura, un antojo por cosas agrias, como solemos tener las
> mujeres. El amor debe ser algo más dulce, más tranquilo. . . . Era
> imposible que yo le quisiera toda la vida. Su genio siempre me ha
> sido antipático. . . . Detesto a los hombres soberbios . . .
> —Es porque tú lo eres. (276)

> ("What I felt for this man cannot be called love. . . . It was a form of
> madness, a craving for something bitter, such as we women have.

Love must be something gentler, calmer. . . . It was impossible for me to love him all my life. I always found his bad temper disagreeable. . . . I detest proud men . . ."
"That's because you're proud yourself.")

The love of Perico Velázquez, the tavernkeeper who is Soledad's lover, is more complex. Velázquez dominates Soledad with a mixture of generosity, arrogance, and physical violence; the more he beats her, the more she adores him and submits to his brutality. But when he, in his pride and indifference, courts other women in her presence and strikes her in front of her friends, she rebels, leaving him and treating him icily.

Now isolated, alone amid the joys of the Carnival of Cádiz, Velázquez seeks Soledad, begging her to return. Back in the tavern, Soledad delights in her new power over her lover, forcing him to kneel before her and rejecting his offers of marriage. Velázquez is now the slave of his love, humiliated, submissive, without pride. The gossips declare that Soledad achieved this sudden transformation by magical skills; feminists *avant la lettre*, they delight in the humiliation of the once proud tavernkeeper:

—¡Al fin llegó tu hora, querida . . . ! Así debe ser: la mujer siempre muy alta. . . . ¿Qué se creen esos tíos? ¿Que porque somos buenas y callamos la mitad de las veces por evitar disgustos se nos ha de tratar como trapos sucios . . . ? ¡Que se limpien . . . ! Ya que le tienes bajo el pie, aprieta, hija, no temas; cuantos más sofocones le des más suavecito le tendrás. . . . Esos malditos son así. . . . (177)

(And so your hour has come, my dear! This is the way it ought to be: the woman always on top. . . . Who do these guys think they are? That because we are good and we keep silent half the time to avoid problems they have to treat us like dirty pieces of rag . . . ? They can go and wipe their own bottoms . . . ! Now you have him beneath your feet, lass, squeeze him hard, don't be afraid; the more grief you give him the gentler he'll be to you. . . . This is what these wretches are like. . . .)

In *Marta y María* (1883), in *El cuarto poder* (1888), and in *El maestrante* (1893), Palacio Valdés had portrayed the perversion of passion. Velázquez's passion, frustrated by Soledad's coldness, suffers a similar distortion. Velázquez derives a secret pleasure from his own degradation:

Entretanto Velázquez seguía exagerando sus rendimientos, no tanto para suavizar la aspereza de su querida como por el íntimo placer que esto le causaba. El placer de antes dominándola, martirizándola, era menos que nada comparado con el que ahora sentía satisfaciendo sus caprichos, uncido, prosternado a sus pies. Y a pesar de su inveterada fanfarronería, cada día le iba importando menos que los amigos se enterasen de su humillación. (178)

(Meanwhile Velázquez continued to exaggerate his submission, not so much to soften his beloved's harshness as for the intimate pleasure that it gave to him. His previous pleasure in dominating and tormenting her was less than nothing when compared with the pleasure he now felt in satisfying her whims, yoked and prostrate at her feet. And in spite of his inveterate boasting, it bothered him less each day that his friends should learn of his humiliation.)

A veces él mismo, acometido de anhelos de adoración, las provocaba, hallando en ellas [las humillaciones] dulzura exquisita, como los ascetas en sus penitencias (198).

(At times he himself, beset with a craving to worship, provoked humiliation, experiencing an exquisite sweetness thereby, such as ascetics find in their penance.)

Increasingly depressed, insulted by his friends, Velázquez wanders at night through the streets of Cádiz, on the edge of an outburst of violence and anger. But at this point his moral development begins, his consciousness of the feelings and rights of others. Challenged by Gabino, the fiancé of Mercedes, whom he had courted as a substitute for Soledad, he realizes that Gabino has a greater right to Mercedes. His moral progress continues. Determined to give Soledad up, he enters her room; she receives him with foul insults. He is able, however, to control himself: "But by making a supreme effort on himself, he let go her arms which he had gripped, took a step back, and suddenly became calm, profoundly calm" (262–3). Conscious of his loss of youth, of his failure in love, and of his loneliness, he decides to emigrate to the New World. The novel could well conclude at this point, at the end of chapter 15 ("Noche Gaditana"), on a tragic note, with the punishment of Velázquez's *hubris*. Palacio Valdés, however, offers a further possibility, one that demonstrates our possession of free will.[16] In a second ending, this time a happy one (chapter 16, "Despedida"), virtue receives its reward.[17] Uceda will marry Soledad, who now recognizes his merits. Mercedes agrees to marry Velázquez, who repents his foolishness. Universal joy and harmony are now established in this, to my mind, finest of Palacio Valdés's novels.

LA ALEGRÍA DEL CAPITÁN RIBOT

La alegría del capitán Ribot (1899) is set in Valencia, a city that—with its pervasive aroma of flowers, blue skies, and healthy sea breezes—is likened, in its privileged position, to classical Greece, (*La alegría del capitán Ribot* [Imprenta de los Hijos de M. G. Hernández, 1899], 67–8). The narrator exclaims at the happiness, serenity, and intelligence of the Valencians (68). The women of Valencia possess an exquisite beauty; their voluptuous eyes suggest the mysteries of love and death (83).

The action is narrated in the first person by the *alicantino* Julián Ribot, the captain of a merchant ship. In his late thirties, the romantic and idealistic Ribot falls in love with Cristina, the young wife of the shipping magnate Enrique Martí. As narrator, he observes the moral failings of others. As in the case of Ceferino Sanjurjo in *La hermana San Sulpicio*, Ribot's self-portrayal contains an occasional note of irony; Ribot's speech is at times hyperbolic and pretentious and smacks of literature, as also does his ecstatic response to the enchantments of Valencia.

Ribot deftly portrays Martí's family and friends. Cristina possesses an attractive combination of "joy and gravity, sweetness and asperity, boldness and timidity" (29); she deeply loves her husband and treats Ribot with reserve when she realizes that his feelings go beyond mere friendship. Enrique Martí, in his late twenties, is a sympathetic figure. He is devoted to his wife and generous and welcoming to others. He risks his capital in ambitious schemes for the development of Spain (the construction of roads, canals, railroads, harbors, artesian wells, etc.). His modernizing, entrepreneurial plans would at first sight appear to answer the practical needs of the nation:

> Spain needs useful men more than philosophers. Don't you think that there is a plethora of theologians, orators, and poets? If we wish to reach the level of the other countries of Europe we must think of opening up communications, building harbors, setting up industries, and exploiting mines. (70)

Other members of the Martí entourage are less engaging. Cristina's brother Sabas is an eccentric whose principal concerns are his dress and his collections of pipes and walking canes. Furthermore, he is a scoundrel who mistreats his wife, is without affection for his children, squanders his brother-in-law's money on actresses and gambling, and maliciously criticizes the family that supports him. Martí's business partner Enrique Castell also provokes Ribot's dislike. Castell disdains others, lives a dissolute life, and believes that there is neither good nor evil, that moral codes are without meaning, and that life is a struggle for personal advantage (245). He is loathsome in his attempt at seducing his trusting partner's wife and in his malevolent reduction of the Martí family to penury when thwarted in his mischievous schemes.

The eccentricities of minor characters are vividly evoked. Cristina's mother, Doña Amparo, is given to tears and fainting fits. The astute Galician businessman Diego Retamoso pretends to defer in his financial dealings to his statuesque wife Clara, who talks loftily of investment schemes. At times, the quirks of minor characters provide a comic element. Doña Clara insists that Ribot speak in English when seeking permission to court her daughter Isabelita. The errant Sabas's flamboyant and histrionic return to his doting family is pure farce.

However, all is not as it seems in the Garden of Eden, as Ribot initially believed the Martí circle to be. Castell is obviously the serpent in Paradise (226). Other characters also offer a false front to the world. The shyly-loving teenager Isabelita Retamoso is presented, by the cynically unreliable witness Sabas, as "simple, modest, well educated, industrious, accustomed to severe economy in a household where a dollar is turned over a hundred times before it is spent, the only daughter and heir of all her father's money" (157–8). Cristina believes Isabelita to be "hardworking, industrious, economical"; Ribot will be able to mold her character in matrimony. But Isabelita is far from being an incipient "angel in the house": a true child of her parents, her interest is in money and position.

Martí represents a case of self-deception. He does not represent the Regeneration of Spain, for he is blind to his own defects (his impracticality, his inability to appreciate his limitations) and to those of others (the treacherous hypocrisy of his "friend"

Castell). His impracticality leads him to squander his resources. His support of his ne'er-do-well brother-in-law, as Cristina indicates, encourages Sabas in his vices. His business ventures, such as his factory to make artificial stone (!) and his brewery, are failures. His impractical trust of others and his generosity are not, however, moral failings; he is therefore worthy of the love and esteem of Cristina and Ribot.

Ribot and Cristina behave in exemplary fashion. Ribot, troubled by his false situation with regard to his friend Martí, obeys the dictates of conscience and renounces temptation. Cristina determines to live, whatever the threat to her social position, with honor and tranquillity. Ribot willingly accepts the imputation of guilt, rather than risk disturbing the peace of Marta's family. Peace of conscience comes before all the joys of earth or heaven, as he piously declares (230). A similar delicacy of feeling leads to the noble decision of Ribot and the widowed Cristina not to marry.

La alegría del capitán Ribot contains a fast-moving plot, skillful character portrayal, and a demonstration of impeccable moral behavior (that of Ribot and Cristina) and vice (Castell). The novel also possesses a fine irony. Characters, whether they wish it or no, follow literary models. The melodramatic villain Castell employs commonplace romantic clichés in his attempts at seduction; he nevertheless indignantly denies that his role is that of a villain in a popular novel.[18] The virtuous roles of Ribot and Cristina also smack of the folletín. A similar interplay of life and literature is evident in Marti's entrepreneurial projects. Marti is not a Costa-like regenerator of Spain but rather a deluded arbitrista (contriver), planning on his deathbed, like Don Quixote, a further folly, the construction of a hydroelectric plant that will provide all of Valencia with inexpensive energy.

In the final chapter, Ribot lives happily in the knowledge of fulfillment of duty.[19] However, the spiritual rewards that he and Cristina obtain by the practice of virtue impress, rather than fully convince, the reader. Indeed, the ending of the novel is inconclusive and ironic. Noble behavior brings its own satisfaction. So also, we must assume, do materialistic goals, for those who use and exploit others (Isabelita, Castell, Sabas) also achieve their aspirations in life.

5

The Later Works

W<small>ITH</small> the exception of *La aldea perdida*, the later works of Palacio Valdés lack the tight construction of his earlier novels. Melodramatic elements persist in *Tristán o el pesimismo, La hija de Natalia, Santa Rogelia*, and *Los cármenes de Granada*. By now, however, they are no more than a shrill mannerism rather than vitally connected to the archetypal universe of the nineteenth-century popular novel. Palacio Valdés also shows an increasing fondness for brief prose (short stories, recollections of his youth, essays, reflections on life). In his essays, Palacio Valdés parades a facile erudition, calculated to impress a middle-brow, conservative newspaper reader. These shorter pieces, which Palacio Valdés composed until the age of eighty-two, are much blander than the works of his prime. It is to this period of his literary career that Palacio Valdés owes his reputation as a "safe" novelist, who presents a rosy-colored vision of the past and who advocates moderation and Christian charity as solutions to life's problems.

La aldea perdida (1903) is a novelistic tour de force, in which Palacio Valdés evokes with nostalgia (but does not idealize) the Asturias of his youth and dramatically portrays the coming of industry to the peaceful rural valleys. The novel is above all remarkable for its all-pervasive irony, as the self-conscious narrator refers the action to a pagan, Hellenic world and brilliantly reworks the myths of Demeter, Persephone, and Pluto in a nineteenth-century setting.

Tristán o el pesimismo (1906) is the worst conceived of Palacio Valdés's novels, tediously long and with an incoherent plot and wooden characters. Its only strength lies in the melodramatic and excessively sentimental dénouement. Angel Jiménez, the alter ego of Palacio Valdés, makes his first appearance in *Papeles del doctor Angélico* (1911), a collection of anecdotes and observations that inaugurates the aging Palacio Valdés's predilection for shorter prose genres. Angel Jiménez teaches the importance of achieving happiness in life and favors feeling over intellect. *La guerra injusta* (1917) is a series of essays praising French civilization written to favor French war propaganda during the First World War.

In *Años de juventud del doctor Angélico* (1918), Palacio Valdés's creative powers are relatively unimpaired. In this ironic novel, Palacio Valdés recreates the Madrid of the early 1870s. In his portrayal of the fate of Natalia, driven to crime and insanity through no fault of her own, Palacio Valdés reveals the same fondness for melodrama of his earlier years.

La novela de un novelista (1921) affectionately portrays Palacio Valdés's childhood in Asturias and early intellectual interests. In the slight first-person novel *La hija de Natalia* (1924), a tale of suicide and attempted sexual assault, Palacio Valdés again reverts to melodrama and, in the person of the aged Angel Jiménez, to sentimentality.

Santa Rogelia (1926) is a curious attempt at portraying the life of a "saint" in the context of the 1860s. With its irony, Dickensian humor, exaggerated melodrama, and a Zolaesque naturalism, the novel continues, in a bizarre combination, many elements of nineteenth-century narrative. The novel *Los cármenes de Granada* (1929) offers, in a superficial setting of Granadan local color, a melodramatic portrayal of neurotic passion, adultery, and suicide.

Palacio Valdés's final works, as he approached and passed the age of eighty, reveal not so much a decline in talent as an increasing mellowing in attitude. In *Testamento literario* (1929), Palacio Valdés meditates on the writer's craft, proclaims his belief in the role of morality in literature, and offers his reflections on life. The novel *Sinfonía pastoral* (1931) contrasts the delights of healthy Asturian rural life with the corruption of the city. *El gobierno de las mujeres* (1931) praises women's ability to rule nations. *Tiempos felices* (1933) are amusing, sprightly evocations of happy scenes of courtship. Finally, in the essays of *Album de un viejo* (posthumously published in 1940), Palacio Valdés proclaims his abhorrence of excess and his adherence to Christ's teaching of charity and love of neighbor.

LA ALDEA PERDIDA

La aldea perdida ("a poem-novel of country customs") (1903) evokes the lost paradise of Palacio Valdés's youth. Although no specific date is mentioned, the action takes place in the late 1850s or early 1860s when the millennial ways of the peaceful valleys of Asturias are brutally disrupted by the exploitation of coal mines and the coming of industry. The setting of the novel is that of Palacio Valdés's childhood, Entralgo in the valley of Laviana. Palacio Valdés evokes with nostalgic affection the dress, food, customs, love of the countryside, simplicity, and loyalty of the peasants of Asturias, the companions of his early years.

Although lovingly treated, the friends of Palacio Valdés's youth are not idealized.[1] Old women can be ill-intentioned witches (the gossiping, spying *sabias* [wise women]) or bad-tempered, bullying wives. Men, including the clergyman Don Lesmes, can be inveterate womanizers; brothers will expel sisters from a household; the wealthy care little for their illegitimate offspring; the "troglodyte" lawyer Don Casiano exploits his clients. Outside of the lush valleys, only incessant labor will produce prosperity from harsh mountain soils. For material gain, peasants will condemn their ten-year-old sons to the slavery of the coal mine.

Compensations for this raw existence are nonetheless many: the bonds of strong affection that link the peasants; the joyful gatherings for *romerías* and dances; the shared tasks of harvest and cider-pressing; the healthy life of the countryside; the religious beliefs of the community. Life outside the magical valley is markedly inferior. When the illegitimate peasant-girl Demetria is carried off in her teens by her mother (whose existence she has never suspected) to the middle-class life of Oviedo, she is unable to adapt. Bullied by her schoolmates and scorned by her mother and aunt, she is desperately unhappy away from her beloved foster family, her friends, and her country tasks.

Characters, although lacking in complexity, are vividly defined by some salient feature. Thus, the priest Don Prisco is enamored of card-playing; Don Antero makes pompous speeches hailing the economic progress—from which he profits—of the valley; the tavernkeeper Martinán is a boring polemicist; the talkative young peasant Celso apes an Andalusian accent and ways in memory of his military service in Sevilla. The leading inhabitant of Entralgo, Don Félix Cantalicio Ramírez del Valle, passionately loves the countryside and opposes industrial "progress." Shattered by the loss of his wife and children, in his loneliness he sensibly recognizes his illegitimate daughter Flora; he will happily see her married to a healthy peasant free from the contagion of consumption that had devastated his family.

With pervasive irony, the distant and self-conscious narrator evokes a lost Arcadia in terms of classical myth.[2] From the initial "Invocation" to the Muses ("Et in Arcadia ego"), the narrator frequently adopts a mock Homeric style. Apostrophe, the attribution of stock epithets (Quino, for example, is, like Odysseus, "ingenioso siempre y fértil en intrigas" [always subtle in wit and full of guile] [La aldea perdida (Madrid: Los Hijos de M. G. Hernández, 1903), 29]), and the narration of the battles between the peasants of Entralgo and those of other villages in terms suited to The Iliad transport us to a vanished heroic world that links Palacio Valdés's memories of childhood with the beginnings of human history. The epic overtones of the dual perspective are reinforced by the frequent impassioned interruptions of the third-person narrator, who laments the passing of the heroes of his youth.

Classical references are numerous. The scholar Don César de las Matas views the universe as a Hellenist, speaks frequently in a high style full of classical allusions, and warns against offending the gods. An apple orchard inspires him to recite Virgil's First Eclogue. Leading characters are presented in terms of Greek mythology. The heroic Nolo is "the image of the god Apollo when he was exiled from Olympus and served as a shepherd in the house of Admetus, the king of Thessaly" (17); Demetria has a "divine smile" (51) and the "high, pure brow of a Hellenic statue" (57); the womanizing Regalado, "surrounded by beautiful youths and skillfully playing the flute," is like "the god Pan amid his nymphs" (204). Chapter 7 ("Nymphs and Satyrs"), in which Flora and Demetria, surrounded by hidden nymphs, wash clothes in the river, before being assaulted by the rude satyrs (the blackened miners Plutón and Joyana), is an obvious recreation of classical myth. Similarly, Nolo's rage (181), his battle with Toribio in which the earth trembles, and the author's appeal to the Muses and apostrophe to the combatants (189–91) are of Homeric inspiration.

The plot of *La aldea perdida* is an imaginative reworking of myths of Demeter (the earth goddess, the goddess of agriculture), of her daughter Persephone (who was carried off to Hades by Pluto), and of Pluto (the god of the underworld). Demetria is kidnapped by the miner Plutón, whose soul is as black as his appearance; after striking Plutón with a sickle, Demetria is lost in the mine. Her devout prayers to the Virgin result in her almost miraculous discovery and rescue from certain death.

Her fiancé Nolo is unwilling to believe that she had been forced into entering the mine with Plutón. Only when she dives into a river (a ritual cleansing?) and he saves her from drowning will Nolo acknowledge her purity and consent to marriage. The novel then proceeds to a predictable happy ending. In the final chapter, during the Fiesta del Carmen, two couples, Demetria and Nolo, Flora and Jacinto, are blissfully united in marriage.

In the final two pages of the novel, however, Palacio Valdés shocks the reader with a totally unexpected and savage dénouement. Plutón's crony Joyana shoots and kills Jacinto. Plutón slashes Demetria in the neck, her life blood gushing out as if she were the victim of a ritualistic sacrifice.

The brutal slayings of Jacinto and Demetria symbolize, on one level, the destruction of the Asturian rural Arcadia by the invasion of industrial civilization, with its corresponding disruption of an age-old pastoral and agricultural society. The violence of the ending represents Palacio Valdés's strong personal feelings at the loss of the earthly paradise of his youth. The loss, or expulsion from Arcadia, is, of course, inevitable, despite the protest of Palacio Valdés's feelings. Throughout the novel, the classicist Don César de las Matas has taught the Heraclitan doctrine of perpetual change: "Todo corre, todo marcha, nada se detiene. . . . No se baja dos veces por el mismo río" (All is change, all is flux, nothing stays put. . . . One cannot twice descend by the same river.) (154)

La aldea perdida has, above all, a religious, mythical import that is Hellenic rather than Christian. The religious devotion of the leading characters is fervent and unquestioned. The cult of the Virgin Mary does not, however, protect its devotees from punishment for hubris. The action of the novel takes place, at its most fundamental level, in a pre-Christian world of jealous gods and demons from the underworld. The apparently eccentric Don César warns against offending the gods by an excess of confidence. In the final chapter, fittingly entitled "The Envy of the Gods," Don César justly fears, despite the mockery of his companions, that the bliss of the young couples will provoke the vengeance of the gods (306).

TRISTÁN O EL PESIMISMO

A lessening of Palacio Valdés's literary talents is evident in the "novel of customs," *Tristán o el pesimismo* (Madrid: Librería General de Victoriano Suárez, 1906). *Tristán o el pesimismo* is lengthy and tedious, with an incoherent structure and wooden characters. The novel purports to demonstrate a moral lesson that can only be described as childish: those who are religious, optimistic, joyful, and charitable to others are more likely to lead happy lives than a mentally deranged, paranoid murderer. To prove this obvious point, Palacio Valdés establishes a series of contrasts: between the countryside (idyllic) and the city (the source of corruption), between optimism (the characteristic of healthy people) and pessimism (which renders human relations impossible),[3] between a happy marriage (that of Cirilo who is lame and Visita who is blind) and an unhappy couple (Tristán and Clara), between a saint (Germán Reynoso, a nature-lover, kindly, compassionate, Christian) and a suspicious, egotistical madman (the embittered, cynical, cowardly Tristán Aldama, an advocate of the doctrines of Buddha and Schopenhauer[4]), between a woman of deep moral beliefs (Clara) and an adulterous coquette (Elena).

Tristán is totally lacking in the magical-lyrical element, of the encounter of an individual with the universe and with his or her unconscious, that we find in such works as *Marta y María*, *El idilio de un enfermo*, and *Los majos de Cádiz*. In *Tristán*, Palacio Valdés presents externally imposed codes of conduct, expressed in banal maxims that are without reference to a transcendental world. The heaviness of Palacio Valdés's novelistic style causes

his attempts to give variety to his narrative—a comic chapter
(15), a potentially tragic chapter (16), a grotesque chapter (17)—
to fail. Palacio Valdés impresses the reader only at the end of
the novel, with the marked melodrama and sentimentality of the
dénouement. Thus, after the melodrama of chapter 21, in which
the Marquesa del Lago curses Tristán (the murderer of her son),
we pass to the final chapter, which in its exaltation reminds us
of the novels of Concha Espina. Elena steals poison, intending to
commit suicide at her husband's feet, and then prostrates herself
before the statue of the Virgin Mary. In the final apotheosis, Reynoso in his goodness proposes to take the unhappy women
(Elena, Clara) to a South American paradise. The pathetic dialogue of the final scenes is worthy of an eighteenth-century lachrymose drama:

> [Clara] Mi conciencia me dice que por encima de todas las conside-
> raciones y de todas las promesas está la ley de la caridad. (My con-
> science tells me that the law of charity is above all other
> considerations and all promises.)

> [Reynoso] Una mano invisible y todo poderoso te ha traído de nuevo
> a mis brazos. Acepto ese don como los acepto todos. Hoy era feliz;
> mañana lo seré también porque nadie, nadie en este mundo puede
> hacerme ya desgraciado! (An invisible and all-powerful hand has
> brought you again to my arms. I accept this gift as I accept all gifts.
> Today I was happy; tomorrow I shall also be happy because no one,
> no one, in this world can now make me unhappy!) (403)

> —¡Tu esposa hasta la muerte y más allá de la muerte!—exclamó
> Elena echándole los brazos al cuello anegada en llanto. ("Your
> spouse until death and beyond death!" Elena exclaimed, tearfully
> flinging her arms around his neck.) (404)

> —Los tres te deberemos nuestra felicidad. Donde tú respiras, la at-
> mósfera se llena de nobles y puros sentimientos. Eres, esposo mío,
> la imagen de Dios sobre la tierra, todo bondad, todo misericordia.
> ("We three shall owe our happiness to you. Where you breathe, the
> air is filled with pure and noble sentiments. You are, my husband,
> the image of God on earth, all goodness, all mercy.") (405)

PAPELES DEL DOCTOR ANGÉLICO

In 1911, Palacio Valdés published *Papeles del doctor Angélico*,
a collection of anecdotes, observations, and aphorisms purport-

edly bequeathed by the saintly philosopher Angel Jiménez.[5] A moral message—the truth of Christian doctrine as established in the thought and experience of Jiménez—illuminates the collection. The teaching is presented for the most part in somewhat tedious dialogues that examine various facets of philosophical questions before arriving at hesitantly expressed, but nonetheless orthodox, solutions. Palacio Valdés's talent lies not in philosophical discourse but in anecdote and in the rapid delineation of character, above all when expressed through dialogue.

Palacio Valdés's anecdotal skill is evident in "Las defensas naturales," the fast-moving tale of a swindler who outwits a pair of greedy bankers. An example of the depiction of character through conversation is the portrayal of the brutal and avaricious *indiano* who had sold his own mistress and sons as slaves before returning to Spain ("Un profesor de energía"). A grotesque element is evident in certain tales. Thus, in "Las leyes inmutables," an insane scientist attempts to play the role of God in his laboratory. In the sinister "Una interviú con Prometeo," a Spanish diplomat meets, while traveling in the Caucasus, Prometheus, who inveighs against man's misuse of the press, industrial arts, and freedom.

Although Angel Jiménez demonstrates a fondness for paradox—perhaps inevitable in a storyteller—he observes human eccentricities without bitterness. He favors feeling, compassion, and conscience over intellect and selfishness. He scorns the hypocrisy and envy that characterize writers. Jiménez, who witnesses an example of child abuse, discusses the problem of the existence of evil and—after summarizing the theories of Schopenhauer, Leibnitz, and Buddha—confirms doctrines of original sin, the goodness of God, collective responsibility for evil, and free will ("Intermedio del editor"). In "Theotocos," he expresses his devotion to the Virgin Mary. In "Ultimo paseo del Doctor Angélico," he declares the necessity of religious faith and of prayer.

A frequent concern of Jiménez, the alter ego of Palacio Valdés, is the achievement of happiness. Happiness is to be found in love of others and, above all, in the love of family. Only when we are ourselves happy can we make others happy; even in this case, we must proceed gently.[6] In the important essay "Terapéutica del odio," Palacio Valdés, continuing the thesis of *Tristán o el pesimismo*, acknowledges that an unbalanced nervous system can destroy the peace of mind of the most virtuous of men. Religion itself can become an obsession for weak natures, leading them to aberration and nightmare (*Papeles del doctor Angélico* [Madrid: Imprenta de Bernardo Rodríguez, 1911], 246).

The essay "El gobierno de las mujeres" is of interest for its trenchant and enlightened defense of feminist values. The septuagenarian poetess Doña Carmen Salazar argues intelligently that women have no marked talent for the arts or for domestic tasks. The cliché roles of "the angel in the house" and of "the rest and recreation of the warrior" merely mean that "woman will continue as before to be an instrument of pleasure" (362). Women have been victimized by men. Woman's true talent is for politics. Women, with their superior capacity for pity and love, should also administer the law courts. The so-called feminine qualities of timidity, mendacity, hypocrisy, and frivolity are merely the consequence of women's enslavement by society (392).

LA GUERRA INJUSTA

With the outbreak of war in 1914, Palacio Valdés immediately expressed sympathy for the allied cause. He was one of four Spanish writers to contribute to *King Albert's Book*, the lavishly produced "Tribute to the Belgian King and People from Representative Men and Women Throughout the World," which the English novelist Thomas Hall Caine assembled in 1914 in the interests of British war propaganda.[7] In March 1915, Palacio Valdés contributed an essay, "Después de la paz," to the influential new journal *España* (which was also subsidized by the British government). In this article, Palacio Valdés contrasts the Latin ideals of morality, virtue, and Christian charity with Germany's cult of force and the state. Palacio Valdés was also a signatory of the "Manifiesto de adhesión a las naciones aliadas," which Spain's intellectual élite published in *España* (9 July 1915).[8]

In 1916, the sexagenarian Palacio Valdés, already suffering from ill health, agreed, for reasons of conscience, to write a series of articles for *El Imparcial* from Paris. These fourteen articles

were later published as a book, *La guerra injusta* (Barcelona/
Paris: Bloud & Gay, 1917).[9]

In *La guerra injusta*, Palacio Valdés offers the wide-ranging
moral and religious reflections of a well-read and thoughtful liberal Catholic rather than an analysis of the war situation. The
essays, intended for a general newspaper audience, may be
faulted as oversimplistic. However, they were intended to create
a sympathetic view of the French, especially among Spanish
Catholics. Palacio Valdés expatiates on original sin, the nature
of optimism, the moral dimensions of Christianity, the primacy
of reason over feeling, and the designs of divine Providence. Despite his marked Anglophilia, Palacio Valdés's admiration for
French culture—its literature and science, its civilizing influence—is manifest in these essays.

Palacio Valdés supports the allied cause as being that of reason
and justice. He acknowledges the many virtues of the French.
The French possess the soldierly qualities of "cunning, joy, manual skill, improvisation" (26). Palacio Valdés corrects many
Spanish misconceptions about the French. The French are neither unduly optimistic nor frivolous; rather, they are an ambitious, calculating nation. They are not immoral and are for the
most part devoutly Catholic. (Spanish women, on the other hand,
are superstitious; few Spanish men attend mass.) French women
of all social classes are fascinating, refined, courteous, and dignified. As part of the war effort, they are doing men's work, as well
as serving as volunteer nurses.

The Germans, despite their solid virtues (tenacity, capacity for
hard work, courage) lack a critical spirit and are therefore over-
impressionable. They are not Christian, but rather worship scientific truth and justify cruelty. Nevertheless, Palacio Valdés
charitably hopes that Germany will again become "the tranquil
nation of philosophers, poets, and musicians that we have always
admired" (149).

Christian teachings of love and charity play a prominent role
in *La guerra injusta*. Palacio Valdés expresses his humanitarian
solidarity with the poor and the exploited (57). The search for a
more just society, however, must be inspired by love and brotherhood, not hatred (59). Palacio Valdés supports the socialists' belief in universal brotherhood and peace, although he is unable

to perceive these qualities in Spanish workers' treatment of strikebreakers.

Although *La guerra injusta* is ostensibly concerned with the First World War, Palacio Valdés harshly castigates, with a moral indignation akin to that of the so-called Generation of 1898, the backwardness and stagnation of contemporary Spain:

> Campos desecados, hombres hambrientos, el nepotismo dictando órdenes, la injusticia erigida en sistema, la frivolidad soltando carcajadas estúpidas, una política mezquina envenenando las inteligencias más altas y los más nobles caracteres . . .
>
> ¡Duerme, pueblo español, duerme! Vale más vivir dormido que despierto y desesperado. (126)

> (Dried-up fields, starving men, nepotism in command, systematic injustice, frivolity cackling stupidly, petty politics poisoning the highest intelligences and the noblest characters . . .
>
> Sleep on, Spanish people, sleep on! It is better to live asleep than awake and in despair.)

AÑOS DE JUVENTUD DEL DOCTOR ANGÉLICO

Años de juventud del doctor Angélico (1918) is a novel in two parts. In the first part, the first-person narrator, Angel Jiménez, recalls his student years in Madrid in the early 1870s. In the second part, taking place ten and sixteen years later, the narrator views the subsequent careers of the group of student friends. Apart from one lengthy extraneous passage—a Chinese diplomat's defense of his country's civilization—the novel, with its sense of irony and compassion, its fast-moving plot, its emotional involvement of the reader, reveals no decline in Palacio Valdés's novelistic skills.

As in the nineteenth-century bildungsroman (Pereda's *Pedro Sánchez*, Palacio Valdés's *Riverita/Maximina*, Flaubert's *L'Education sentimentale*), the characters' development takes place within a historical context. Accounts of a revolutionary *tertulia*, of student riots, of the materialistic dogmas held by medical students, of the incompetence of university professors, numerous details of the daily life of the period, and the summary of the career of the revolutionary general Luis de Reyes fittingly establish the disturbed atmosphere of the Madrid of the early 1870s. In a wider context, characters refer to the corruption of Spanish rule in the Philippines and the continuation of slavery in Cuba. Regenerationist impulses are evident in the practical reforms—the establishment of schools, the inauguration of a sanatorium for sick children—set in motion by the millionaire Pérez de Vargas. For Pérez de Vargas, such ills as the hatred and ignorance that fill the hearts of Spanish workers are to be remedied by moral, rather than technical, education; his emphasis on the education of an outstanding man (a new Socrates, Shakespeare, Spinoza, or Cervantes), suggests the influence of Joaquín Costa (*Años de juventud del doctor Angélico* [Madrid: Librería General de Victoriano Suárez, 1918], 243).

Palacio Valdés sketches skillfully the inhabitants of the student lodging house. These include, among others, the kindly landlady, the young scholar and bibliophile Pasarón (a barely disguised portrait of Marcelino Menéndez Pelayo[10]); two enchanting young seamstresses (Lolita and Rosario); their garrulous, pretentious mother; the law student Sixto Moro (the son of a humble cobbler, a nonconformist with a gift for words and remarkable for his romantic locks); and the eccentric Carlos de Jáuregui, with his mania for spiritualism. Other characters of interest are the bluff General Luis de Vargas (a friend of Angel Jiménez's father), his second wife (the duplicitous Brazilian, Guadalupe), and his virtuous daughter Natalia. The extent to which their careers and sentimental lives are controlled by economic factors is stressed by Palacio Valdés. Women, indeed, are especially trapped by social situations.

Although the characters initially appear unremarkable, their passions devastate their lives. Rosarito is brokenhearted when the enamored Pasarón coldly breaks off relations to pursue a university chair. Natalia, treated coldly by her stepmother, horrified by her stepmother's adultery, physically assaulted by her father who, although loving, fails to understand her situation, and the prey of nervous problems, is forced at the age of sixteen into marriage with the wastrel Céspedes. Her distraught admirer Sixto Moro attempts suicide on her wedding day. The maniac Jáuregui, following the counsel of spirits, marries in horror an ugly, ignorant laundress.

The ironies of life and the futility of many of our ambitions are apparent when we meet the characters ten and sixteen years later. Three characters, at least, have lost their youthful illusions. The scholar Pasarón dies of tuberculosis in squalid surroundings, bitterly regretting his sterile and loveless life of scholarship; his final teaching, of the vanity of fame, is expressed as: "Don't delude yourself, Jiménez! Enjoy yourself, enjoy yourself!" (253). Pérez de Vargas, a geologist now wealthy through his wife's fortune, has abandoned his dreams of socialism; working as a servant and as a laborer, he had learned through painful experience the venality, selfishness, ignorance, and violence of Spanish workers. Only in the case of Jáuregui has the loss of illusion had totally happy consequences: his ugly laundress has borne him twelve children; with the healthy life of the countryside and the joys of family, he has abandoned his mania for spiritualism.

Palacio Valdés's novelistic skills, as emotionally melodramatic as in his earlier works, are starkly apparent in his treatment of Natalia. Reduced to penury, physically abused, and her body offered for sale by her degenerate husband, in desperation she hurls vitriol in the face of her oppressor. After a trial scene full of suspense, she is freed from jail by the forensic skills of Sixto Moro. After a period of happiness living with Sixto Moro, whose daughter she bears, Natalia is pursued again by the Fates. Tormented by remorse, haunted by visions of a blind beggar, believing that church images close their eyes to her, she dies of guilt, after becoming reconciled to the Church.

Años de juventud del doctor Angélico is ironic, rather than pessimistic or optimistic, in its conclusions. An exaggerated devotion to learning has led to the waste of Pasarón's life; Natalia, with her natural goodness and spontaneity, is driven to crime and insanity by the abuse of others; the kindly landlady Doña Encarnación is ruined by her generosity; the wretched Jáuregui by chance makes a marriage that brings him domestic bliss. Family life also brings happiness to lesser characters (the two seamstresses, the Mezquita cousins). In the last lines of the final chapter ("Isla de reposo"), Palacio Valdés offers an ironic ending, one of sadness and joy (like life itself), as Sixto Moro offers a toast not only to friendship and memories of youth but also to the hope that God will allow him to be reunited with Natalia: "Bebió. Una lágrima bajó rodando por sus mejillas y cayó en la copa del champaña. El símbolo del dolor se mezcló al de la alegría. Lo mismo que en la vida." (He drank. A tear rolled down his cheek and fell into the glass of champagne. The symbol of pain mingled with the symbol of happiness. Just like life.)

LA NOVELA DE UN NOVELISTA

In *La novela de un novelista* (1921) Palacio Valdés offers fond memories of an idyllic childhood spent in the village of Entralgo, in the small town of Avilés, and in Oviedo, where he studied for the *bachillerato*. Although Palacio Valdés acknowledges the presence of bandits, bullies, and death, his Asturian childhood was a time of happiness, a Paradise from which he was expelled just before the age of seventeen, when he left to study law in Madrid. His early years in Entralgo, with memories of kindly peasants, of animals, and childish escapades, are presented through rose-colored spectacles. Palacio Valdés's schoolboy days in Avilés and Oviedo are evoked in more factual manner, with descriptions of local customs and excellent vignettes of his neighbors, friends, and teachers, with their various eccentricities.

Palacio Valdés's fondness for anecdote, and corresponding skill in converting experience into literature, is evident. Thus, "El suicidio de Anguila" is a picaresque account of the stratagems of a youth who ran away to Madrid. A favorite device of the nineteenth-century popular novel, the emotional involvement of the reader in a tale of abused innocence, is present in "Historia triste de mi amigo Genaro," the account of an adolescent who, unjustly suspected of theft, was savagely beaten by his father and finally banished to Cuba, where he died of yellow fever.

La novela de un novelista affords useful information on Palacio Valdés's formative years. His mother, although delicate in health, was the strong character in the family; his father, physically strong, was sensitive and inclined to melancholy; he was enlightened in the freedom that he granted to the young Palacio Valdés. Palacio Valdés recalls his youthful readings: (at age eight) such popular novelists as Pérez Escrich, Dumas, Fernández y González, and Chateaubriand; (in his early adolescence) the romantics, Bulwer Lytton, Tasso, Ariosto, and Camoens. Later, he developed an interest, which he never abandoned, in history, philosophy, economics, and social science; he was greatly impressed by François Guizot's *Histoire de la civilisation en Europe*. The fifteen-year-old Palacio Valdés was also interested in the theater and in opera, especially in Donizetti and the *zarzuela* (light musical drama). Palacio Valdés gives his recollections of his two closest friends, Leopoldo Alas (too cruelly satirical) and Tomás Tuero. His account of the Revolution of 1868 in Oviedo and of the ingenuousness of working-class republicans is both comical and a useful document of the times.

La novela de un novelista, despite its popularity with the reading public, is blemished by the archness of its account of Palacio Valdés's years in Entralgo. The passages dealing with Oviedo, when Palacio Valdés no longer portrays the world through the eyes of a small child, are more effective. In one chapter ("Paréntesis"), Palacio Valdés movingly confesses his fear of death and his sense of loss at the deaths of the friends of his youth. Philosophy is no consolation; he finds joy only in his Christian belief in Heaven.

LA HIJA DE NATALIA

La hija de Natalia (1924), subtitled "Ultimos días del doctor Angélico," is narrated in the first person by the quinquagenarian Angel Jiménez. The novel takes place, at some unspecified period in the final decade of the nineteenth century, in Madrid, the country estate (Los Jarales) near to Madrid belonging to the wealthy Martín Pérez de Vargas and to his devoted wife Leonor, and in Paris.

The novel is heavily melodramatic. In the first part, the self-sacrificing and honorable Sixto Moro is hounded to his death by the machinations of duplicitous politicians. His daughter Natalia (Lalita), raised in luxury but now impoverished, is welcomed into the home of the Pérez de Vargas. Martín Pérez de Vargas becomes enamored of the beautiful and capricious Lalita; his wife, in her jealousy, commits suicide. A year later, in Paris, Angel Jiménez meets by chance Lalita, who is the tutor of the family of a wealthy Mexican. The Mexican, Bernal (described as an Indian with the teeth of a carnivore), attempts to assault Lalita sexually; she is saved only by the physical intervention of the Mexican's energetic son, Enrique Bernal. Only in the conclusion of *La hija de Natalia* does melodrama give way to sentimentality. Jiménez, with the greatest of delicacy, protects Lalita, who is now a "serious, sensible, industrious little woman" (*La hija de Natalia* [Madrid: Librería General de Victoriano Suárez, 1924], 271). Jiménez, himself in love with Lalita, generously sacrifices himself to her interests, enabling her to marry the man she loves, Enrique Bernal.

A further element of interest lies in Angel Jiménez's self-portrait. Jiménez presents himself, somewhat archly, as on the threshold of old age and of fragile health. He portrays himself favorably: he possesses a keen sense of humor, is altruistic, is capable of winning the love of a younger woman, and is a true friend. A devotee of the Latin classics, Jiménez preaches the futility of ambition and of all excess. Nevertheless, Jiménez's philosophy is only superficial. Jiménez is as capable of passion as any youth; his strong sense of decorum, and a certain inability to take decisive action without prolonged thought, preserve him from the excesses and loss of self-control of his friend Pérez de Vargas.

Although Jiménez propounds the same philosophy of gentleness and moderation as that advocated by the aged Palacio Valdés in his *ABC* articles of the 1930s, only the unwary reader will assume that Palacio Valdés is depicting his "true" self in the flattering portrayal of Angel Jiménez, rather than a mask, akin to that which he cultivated as "the patriarch of Spanish letters" in the 1920s.

Despite its criticism of Spanish political corruption and its powerful depiction of the ravages of passion in the middle-aged Pérez de Vargas, *La hija de Natalia* nevertheless remains a slight novel, its major defects being the overidealized and sentimentalized portraits of Jiménez and of Lalita. In his review of *La hija de Natalia*, Enrique Díez-Canedo justly indicated that the novel is mainly of interest as an example of Palacio Valdés's somewhat old-fashioned narratorial skills; Palacio Valdés emphasizes plot, rather than the experimentation that was becoming fashionable in the 1920s, to create "a story from the *Arabian Nights* scarcely concealed in a humble bourgeois novel."[11]

SANTA ROGELIA

The penultimate novel of Palacio Valdés, *Santa Rogelia* ("From the Golden Legend") (1926), is, in the preliminary words of the author, "a story of modern times which seems to be from the Middle Ages." This curious novel is certainly of greater literary interest than *Tristán o el pesimismo*. It is the tale of Rogelia, a "zagala gallarda" (lively lass) from the working class, who marries a despotic and quarrelsome miner (Máximo). After committing murder, Máximo is sent to prison. Rogelia falls in love with a young doctor (Vilches), who takes her to Paris, where they live happily. They have a child. Vilches becomes famous. Rogelia obtains an education and meets such scholars as Renan and Flammarion.

But now the novel changes in tone, becoming a hagiography rather than a realistic work. Back in Madrid, Rogelia, influenced by a dying novice (the Marquesita Cristobalina) and her confessor ("fervent and austere"), begins to repent her sin: "La Gracia golpeaba ya sordamente en su corazón como la crisálida dentro del tronco antes de salir" (Grace was now pulsating silently in her heart like a chrysalis inside the cocoon before emerging [*Santa Rogelia* (Madrid: Imprenta Helénica, 1926), 184]).

In part 3 of the novel, Rogelia, the slave of her religious duty, feeling the presence of God inside her soul, goes to the penal colony of Ceuta. She tries, amid numerous privations and indignities, to lead her foul and repugnant husband to God. In the end, Máximo hangs himself, thus fulfilling "God's high purposes." The happy Rogelia rejoins Vilches and her son, who understandably exclaims, in the last line of the novel: "Mummy, I don't want you to go back to Heaven."

Part of the literary interest of *Santa Rogelia* lies in the plot, full of suspense. The settings are varied: the sordid world of workers and peasants brutally exploited by capitalists and *caciques*; the cultivated milieu of Paris during the Second Empire; the atrocious conditions of the convicts in Ceuta. Palacio Valdés portrays the violent, impoverished, starving lives of the Asturian miners and of the convicts with the frankness and naturalism of Zola. The idyllic life of the two lovers in Paris, on the other hand, recalls the happy ending to Benito Pérez Galdós's *episodio nacional, La de los tristes destinos* (1907); both Galdós's *episodio* and Palacio Valdés's novel are implicitly condemnatory of Spain, for in both cases amatory bliss can credibly be portrayed only in a French setting.

The greatest interest of the novel lies not so much in its realistic narrative as in the fine irony with which the exemplary life of Rogelia is presented.[12] The comic description of the "artistic family" (chapters 4 and 5 of part 3) and of their ill-treatment of the unhappy Rogelia recall the comic exuberance of Dickens. Above all, *Santa Rogelia* reminds us of Galdós's *Nazarín* in the exaggerated hagiography of Rogelia. As in Galdós's novel,[13] throughout part 3 of *Santa Rogelia* the great tribulations and outstanding virtues of the saint are related in an ironic and ambiguous manner. Like Nazarín, Rogelia, imitating Christ, rejoices when she is maltreated (255). Irony is present in the highly exaggerated and melodramatic presentation of the pious Rogelia's reaction to her friend Baldomera's attempt to sell her to a seducer:

> —Vas a vender por un puñado de oro la honra de una desgraciada que ningún mal te ha hecho, de una amiga, casi de una hermana, que contigo comparte el trabajo y el pan. ¡Vas a seguir los pasos del traidor Judás para juntarte después con él en el infierno!
>
> Baldomera, aterrada, imaginando que su amiga había tenido una comunicación celestial, cayó de rodillas.
>
> —¡Perdón!, ¡perdón!
>
> Rogelia, con exaltación y gesto de iluminada, le gritó:
>
> —¡No me lo pidas a mí, que soy una miserable criatura digna de ser pisoteada! Pídeselo a ese Mártir Divino, en cuya frente has querido clavar una espina más.
>
> Y sujetándole las manos la arrastró con fuerza hasta los pies del Crucifijo.
>
> —¡Perdón, perdón!—volvió a exclamar la viuda, ahogada por los sollozos. (284)

("You are going to sell for a fistful of gold the honor of a poor woman who has done you no harm, of a friend, almost a sister, who shares her bread and labors with you. You are going to follow in the steps of the traitor Judas and join him later in Hell.''

The terrified Baldomera, imagining that her friend had received a communication from Heaven, fell to her knees.

"Forgive me! Forgive me!"

Rogelia, exalted and with the gesture of one inspired, cried out:

"Don't ask me to forgive you. I'm a poor wretch who deserves only to be trampled under. Ask this Divine Martyr, on whose brow you wished to nail one more thorn."

And grabbing her by the hands, she forcefully dragged her to the feet of the Crucifix.

"Forgive me, forgive me!" the widow again exclaimed, overcome with sobs.)

The same exaggeration—accompanied by a certain ironical distancing on the part of the author—continues in the description of Rogelia's faith:

Horas terribles en que el alma brama dentro del pecho con sordos mugidos de volcán en erupción y termina por vomitar la lava de las lágrimas que escalda las mejillas. Pero supo vencerlos con su voluntad indomable y su fe casi sobrenatural. De cada una de estas crisis salía más fuerte y animosa, como el acero que una y otra vez entra en el fuego para templarse. Y volvía a dormir su piadoso sueño de amor divino, de esperanza y celestial alegría. (287–8)

(Terrible hours in which the soul rages within the breast with the muffled roar of an erupting volcano that finally vomits its lava of tears to scald her cheeks. But she succceeded in overcoming [temptation] with her indomitable will and almost supernatural faith. From each crisis she emerged strengthened in spirit, as steel that is repeatedly tempered by fire. And she could again sleep with her pious dream of divine love, hope, and celestial joy.)

Rogelia's sufferings end with a miracle (this in a novel that is apparently realistic), when the image of Christ speaks to her in the Cathedral of Ceuta, to tell her that her sufferings are over. The miracle, however, is not the repentance and conversion of Máximo, but rather his suicide. In a final manifestation of "holiness," the horrified Rogelia, with the help of God, kisses the corpse of her monstrous husband.

The moral of *Santa Rogelia* is elusive. The account of Rogelia's deeds amazes, but does not edify, the reader. Rogelia does not love her vile husband; she follows him only out of religious duty. She does not redeem him; rather, she offers him further opportunity to commit evil. As in the case of Galdós's Nazarín, the holy conduct of Rogelia inspires neither her companions nor the reader to imitation. She is portrayed ironically and at a distance by the narrator. In spite of the admiration (or rather, wonder) that we may feel for her courage, Rogelia has much in common with the pathological cases that Palacio Valdés depicts in so many of his novels.

LOS CÁRMENES DE GRANADA

The novel *Los cármenes de Granada* (1929) takes place in Granada in the late nineteenth century. Apart from descriptions of fashions in women's clothing, Palacio Valdés is little concerned with the historical moment. The local color is also mainly external, being limited to Granadan place names and one brief passage in which gypsy dialect is reproduced. Lengthy passages, barely linked to the narrative, chronicle the history of Moorish Granada.

Apart from vivid sketches of minor characters (the eccentric Pedro Venegas, who dresses as a Moor, the sordid moneylender Crispín Garrido, the scoundrel Rafael Izquierdo, the hunchback Quasimodo, and the bluff, former military officer Don Enrique de Aguilar), the novel is concerned above all with the loves of the naive and self-centered young poet Alfonso Aguilar. Aguilar, exalted by his readings of romantic poets, breaks his engagement with the loving Ana María, who is too simple for his refined imagination. "He had not yet experienced, nor perhaps ever would, the attraction of the tender, modest, and serene woman who assures the happiness of the home" (*Los cármenes de Granada* [Madrid: Librería General de Victoriano Suárez, 1927], 207).

Instead, Alfonso is obsessed by the romantic behavior and speech of Alicia Izquierdo. Neurotic, degraded by his passion (Alicia, to mark her despotism, forces him to kiss her feet, 229, 262–3), he is ruined by his marriage. His father dies of a broken heart; his fortune is plundered by Alicia and her father; he is cuckolded by a money grubbing "friend." In despair, after attempting to strangle his unfaithful wife, Alfonso hangs himself. Palacio Valdés ends this gruesome cautionary tale with an epilogue from Richter: "Happy is he whose heart seeks only another heart and who yearns not for a park in the English style, music by Mozart, paintings by Raphael, lunar eclipses, moonlight, novelistic scenes or the realization of the latter in real life."

The only lengthy critical discussion of *Los cármenes de Granada* is that of Padre Félix García, who found the novel to lack subtlety and dramatic movement and to be little more than an extended anecdote, with lifeless characters and excessive reference to history.[14]

TESTAMENTO LITERARIO

Testamento literario (1929) contains Palacio Valdés's reflections on art and the writer's craft. Discussing the novel, Palacio Valdés repeats the ideas, and on occasions the words, of the prologue to *Los majos de Cádiz*. The novel does not depend on the poetic sensitivity or the romantic posturing of the novelist. Rather, the novelist should choose an appropriate theme, use simple language, and portray with verisimilitude decisive characters. Palacio Valdés's dislike of "insignificant" characters leads him to condemn *L'Education sentimentale* of Flaubert (whom he considers head of the "so-called naturalistic school") as one of the most cloying novels he has ever read (*Testamento literario* [Madrid: Librería General de Victoriano Suárez, 1929], 73). In treating character, the novelist should reproduce actions and speech. The procedure of the Goncourt brothers in *Germinie Lacerteux*, in reproducing at length the thoughts of the protagonist, strikes Palacio Valdés as false. The modern cult of originality is also harmful; Palacio Valdés prefers the Hellenic ideal of moderation.

A central feature of *Testamento literario* is Palacio Valdés's insistence on morality in art and in the novelist's life. The novelist should avoid the deadly sins, especially those of pride, envy, and melancholy. As a remedy for "neurasthenia," the writer should have contact with others, but will find no profit in the backbiting of literary *tertulias*. The novelist should read the works of balanced writers ("men healthy in body and spirit"), such as Plato, Leibnitz, Sophocles, Goethe, Shakespeare, Petrarch, Bossuet, and Saint Francis de Sales. The writer should be joyful, work hard ("Laborare est orare"), avoid the use of stimulants, exercise his body, and be tolerant of others. Love and happiness are synonyms. Glory, political ambition, and the desire for wealth are traps for the writer. It is healthier to avoid suffering than to seek pleasure (267).

Apart from the ponderous discussion of novelistic aesthetics, *Testamento literario* contains much of interest. Palacio Valdés's advice on the conduct of life is sane, if unromantic. *Testamento literario* also gives much information, unobtainable elsewhere, on Palacio Valdés's life: his loss of religious faith in his teens; his almost obsessive youthful studies of the history of philosophy; his interest in Spinoza, Fichte, Kant, Hegel, and above all Schopenhauer; his increasing reliance on intuition, rather than reason alone; his recovered faith in Christianity and acceptance of Catholic teaching; his happiness in marriage; his belief in spiritual love, rather than the deceptions of carnal attraction; his friendships with the novelists Pérez Galdós and Pereda and with the statesman Emilio Castelar, whom he greatly admired; his political scepticism (he was a "republican who did not believe in the republic"); the aversion he felt for the overly-critical stance of his early friends Leopoldo Alas and Tomás Tuero; the breakdown of his health in his student years, from which he recovered by bodily exercise and by seeking fresh air; his belief in the dignity and redemptive power of manual labor (239); his claim that the world is symbol or appearance, not reality (256); the happiness he found in reading and writing (273–4); his belief that ethical conduct is the prerequisite for happiness; the influence on him of Montaigne and Goethe.

The reader should, however, be alerted to the self-serving nature of Palacio Valdés's "literary testament." His portrayal of his "friendship" with Pérez Galdós and Pereda, for example, should be examined in the light of his vicious attacks on these same novelists in his interview (circa 1921) with Alberto Guillén.[15]

A CARA O CRUZ

A cara o cruz (1929) is an extended short story, pleasantly written but of slight literary significance. The writer Julio

Samper is acquainted with an affable giant, Macrino Salcedo; Salcedo is dominated by his despotic wife, the dwarf Rosario. Rosario scorns her husband, who commits suicide. Samper in his turn loves the dwarf twin sisters of Rosario. After tossing a coin, Samper marries one twin, Angelita; on her death, he finds equal happiness in marriage with the other twin, Fernandita.

SINFONÍA PASTORAL

In the introduction to Sinfonía pastoral ("a novel of country customs") (1931), Palacio Valdés protests against the deformed vision of rural life presented by French naturalists, who could see only "blackness, monsters of malevolence, lewd women, lustful males, dark intrigues, foulness and abominations of every kind" (Sinfonía pastoral [Madrid: Librería General de Victoriano Suárez, 1931], 8). Living in the country, Palacio Valdés had encountered less serious vices (selfishness and petty materialism) than those attributed by Zola. He had found considerable pleasure not only in the beauty and calm of the countryside, but also in the many comic incidents provoked by rural ignorance.

Sinfonía pastoral is, like La aldea perdida, set in the Asturian Valley of Laviana. The action takes place in the final third of the nineteenth century. The novel is pleasantly written and evenly paced, with short sentences and much conversation. There is an almost fairy-tale atmosphere to the plot. Angelina Quirós, despite her father's millions, is a bored, neurotic nineteen-year-old, who refuses to eat and is given to temper tantrums. She becomes engaged to the fortune-hunter Gustavo Manrique, who uses the hollow phrases of romantic novels to further his seductions. To save his daughter's health, Angelina's father, the bluff, simple-living Antonio Quirós, with the advice of his friend the Cardinal Archbishop of Seville, feigns financial ruin and sends Angelina to his brother's farm in Asturias.

Angelina is most warmly received by her relatives. Courageously, she voluntarily assists in the daily tasks of the farm, haymaking, milking cows, and herding. She now sleeps soundly; her appetite is so hearty that in a year she gains twenty-two kilograms in weight. Angelina also enjoys the social life of the region, becoming popular as she vigorously takes part in local dances, delights the rustics by singing the songs of the region and of Madrid, and reads aloud the novels of Pérez Escrich and Fernández y González during the *esfoyazas* (corn-husking bees). Religious, she follows the advice of the local priest and accepts with resignation her changed status. She is generous and kind to others. When her father reveals his true wealth, the reader is hardly surprised by Angelina's determination to stay in the village and marry her ignorant but loving cousin Telesforo.

The novel conveys with charm the delights of rural life, the honest virtues of Angelina's family, and the eccentricities of many of the peasants. Evil, in the shape of the jealous family of the jilted Sinforosa and of the vile Manrique who returns when he scents money, is present but can be thwarted by constant and courageous hearts. The poor parish priest, Don Tiburcio, teaches that wealth is of little importance if one has spiritual and physical health; Angelina's career proves, of course, the wisdom of Don Tiburcio's views. Examples of individual acts of charity and generosity by the poor abound. The frugal lives of the banker Antonio Quirós and of the Cardinal Archbishop of Seville attest to the irrelevance of luxury. Palacio Valdés's contempt is reserved for those whose moral degradation corrupts others. The oily Manrique is loathsome in his behavior; the village seducer Ramón dies mourned by none. By way of contrast, the world loses by the death of the eccentric and impoverished dwarf Faz, the best *gaitero* (bagpipe player) in the region.

EL GOBIERNO DE LAS MUJERES

El gobierno de las mujeres (1931) is a series of essays that attempt to demonstrate that women have proved better rulers than men. Combining history and anecdote, Palacio Valdés praises the good sense, courage, prudence, energy, sense of justice, and civic virtues of such women as Isabel I of Castilla, María de Molina, Elizabeth I of England, Mary Stuart, Margaret of Austria, Christina of Sweden, the Tsarinas, Catherine II of Russia, Maria Teresa of Austria, Queen Victoria, and the two María Cristinas who were regents of Spain in the nineteenth century. The essays are remarkable for their tolerance. Palacio Valdés inveighs against the Inquisition, the expulsion of the Jews, and religious fanaticism; he shows no hostility to Protestantism. He highly praises the individualism, sense of duty, Christian charity, and good humor of the English.

Curiously, Donald L. Shaw describes *El gobierno de las mujeres* as an antifeminist tract; similarly, Arturo Berenguer Carisomo conjectures that, given the sly humor of Palacio Valdés, the work is possibly ironic.[16] Palacio Valdés's sincerity cannot, however, be doubted. In February 1912, he had written to William Dean Howells: "I am very glad that we are in agreement about the public talents of women. I am convinced that within two hundred years power and justice will have fallen into women's hands"; in the same letter he praised Catherine II of Russia as "a prodigy of insight, justice, tact, clemency, intrepid courage, patience, hard work, physical and moral balance."[17] The teaching of *El gobierno de las mujeres*—the civilizing, moral influence of a woman who rules her household—would be repeated in "Comó se casó Tejero" (*Tiempos felices*).

TIEMPOS FELICES

Tiempos felices ("Escenas de la época esponsalicia") (1933) contains eight tales of courtship in which love and virtue triumph. These evocations of scenes of happiness, Palacio Valdés explains in his brief introduction, were written to relieve feelings of sadness a few months before he completed his eightieth birthday.[18] In each chapter, a narrator urbanely relates his tale to Palacio Valdés. The stories include memories of Palacio Valdés's youth (the school he attended in Oviedo, the joys of rural life in Asturias, the Ateneo, and his meetings with friends in the Cervecería Inglesa in the 1870s). Palacio Valdés's mastery of the short genre is manifest in his skillful use of dialogue, sense of humor, and rapid delineation of character and social setting. At times, Palacio Valdés continues themes of previous works; thus, the opposition of *gallego* and Andalusian traits of *La hermana San Sulpicio* is repeated in "Cómo se casó Brañanova"; the low life of Sevilla, portrayed in *La hermana San Sulpicio*, is recreated in "Cómo se casó el marqués de Guadaira."

The first tale ("Cómo se casó Pedraja") is framed by an initial rejection of Nietzsche's theories of the superman and of the eternal return. The anecdote contrasts, in lively dialogue, courtship customs in the closing years of the eighteenth century with those of the mid-nineteenth century. The female characters (Juanita and her mother) possess much greater strength and energy than the males.

"Cómo se casó Brañanova" begins with Brañanova's joy in country life, in the popular customs of Madrid, and in his school-days in the Instituto of Oviedo. In the amusing anecdote, the young Brañanova is rejected for his *gallego* origin; after three years in Sevilla, he can pass for an Andalusian and thus wins the heart of his bride and her family, who are all addicted to *flamenquismo*.

"Cómo se casó Tejero" portrays, with the approval of the author Palacio Valdés, the dictatorial, but beneficial, rule of the young Mimí over her middle-aged husband to produce "a tranquil home, where honor, order, fidelity, affection, and well-being reign" (*Tiempos felices* [Madrid: Librería General de Victoriano Suárez, 1929], 29). By way of contrast, the next tale, "Cómo se casó Izaguirre," relates the deep love of a Spaniard for an older Frenchwoman, his former teacher.

"Cómo se casó Montejo" is framed by Palacio Valdés's evocation of conversations in the Cervecería Inglesa with Mariano de Cavia, Sánchez Guerra, Tomás Tuero, and Luis Taboada; the anecdote relates in lively manner the courtship of a rustic deputy and his aristocratic cousin, Asunción. The pert Asunción arranges the elopement of the enamored couple; Asunción's mocking, capricious character, however, was such that Montejo was unable to support married life with her; both nevertheless, although separated, continue to love each other. "Cómo se casó Montejo," besides its elegant portrayal of a nonconventional relationship, also deftly satirizes, in the person of the ridiculous Count of Arnedo, the pretensions of aristocrats.

"Cómo se casó Taulet" relates the case of a Catalan lawyer who married a shopkeeper's daughter who showed compassion when he was wrongly arrested; the tale contains interesting sketches of life in a Madrid prison in 1843. In a similarly class-based story, "Cómo se casó Laplana," a wealthy, young man-about-town, disgusted with the immorality of the Madrid aristocracy, marries a virtuous, orphaned servant girl, whom he had previously known as the five-year-old daughter of his lodging-house keeper.

The final tale, "Cómo se casó el marqués de Guadaira," begins with an affectionate portrayal of an Asturian spa in the 1870s; Palacio Valdés notes the strong sense of the ridiculous possessed by Asturians. The anecdote, set in Sevilla, offers the strange case of an act of violence that leads to a family's peace and happiness. The young marqués Jaime de Guadaira, despite his noble sentiments, becomes a wastrel and frequents the low taverns of Sevilla. Guadaira, defying social convention, marries the beautiful Josefina, the daughter of a tailor. The seamstresses from her father's workshop, learning that the drunken Guadaira physically mistreats Josefina, give the marqués a beating; as a result, Guadaira repents and becomes a model husband.

LOS CONTRASTES ELECTIVOS

The lengthy short story Los contrastes electivos (1936) explores the attraction felt by two sets of fiancés, a pair of vivacious Andalusians and a pair of shy Basques, towards their sexual counterparts of contrasting temperaments and cultures. Despite the lightness of the plot and the stereotypical presentation of Basque and Andalusian, the story is pleasantly written in fast-paced dialogue. The interest of the tale lies above all in Palacio Valdés's appearance in the person of the wise uncle of Rosarito. Creating a play of mirrors, Rosarito, in the final paragraph, proposes that, to oppose Goethe's thesis in Elective Affinities, the uncle compose a novel entitled Los contrastes electivos.

ALBUM DE UN VIEJO

Between 1932 and 1936, Palacio Valdés published twenty-eight articles in the monarchist newspaper ABC; nine of these articles were later reprinted in Album de un viejo.[19] In the ABC articles, written in the polarized political climate of the Second Republic, Palacio Valdés exalts moral and spiritual values as the basis of life. Declaring that love is the law of the universe, Palacio Valdés protests social injustice ("Intelectuales y obreros, I," ABC,

2 April 1932; "Extremismos," *ABC*, 19 January 1935) and also strongly attacks the anticlerical policies of the Second Republic ("El despido," *ABC*, 28 May 1932; "La ola negra," *ABC*, 6 August 1932).

Album de un viejo (the "Second Part of *La novela de un novelista*") was published posthumously in 1940. The octogenarian Palacio Valdés offers in urbane, if somewhat simplistic, manner, his reflections on such diverse topics as love, the joys of conversation, the divine nature of matrimony and the family, friendship, the need for common sense in daily life, and his belief in moderation as the key to happiness (the "Nothing in Excess" of the temple of Delphi) (*Album de un viejo* [Madrid: Librería General de Victoriano Suárez, 1940], 101). In literature, he eschews the craving for originality; he admires Espronceda; he dislikes modern literature, art, and music ("Inspiración y tecnicismo"). Palacio Valdés's musings are enlivened by anecdotes and quotes drawn from his readings in literature and philosophy and by recollections of his youth in Oviedo and Madrid ("Historia de un ramillete"). One chapter—"Una amigable separación (escena dramática)"—is a brief, one-act play.

The essays are illuminated by Palacio Valdés's faith in Christ's teachings of charity and brotherly love. For Palacio Valdés, our sense of beauty and our awareness of God come from within ("Organillos callejeros," 161; "Divagando," 180–1). The world is only appearance. Many of Palacio Valdés's statements in *Album de un viejo* are expressed in the form of aphorisms: "In this world we receive only what we have given" ("El sentido común," 22); "Optimism and pessimism are both the result of suggestion. He who believes himself to be happy is happy, and he who believes himself to be miserable is miserable" ("Optimismo," 144); "Any truth when exaggerated becomes a falsehood" ("Divagando," 179); "In reality, only he who loves lives and is happy; he who hates is dead" ("La iluminación," 236).

6

Conclusions

Palacio Valdés's ideological and literary sympathies were defined at the beginning of his career, in the articles published in the *Revista Europea*. In his discussion of contemporary novelists and poets, Palacio Valdés extols values of spontaneity, energy, and verisimilitude. He abhors theological systems and seeks a Christianity based on tolerance and love. His iconoclasm is apparent in his brash, sarcastic treatment of the orators of the Ateneo. His praise of the romantics, both Spanish and foreign, and recollections of his adolescent enthusiasm for the popular novel foreshadow his later novelistic tendency to portray extreme situations. The imaginative, romantic note is strongly apparent in *Crotalus horridus* (1878), a macabre tale that, with its heavy melodrama and theme of diabolical woman and male victim, introduces elements that remained constant in Palacio Valdés's works until the novelist reached old age.

For lack of a more convenient label, critics often group—albeit with caveats—Palacio Valdés among Spain's "realistic" novelists.[1] Palacio Valdés has a Balzacian sense of the importance of money and, like Balzac, depicts the middle classes. (Palacio Valdés explained the critical failure of *Los majos de Cádiz* by the proletarian setting of the novel.) In his novels, Palacio Valdés provides realistic details of physical setting and of daily life in the dreary small towns of Asturias. In *Riverita* and *Maximina*, he portrays in detail an urban bourgeois society. However, save in the case of his first novel, *El señorito Octavio*, Palacio Valdés's descriptions tend to be brief and disappear in his later works. Although the milieus are adequately evoked, the historical moment is (if we except *Marta y María*, *Riverita*, *Maximina*, and *Años de juventud del doctor Angélico*) much less accurately defined; the action of most of his novels takes place in a Spain o the 1860s or 1870s (Palacio Valdés's formative years) only remotely connected to national history. The greatest "realism" is to be found in the autobiographical sections of *Riverita*, *Maximina*, and *Años de juventud del doctor Angélico*.

Despite his humor and irony, Palacio Valdés's realism has much in common with Zola's naturalism. Thus, in *El idilio de un enfermo*, the protagonist Heredia's parentage, ill health, and economic circumstances are presented with scientific precision. Moreover, the novel portrays peasant lust, cruelty, and violence. Naturalistic themes of suicide, rape, and madness are frequent in Palacio Valdés's novels. Naturalistic also are the evocations of the drunkenness and violence of the poor of Sevilla (*La hermana San Sulpicio*), the grotesque appetites and vulgarity of the banker Salabert (*La espuma*), the sexual pathology of Obdulia (*La fe*), and the sordid lives of miners and convicts (*Santa Rogelia*). Furthermore, Palacio Valdés depicts psychologically and physically deformed characters; however, these portrayals, such as that of the gruesome "man of the gallows" (*Aguas fuertes*), owe as much to the romantic grotesque as to naturalism.[2]

Social criticism plays a far greater role in the works of Palacio Valdés than in those of his more famous contemporaries, Benito Pérez Galdós and Leopoldo Alas. In his first novel, *El señorito Octavio* (1881), Palacio Valdés contrasts the harsh life of a peasantry on the verge of starvation with the gratuitous cruelty of the aristocracy. *Riverita* (1886) exposes, if only in passing, the wretched living conditions of single mothers. Palacio Valdés touches frequently on the difficult life of the working classes: the exploitation of workers in mercury mines in *La espuma* (1890) (a novel criticized by William Dean Howells for its exposition of socialist doctrines); the cruel sufferings of peasants, miners, and convicts in *Santa Rogelia* (1926). Class resentments and differences are readily acknowledged in *El señorito Octavio*, *Riverita*, *Maximina*, *El cuarto poder*, *La hermana San Sulpicio*, *La espuma*, *Los majos de Cádiz*, and *La aldea perdida*.

The ideological content of Palacio Valdés's novels is notable. Despite the self-serving, pious declarations added to twentieth-century editions of *Marta y María* and *La fe*, Palacio Valdés is strongly anticlerical in his early works. Thus, in *El señorito Octavio*, *Marta y María*, *La espuma*, and *La fe*, he condemns clerical intervention in politics, the trivialization of religion, the superstition of many Catholics, the perversion of religious sentiment by the narrow-minded, and the ignorance, hypocrisy, manipulativeness, and violence of the clergy. Like the Galdós of *Doña Perfecta*, Palacio Valdés (before his "conversion" to Catholicism in 1899) defends values of love of neighbor and acceptance of secular society, rather than adherence to Church practices that— as described in *Marta y María, La espuma*, and *La fe*—can interfere with genuine spiritual life. A later novel, *Tristán o el pesimismo* (1906), with its strident defense of an exalted Catholicism, is much less convincing to the reader than the earlier anticlerical works.

As a parallel to his attacks on Catholic bigotry, Palacio Valdés also satirizes the fatuous and simplistic theories of progressive reformers. He mocks Krausist philosophy and jargon (*El señorito Octavio*), the cliché-ridden prose of journalists (*Riverita, Maximina, El cuarto poder*), political corruption and hypocrisy (*Riverita, Maximina, Años de juventud del doctor Angélico*), a simplistic belief in science (*La fe, El origen del pensamiento*), and the impracticality of Regenerationist schemes (*La alegría del capitán Ribot*). The pretensions of the half-educated middle classes are exposed in *El cuarto poder* and *El origen del pensamiento*; the vulgarity and immorality of the upper classes are scathingly treated in *La espuma*.

Connected with the attack on the dangers inherent in ideological narrowness (whether religious or "progressive") is Palacio Valdés's criticism of values derived from literature rather than from life. The eponymous protagonist of *El señorito Octavio* leads a second-hand existence based on his readings of mediocre French novels; whereas Octavio's passion for Laura is distorted by bookishness, the girls of Vegalora represent, in their gaucherie and down-to-earth practicality, reality rather than fantasy. María, who imitates the heroines of romantic novels and of hagiographies, has little contact with "reality" and is unfavorably contrasted with her sister who bases her life on feeling (*Marta y María*). Heredia's juvenile lachrymose verses bear no relation to his behavior (*El idilio de un enfermo*).

In "El último bohemio" (*Aguas fuertes*), Palacio Valdés attacks the falsity of the romantic theory of inspiration. Lucía Población wraps her sexual desires in romantic rhetoric (*Riverita*). Belinchón is corrupted by his readings (*El cuarto poder*)[3] and Padre

Gil is led by his studies of the mystics to treat the hysterical Obdulia as a possible saint (*La fe*). Romantic cliché, scientific jargon, and heady ecclesiastical prose are parodied in *El origen del pensamiento*. Romantic readings lead the exalted Alfonso Aguilar to break his engagement to the loving Ana María and to wed the neurotic and despotic Alicia Izquierdo (*Los cármenes de Granada*). Gustavo Manrique uses the hollow phrases of romantic novels to further his seductions (*Sinfonía pastoral*).

The ironic, Cervantine use of literature to undermine literature is most apparent in *La hermana San Sulpicio*, in which the self-conscious "poetic" approach to the Andalusia of legend is undercut by the prosaic values of the first-person narrator. The Cervantine vein is equally apparent in *La alegría del capitán Ribot*. Ribot's ironic self-portrayal is literary and pretentious; the interplay of life and literature is evident in Enrique Martí, the deluded Quixote of Regeneration. The all-pervasive irony of *La aldea perdida* derives in large measure from the narrator's intrusive comments and from the overt reworking of the myths of Demeter, Persephone, and Pluto in the context of the Asturias of the 1860s. The markedly literary nature of Palacio Valdés's narrative is also evident in the contrived—although artistically fitting—double dénouements to *Los majos de Cádiz* and *La aldea perdida*.

Palacio Valdés offers at one and the same time an acceptance of and a criticism of romantic values.[4] He extols spontaneity, emotional warmth, and simplicity (i.e., the praise of working-class and rural values in such novels as *Maximina* and *Sinfonía pastoral*). His portrayals of cosmic despair (Rivera's in *Maximina*, Mario's in *El origen del pensamiento*) represent the narrator's "romantic" self-indulgence. A critique of romantic exaltation, on the other hand, is apparent in the commonsense, "realistic" solutions to his characters' situations. María receives not martyrdom but release on bail (*Marta y María*); the jilted Rosa does not despair but settles for a servant's job (*El idilio de un enfermo*); recourse to the judicial system enables José (*José*) and Sanjurjo (*La hermana San Sulpicio*) to wed their brides. A similar practicality is evident in *El origen del pensamiento* when the foul-mouthed *chula* Concha terrorizes her aged seducer into matrimony. Palacio Valdés is equally unromantic in the philosophy of life he propounds in his old age: the finding of happiness

in love of family (*Papeles del doctor Angélico*), the search for
health in bodily exercise, fresh air, and the avoidance of suffering
(*Testamento literario*), and the refusal of all excess (*Album de
un viejo*).

Although Palacio Valdés's novels contain realistic elements,
their most noticeable feature is the recourse to extreme situations
and characters; they are, indeed, the direct descendants of those
same popular novels or *folletines* that Palacio Valdés affected to
despise in his literary criticism.[5] In Palacio Valdés's novels, the
forces of good battle the forces of evil in an archetypal universe.
Unidimensional characters represent moral qualities, in exaggerated fashion. The Count of Trevia is a sadistic, pathological murderer (*El señorito Octavio*). The fiendish seducer Alfonso
Saavedra deliberately ruins the warm-natured Julia (*Maximina*).
El cuarto poder is a novel of adultery, violence, vengeance, madness, and suicide, portraying a cosmic struggle in which evil
(incarnated in the diabolical Venturita and the spiteful cuckold
the Duque de Tornos) vanquishes good (the angelic Cecilia).

La hermana San Sulpicio, as Daniel Henri Pageaux has indicated, relies for its irony on the conscious recourse to the phrases
and stereotypes of the popular novel. In *La espuma*, the grotesque
appetites and final syphilitic madness of the banker Salabert
exemplify that very *efectismo* that Palacio Valdés, under the urg-
ings of William Dean Howells, theoretically rejected. *La espuma*
also reveals a mannerism of the popular novel in the authorial
attribution to the reader of an exaggerated physical reaction; for
example, the suggestion that the reader's hair would stand on
end at the description of a barbaric deed (*La espuma*, 1: 159).

El maestrante markedly exemplifies the universe of the *folletín*. The narrator, writing from a perspective of moral outrage
cruelly plays with the emotions of the reader who regards with
anguish and horror as an innocent child is tortured to death
perversion and insanity are the motivating factors for the leading
characters of the novel. Similarly, the insane Pantaleón Sánchez
(*El origen del pensamiento*), the villainous Castell and the virtuous Ribot and Cristina (*La alegría del capitán Ribot*), and the
exalted Clara, Elena, and Reynoso (*Tristán o el pesimismo*) all
belong to the world of the popular novel.

Melodrama is also strongly apparent in the later novels. *Años de juventud del doctor Angélico* portrays lives devastated by passion; the good and spontaneous Natalia, offered for sale by her wastrel husband, hurls vitriol in his face and later dies insane. *La hija de Natalia* is a novel of suicide and sexual assault. *Santa Rogelia*, a curious mixture of exaggerated sentiments, Zolaesque naturalism, and hagiography, contains murder, suicide, a miracle, and—a final grotesque touch—Rogelia's kissing the corpse of her monstrous husband. *Los cármenes de Granada* portrays a degraded, neurotic passion, adultery, and suicide.

Whereas Palacio Valdés's male characters lack force,[6] his female characters often possess the exaggerated virtues and vices of protagonists of popular novels.[7] The portrayals of Maximina (*Riverita, Maximina*) and Cecilia (*El cuarto poder*), for example, are markedly oversentimentalized. Women in Palacio Valdés's novels are frequently presented as self-centered, insane, or evil. The cruel Baroness Zohiloff demands that her lover murder his wife (*El señorito Octavio*); María is emotionally cold (*Marta y María*); the duplicitous Isabel schemes to prevent her daughter's happiness (*José*); Angela Guevara mistreats the child she loves (*Riverita*); Venturita is a lying adulteress (*El cuarto poder*). The female characters (Gloria Bermúdez excepted) of *La hermana San Sulpicio* take pleasure in humiliating the men who love them. In *La espuma*, Salabert's daughter Clementina (who as a child was tortured by a cruel mother) is cold and capricious; the whore Amparo loots Salabert; Pepa Frías seduces her daughter's husband. In *La fe*, Alvaro's treacherous and adulterous wife manipulates Padre Gil; in the same novel, Obdulia's hysterical sexual frustration leads her to attempt the violation of Padre Gil; subsequently, she lies to ruin the priest. In *El maestrante*, Fernanda observes the suffering of her former fiancé with delight; the demonic Amalia obtains a perverse sensual pleasure as she fiendishly tortures her daughter. In *Años de juventud del doctor Angélico*, Natalia's stepmother is adulterous and cruel. Alicia Izquierdo commits adultery and drives her husband to suicide (*Los cármenes de Granada*).

The portrayal of diabolical women, a stock feature of the popular novel, accompanies a moral teaching, that of the degradation of passion. The Count of Trevia is enslaved by his passion for the exotic Baroness Zohiloff (*El señorito Octavio*). María's religious "humility" is a disguise for her perverted sexuality (*Marta y*

María). Miguel Rivera takes pleasure in the humiliations imposed on him by the laundress Petra (*Riverita*). Gonzalo is still bound by his degraded passion for Venturita, even after the discovery of her adultery (*El cuarto poder*). Paca and her husband mutually abuse each other (*La hermana San Sulpicio*). Salabert is the grotesque slave of the prostitute Amparo (*La espuma*). Soledad recognizes the perverse nature of her passion for Velázquez; later, Velázquez takes a secret pleasure in his own degradation (*Los majos de Cádiz*). Alfonso Aguilar is the pathetic creature of his despotic, neurotic wife (*Los cármenes de Granada*).

Palacio Valdés not only presents archetypal moral struggles and larger-than-life characters. At times—and this is one of the strengths of Palacio Valdés's fiction when compared with that of Spanish contemporary novelists—his novels will suddenly abandon realism to enter an otherworldly realm of the unconscious or of myth. His first novel, *El señorito Octavio*, portrays a hauntingly magical romería, the nightmares of Octavio, and the search for a Paradise Lost. In *Marta y María*, Marta's passage to puberty is conveyed by a journey through a narrow tunnel (vaginal), culminating in the sexuality of the beach scene and her attempted suicide in the ocean. *El idilio de un enfermo* is remarkable for its magical scene of elopement and for its creation of an archetypal universe of Nature and of Greek tragedy. Similarly, a sacred Edenic quality accompanies the romería in *El cuarto poder*. The superficial Ceferino Sanjurjo is emotionally shaken, his love mingled with a death wish, when Gloria Bermúdez sings; there is also a dark side to Gloria Bermúdez (her physical assaults on the nuns, her nervous attacks, her attempted suicide, her jealousies) (*La hermana San Sulpicio*). María (*Marta y María*), Obdulia (*La fe*) and Pantaleón Sánchez (*El origen del pensamiento*) are dominated by unconscious drives.

The most magical of Palacio Valdés's works is *Los majos de Cádiz*, which takes place outside of time, in a universe that combines the myths of ancient Greece and of Andalusia. Similarly, *La aldea perdida* refers us to a wider dimension of classical mythology. Classical themes of cosmic indifference and of the disappointment of human aspirations provide the elegiac quality to Palacio Valdés's autobiographical novels (*Riverita, Maximina,*

Papeles del doctor Angélico), with their pointless waste of young lives (Utrilla, Maximina, Natalia).

Accompanying the exaggerated melodrama of the popular novel and the occasional dazzling suggestions of myth and of the unconscious are affectionate portrayals of everyday life. Palacio Valdés places his characters in social settings, reproduces their conversations, and illustrates their foibles by anecdote. Palacio Valdés stresses the happiness of family life and pities those who must live in loneliness (Riverita in *Maximina*, Luis in *El maestrante*); he reserves his greatest contempt for seducers and adulterers who would destroy the content of others. Charity towards neighbor, compassion, the avoidance of excess, the joys of country life, and the identification of love, health, and happiness are among the practical teachings of Palacio Valdés. Noteworthy also is Palacio Valdés's respect for those women who give primacy to feeling and love of family. His claim, expressed in *El gobierno de las mujeres* but formulated decades previously, that the so-called feminine qualities of timidity, mendacity, hypocrisy, and frivolity are the consequence of woman's victimization by a male-oriented society is surprisingly modern.

Palacio Valdés was one of the most talented Spanish writers of his generation. Literary fame came to him early in life; he was editor of the *Revista Europea* in his early twenties and published the successful novels *El señorito Octavio* and *Marta y María* before he was thirty. At his best, Palacio Valdés could create—in *Los majos de Cádiz*—a magical universe combining, in a highly controlled narrative, feeling, unconscious motives, and moral decision. A similar richness of perspective is evident in *La aldea perdida*. He attempted, in the bildungsroman *Riverita* and *Maximina*, a major literary theme neglected by his Spanish contemporaries, that of the disappointment of human aspirations.

Palacio Valdés's universe was above all that of the popular novel. Much of his novelistic power, like that of Balzac and of Pérez Galdós, had its roots in the archetypal world of the *folletín*. Rather than creating complex characters placed in a realistic milieu, Palacio Valdés presented grandiose struggles between good and evil, portrayed unifaceted and often grotesque characters, and emphasized plot. There was, indeed, in Palacio Valdés an element of excessive self-indulgence such as that found in a bright undergraduate who would never achieve full literary maturity. Throughout his literary career, from *El señorito Octavio* (1881) to *Los cármenes de Granada* (1929), Palacio Valdés relied on the shock effect of exaggerated emotions and plot. Even the more subdued and ironically "realistic" *Riverita* and *Maximina* are flawed by the melodramatic portrayal of Julia's seduction, by the pathos of Maximina's death, and by Rivera's excessive cosmic despair. The stridency and incoherence of *Tristán o el pesimismo* similarly grate on the reader. A certain negligence of composition can also be observed in *La espuma* and *La fe*, where disparate themes are barely connected. An occasional carelessness of style—inappropriate choice of vocabulary, even grammatical incoherence—and a tendency to pretentiousness and pose also mar Palacio Valdés's works.

Palacio Valdés's novels do not merit the critical disrepute into which they have fallen. Palacio Valdés is too often associated with the anodyne philosophies of his old age, when he cultivated his reputation as the "patriarch of Spanish letters," a Spanish Catholic equivalent of the mature Anatole France. The novels of his maturity—those written in the nineteenth century—combine "realistic" traits of ironic observation and ideological commitment with sudden excursions into an archetypal universe of myth. Despite the clumsy composition of many of his works, Palacio Valdés—like Benito Pérez Galdós, who explored the collective and individual madness of his fellow-countrymen, and Leopoldo Alas, who offered a powerful treatment of frustration in *La regenta*—escaped the limitations of a narrow "realism" to suggest a further "reality" of the unconscious. Palacio Valdés's finest novels—*Marta y María, El idilio de un enfermo, Riverita, Los majos de Cádiz, La aldea perdida*—certainly deserve rescue from critical oblivion.

Notes

CHAPTER 1. INTRODUCTION

1. Carlos María Abad, "Novelistas católicos. II. Armando Palacio Valdés," *Razón y Fe* 68 (1924): 45–63. E. Fernández Almuzara, "Palacio Valdés (1853–1938)," *Razón y Fe* 113 (1938): 422–34. Angel Cruz Rueda's *Palacio Valdés* (Granada: Editorial y Librería Prieto, 1938) is full of praise for Franco's "Crusade." Franco sympathizers also attempted to claim, on the grounds of his patriotism, the anticlerical novelist Pérez Galdós for their cause; see Brian J. Dendle, "The Second Republic, the Spanish Civil War, and the *episodios nacionales*," *Crítica Hispánica* 13 (1991): 141–55. Manuel Altolaguirre, on the other hand, curiously claimed, in the republican literary journal *Hora de España* (February 1938), that Palacio Valdés was a "defender of democracy." For Palacio Valdés's sympathy with Italian fascism, see Note 15.

2. Gerald Brenan, *The Literature of the Spanish People* (Cambridge: Cambridge University Press, 1953), 410.

3. Apart from his contributions to the *Revista Europea* in the 1870s and to *ABC* in the 1930s, Palacio Valdés's journalism has been insufficiently studied. Palacio Valdés contributed also to *El Eco de Avilés* (his first article, 22 July 1869), *Rabagás* (with Leopoldo Alas and Tomás Tuero), *El Cronista* (of which he was editor and for which he reported on foreign news for three months), *La Política, Ecos del Nalón* (1878), *Revista de Asturias* (1878–1880), *El Imparcial* (1879), *La Ilustración Gallega y Asturiana* (1881), *El Día* (1880–1881), *Arte y Letras* (1883), *La Epoca* (1884), *España Moderna* (1889–1890), *Revista de la Unión Ibero-Americana* (1904), *España* (1915), *La Esfera* (1918), *Blanco y Negro* (1932), and *El Debate* (1932). Between 1881 and 1931, Palacio Valdés's contributions to the press were only occasional.

4. Camille Pitollet, "Recuerdos de don Armando Palacio Valdés," *Boletín de la Biblioteca Menéndez Pelayo* 33 (1957): 107.

5. Angel Cruz Rueda dates the fracture of the femur, which endangered Palacio Valdés's life, as occurring in February 1928 (*Armando Palacio Valdés* [Madrid: SAETA, 1949], 197). The less-reliable Pitollet dates the accident in 1926 ("Recuerdos," 103).

6. See Angel Cruz Rueda, *Armando Palacio Valdés* (Madrid: 1949), 99–101.

7. His affection for Asturias was expressed, in fulsome terms, in the speeches he delivered in the "Homages" at Avilés (in 1918) and Oviedo (1926). Although he proclaimed his desire to retire to Avilés (Jesús-Andrés Solís, *Homenajes a Palacio Valdés en Asturias* [Candás: Imprenta El Faro, 1976], 39–41), he nonetheless chose Cap Breton for his second residence.

8. For Palacio Valdés's life in Cap Breton, see Leah R. Wagenheim, "A Chat with Armando Palacio Valdés on Feminism," *Hispania* 12 (1929): 439–46. For his admiration for France, see Brian J. Dendle, "Armando Palacio Valdés y Francia," *Estudios de Investigación Franco-española* 4 (1991): 79–90.

9. Pitollet, "Recuerdos," 99.

10. Quoted by Edmund Gosse in the introduction to Armando Palacio Valdés, *Froth* (London: William Heinemann, 1891), xii. The information, in the form of a brief biographical sketch, was included in a letter of 8 November 1890 sent by Palacio Valdés to Gosse; see Brian J. Dendle, "Diez cartas inéditas de Armando Palacio Valdés a Edmund Gosse y a William Heinemann," *BIEA* 47 (1993): 303–13.

11. Matilde Muñoz, "Como vive el patriarca de las letras españolas," *Estampa*, 3 January 1928. With regard to Palacio Valdés's diet, Pitollet notes that the novelist would eat fish but, after gastric disturbances in the 1880s, had long since renounced meat ("Recuerdos," 101). Palacio Valdés, however, in a letter to Betancourt of 16 May 1898, refers to the beefsteak that he had eaten the day before; see Manuel Fernández Rodríguez-Avello, *Vida y obra literaria de Juan Ochoa Betancourt* (Oviedo: Instituto de Estudios Asturianos, 1955), 167.

12. Manuel Altolaguirre, "Don Armando Palacio Valdés," *Hora de España* 14 (February 1938): 90.

13. Jules Laborde, "Préface," to Armando Palacio Valdés, *La Foi* (Paris: Librairie des "Annales Politiques et littéraires," 1910), xiv.

14. Palacio Valdés was an adept name-dropper. For example, he bolstered his arguments in the articles in *Album de un viejo* with references to Aeschylus, Aristotle, Bécquer, Jacob Boehm, Boileau, Bossuet, Bunyan, Carlyle, Alexis Carrel, Cicero, Dante, Emerson, Epicurus, Fichte, Flammarion, Flaubert, Fontenelle, Franklin, Goldsmith, Gracián, Hegel, Heine, Homer, the abbé Huc, Hurtado de Mendoza, Kalidasa, Kant, Leibnitz, Lope de Vega, Novalis, Pascal, Plato, Pliny, Renan, the *Rig Veda*, Saint Augustine, Saint Clement of Alexandria, Saint Francis of Assisi, Saint François de Sales, Saint Paul, Saint Teresa, Sainte Beuve, Schopenhauer, Shakespeare, Socrates, Spinoza, Stendhal, Taine, Tolstoi, and Zola. He refers unfavorably to Ibsen ("Originalidad") and Nietzsche.

15. Beatrice Palumbo Caravaglios quotes from Palacio Valdés's letters to her: "I follow with emotion the success of Italian arms and am pained by the League of Nations' injustice toward Italy. . . . I avidly seek news from Italy. There is no Spaniard with a heart who is not at this moment supporting our sister nation. My strongest wishes are for the glory of Italy" (19 October 1935). "On Sunday the 16th it will be decided whether we are going to be a free and civilized nation or a second Russia" (February 1936). "The situation of my country is most painful. We are living in total anarchy; how I envy the Italian nation! Today it is the happiest nation on earth" (June 1936). See Beatrice Palumbo Caravaglios, *Armando Palacio Valdés* (Aquila: Officine Tipografiche Aquilane, 1938), 17–8.

16. See Guadalupe Gómez-Ferrer, "Palacio Valdés en los años noventa: la quiebra del positivismo," in *Clarín y "La Regenta" en su tiempo* (Oviedo: Universidad de Oviedo, 1987), 1064–5.

17. Luis Antón del Olmet and José de Torres Bernal, *Palacio Valdés* (Madrid Imprenta de Juan Pueyo, 1919), 11–20.

18. Angel Cruz Rueda, *Armando Palacio Valdés. Su vida y su obra* (Paris Madrid, Lisbon: Agence Mondiale de Librairie, 1925; rev. 2d ed., Madrid SAETA, 1949).

19. Constantino Cabal, "Esta vez era un hombre de Laviana . . . ," *BIEA* 7 (1953): 168–278.

20. The references in this paragraph are respectively to: Peter A. Bly, "La fe y Galdós," in Brian J. Dendle and Stephen Miller, eds., *Estudios sobre Armando Palacio Valdés*, 62–73; José F. Montesinos, *Pereda o la novela idilio* (Madrid

Castalia, 1969), 287; María José Tintoré, *"La Regenta" de Clarín y la crítica de su tiempo* (Barcelona: Editorial Lumen, 1987), 58; Mariano Gómez-Santos, *Leopoldo Alas "Clarín." Ensayo biobibliográfico* (Oviedo: Instituto de Estudios Asturianos, 1952), 81, 186–7; Adolfo Alas, *Epistolario a Clarín* (Madrid: Ediciones Escorial, 1951), 118–9.

21. Alberto Guillén, "Armando Palacio Valdés," in his *La linterna de Diógenes* (Madrid: Editorial América, n. d.), 33–40. Although Guillén's work bears no publication date, internal evidence suggests that it was published in 1921.

22. See Pío Baroja, *Desde la útima vuelta del camino, Obras completas* (Madrid: Biblioteca Nueva, 1949), 7: 762–3, 784, 806, and *Nuevo Tablado de Arlequín, Obras completas* (Madrid: Biblioteca Nueva, 1948), 5: 128.

23. Pitollet, "Recuerdos," 77–8. For an account of Pitollet's eccentricities and stormy relations with his French colleagues, see Marie-Françoise Segut, *Les mémoires manuscrits de Camille Pitollet à la Bibliothèque Municipale de Dijon* (Dijon: Université de Dijon. Faculté de Langues et Civilisation Etrangères, 1979–1980).

24. Enrique Gómez Carrillo. *Treinta años de mi vida.* Vol. 3 (*La miseria de Madrid*) (Madrid: Sociedad Española de Librería, 1921), 173.

25. César Barja, *Libros y autores modernos* (Los Angeles: Campbell's Book Store, 1933), 381.

26. Rafael Narbona, *Palacio Valdés o la Armonía* (Madrid: Librería General de Victoriano Suárez, 1941), 5 and 13.

27. Edwin H. Cady, "Armando Palacio Valdés Writes to William Dean Howells," *Symposium* 2 (1948): 19–37.

28. José María Roca Franquesa, *Palacio Valdés, técnica novelística y credo estético* (Oviedo: Instituto de Estudios Asturianos, 1951), 41.

29. Maria Romano Colangeli, *A. Palacio Valdés Romanziere* (Lecce: Libreria Editrice Milella, 1962), 116.

30. Manuel Pascual Rodríguez, *Armando Palacio Valdés. Teoría y práctica novelística* (Madrid: Sociedad General Española de Librería, 1976), 84, 154.

31. Ibid., 134.

32. Ibid., 193–9.

33. Ibid., 230–1.

34. José María Roca Franquesa, *Clases sociales y tipos representativos en la novelística de Armando Palacio Valdés* (Oviedo: Instituto de Estudios Asturianos, 1980).

35. Guadalupe Gómez-Ferrer, *Palacio Valdés y el mundo social de la Restauración* (Oviedo: Instituto de Estudios Asturianos, 1983), 67.

36. Ibid., 119.

37. Ibid., 126.

38. Ibid., 370–1.

39. For Palacio Valdés's hostile treatments of the Krausists, see Brian J. Dendle, "Armando Palacio Valdés, the *Revista Europea*, and the Krausist Movement," *Letras Peninsulares* 4 (1991): 25–33.

40. Gómez-Ferrer takes at face value the pretensions of the Krausist Homobono Pereda of *El señorito Octavio* (372, 378, 382–3), who is, nevertheless, in the context of the novel (and above all in the first edition, which Gómez-Ferrer has obviously not consulted), a fool whose inane beliefs Palacio Valdés satirizes. Similarly, she attempts to make of Palacio Valdés an antimilitarist; she thus assumes that Cristóbal Mateo's opposition to the army in *El maestrante* represents the author's opinion (376–7) rather than a character's comic idiosyncrasy; Gómez-Ferrer does not consider Palacio Valdés's obvious approval of the

devotion to duty of the army officer Ricardo, the Marqués de Peñalta, in *Marta y María*.

41. Laura N. de Villavicencio, "El estilo de época y la expresión personal en las descripciones de Pereda, Pardo Bazán y Palacio Valdés," *Hispanófila* 60 (1977): 21–44.

42. Gilbert Paolini, "La Psicopatología en la Literatura Italo-española: D'Annunzio y Palacio Valdés," in Americo Bugliani, ed., *The Two Hesperias. Literary Studies in Honor of Joseph G. Fucilla* (Madrid: Porrúa Turanzas, 1978), 275–89.

43. Guadalupe Gómez-Ferrer Morant, "La imagen de la mujer en la novela de la Restauración: Ocio social y trabajo doméstico I," in Rosa María Capel Martínez, ed., *Mujer y sociedad en España 1700–1975* (2nd ed.) (Madrid: Ministerio de Cultura, Instituto de la Mujer, 1986), 147–73.

44. Noël M. Valis, "Palacio Valdés' First Novel," *Romance Notes* 20 (1980): 317–21; Brian J. Dendle, "Las variantes textuales de *El señorito Octavio*, de Armando Palacio Valdés," *BIEA* 41 (1987): 463–74.

45. Brian J. Dendle, "Erotismo y anticlericalismo en la primera edición de *Marta y María*, de Armando Palacio Valdés," *BBMP* 65 (1989): 305–6.

46. Daniel Henri Pageaux, "Eléments pour une lecture de *La hermana San Sulpicio* de Armando Palacio Valdés," *Iberoromania* 16 (1982): 95–109.

47. Jesús Fernández Alvarez, "Un probable eco de Henry Fielding en *La fe* de Armando Palacio Valdés," *Filología Moderna* Nos. 33–34 (October 1969): 101–08; Jennifer J. Wood, "Armando Palacio Valdés's *La Fe*: Providential Novel," *Hispanic Journal* 7 (1985): 51–57; Peter A. Bly, "*La fe*: Palacio Valdés Looks Back to Alas and Forward to Unamuno," *Romance Quarterly* 35 (1988): 339–46; D. J. O'Connor, "Filiation, the Eucharist and the Grotesque in Palacio Valdés' *La fe* (1892)," *Letras Peninsulares* 1 (1988): 51–69; D. J. O'Connor, "Mrs. Humphrey Ward's *Robert Elsmere* (1888) and Palacio Valdés's *La fe* (1892)," *Romance Quarterly* 37 (1990): 331–36.

48. D. J. O'Connor, "Parallel Plots and Fates in Palacio Valdés' *El origen del pensamiento* (1894)," *España Contemporánea* 3 (1990): 105–15.

49. Francisco Caudet, "Armando Palacio Valdés: alcance ideológico de *La aldea perdida*," *Diálogos Hispánicos de Amsterdam* 4 (1984): 109–23; Jean-François Botrel, "Paysages et industrialisation: Les visions d'Armando Palacio Valdés dans *La aldea perdida*," in Claude Dumas, ed., *L'Homme et l'espace dans la littérature, les arts et l'histoire en Espagne et en Amérique Latine au XIXe. siécle* (Université de Lille III, 1985), 157–69.

50. Gilbert Paolini, "Resonancia armónica del mundo mágico creadora del porvenir en *La alegría del Capitán Ribot*," in Juan Fernández Jiménez, José J. Labrador Herraiz, and L. Teresa Valdivieso, eds., *Estudios en Homenaje a Enrique Ruiz Fornells* (Erie, Pennsylvania: ALDEEU, 1990), 479–85.

51. Brian J. Dendle, "Los artículos de Armando Palacio Valdés en *ABC*, 1932–1936." *BIEA* 44 (1990): 233–79.

52. Brian J. Dendle and Stephen Miller, eds., *Estudios sobre Armando Palacio Valdés* (Ottawa: Dovehouse Editions, Canada, 1993).

53. William Dean Howells, *Harpers* 76 (January 1888): 320.

54. The quotes are respectively from: the review of *Riverita*, *Harpers* 73 (1886): 964; and the review of *Maximina*, *Harpers* 76 (January 1888): 320. Howells's cliché-ridden and overly benevolent criticism of Palacio Valdés has recently been usefully studied by Angel Capellán González, "William Dean Howells and Armando Palacio Valdés: A Literary Friendship," *Revista de Estudios Hispánicos* 10 (1976): 451–71.

55. Sylvester Baxter, "A Great Modern Spaniard," *Atlantic Monthly* 85 (1900): 546–9. Grant Showerman, "A Spanish Novelist," *The Sewanee Review* 22 (1914): 404.

56. Pío Baroja, *Nuevo Tablado de Arlequín, Obras completas* (Madrid: Biblioteca Nueva, 1948), 5: 128; José María Carretero, "Palacio Valdés," *La Esfera*, No. 2, 10 January 1914; Luis Antón del Olmet and José de Torres Bernal, *Palacio Valdés*, 30; Ramón Martínez de la Riva, "La novela españolista," *Blanco y Negro*, 9 February 1919; Camille Pitollet, "Don Armando Palacio Valdés," *Bulletin Hispanique* 40 (1938): 203.

57. José A. Balseiro, *Novelistas españoles modernos* (7th ed.) (New York: Las Américas Publishing Co., 1963), 444, note 21.

58. L. Bordes, "Armando Palacio Valdés," *Bulletin Hispanique* 1 (1899): 45–76; F. Vézinet, "A. Palacio Valdés," *Les maîtres du roman espagnol contemporain* (Paris: Hachette, 1907), 167–202.

59. H. Peseux-Richard, "Armando Palacio Valdés," *Revue Hispanique* 42 (1918): 314.

60. Jean Sarrailh, "Palacio Valdés," *Prosateurs espagnols contemporains* (Paris: Librairie Delagrave, 1927), 78.

61. Pitollet, "Recuerdos," 115.

62. See Philine Burnet, "*La Novela de un Novelista*," *L'Express du Midi*, 3 April 1922, and "Nos amis d'Espagne," *L'Express du Midi*, 22 April 1924; and Paul Mathiex, "Souvenirs d'Enfance," *L'Express du Midi*, 6 February 1924.

63. José Martínez Cachero, "40 fichas para una bibliographia 'sobre' Armando Palacio Valdés," *BIEA* 19 (1953): 467–78.

64. I have been unable to locate in the respective journals the following items listed by Pitollet ("Recuerdos," p. 120): *L'Express du Midi*, 20 September 1920 and 16 April 1925; *La Garonne*, 21 March 1938.

65. For example, Gómez-Ferrer lists an article on *La aldea perdida* by J. H. Abbot; Professor Abbot denies any knowledge of such a publication (letter of 19 December 1990). Even more curious is the listing by both Manuel Pascual Rodríguez (*Armando Palacio Valdés, Teoría y práctica novelística*) and Guadalupe Gómez-Ferrer of a book by P. Barberis, *Palacio Valdés, le roman possible. Théories, thèmes, techniques* (Paris: Corti, 1969). I can find no trace of the existence of this work; the Librairie José Corti informs me that "we have published no work by Barberis and nothing on Palacio Valdés" (letter of 21 December 1990).

66. For example, the Aguilar edition suppresses, perhaps because of its sexual connotations, the essay "Las caderas" (*Album de un viejo*).

CHAPTER 2. THE LITERARY APPRENTICESHIP, 1875–1881

1. In the second paragraph of his essay on Revilla, Palacio Valdés declared that he had already treated Revilla in *La Política*. My search of *La Política* between July 1874 and December 1875 reveals only one article by Palacio Valdés: "Los oradores del Ateneo. Don José Moreno Nieto" (*La Política*, 15 June 1875); the text resembles, but is not identical to, that of the *Revista Europea* version.

2. The essay on Galdós was omitted in 1908 from *Semblanzas literarias*, possibly because its heavy anticlericalism no longer reflected the views of Palacio Valdés, as Noël M. Valis argues ("Una opinión de Palacio Valdés," *BIEA* 82 [1982]: 691–714). However, the mature Palacio Valdés certainly recalled the

essay as Christian in spirit: "You say that you and others speak of my *conversion*. This is an impossibility because I have never ceased to be a Christian in theory, and I cite my 'semblanza' [likeness] of Galdós written when I was twenty-four" (letter of 11 April 1906 to Maximiliano Arboleya, cited by José María Roca Franquesa, *Clases sociales y tipos representativos en la novelística de Armando Palacio Valdés*, 51).

3. A further adolescent reading was of Chateaubriand's *Atala* and *Les Natchez*; see Armando Palacio Valdés, "La novela en América," *Revista de la Unión Ibero-Americana* 20 (1 March 1906): 26–7.

4. For a fascinating discussion of the theme of the femme fatale in nineteenth-century European literature, see Mario Praz, "La Belle Dame sans Merci," in his *The Romantic Agony* (Cleveland: The World Publishing Co., 1967), 187–286. Although Professor Praz makes no reference to Spanish literature, Anita of *Crotalus horridus* would fully exemplify his thesis.

5. See Palacio Valdés's letter of 14 November 1880 to Galdós, reproduced in Sebastián de la Nuez and José Schraibman, *Cartas del archivo de Galdós* (Madrid: Taurus, 1967), 110–2.

6. Publicity for the novel also resulted from the attacks by Aniceto Valdivia in *Madrid Cómico* in March and April 1881 and Palacio Valdés's consequent challenge of Valdivia to a duel (*Madrid Cómico*, 24 April 1881). I am indebted to Professor Noël M. Valis for drawing my attention to the feud with Valdivia.

7. Noël M. Valis, "Palacio Valdés' First Novel," *Romance Notes* 20 (1980): 317–21.

8. Nevertheless, in her vitality, good health, and refusal to heed Octavio's attempts to convert her into a character from a novel, Carmen meets with the narrator's approbation and is a forerunner of the Marta of *Marta y María*.

9. For a full discussion of the changes in the 1896 edition, see Brian J. Dendle, "Las variantes textuales de *El señorito Octavio*, de Armando Palacio Valdés," *BIEA* 41 (1987): 463–74.

CHAPTER 3. THE NOVELS OF THE 1880s:
FROM ASTURIAS TO SEVILLA

1. For the regional aspects of Palacio Valdés's novels, see Jesús-Andrés Solís, *La Asturias de Palacio Valdés* (Avilés: Graf. Careaga, 1973) and José González Fernández, "Aspectos regionales en Jovellanos, Palacio Valdés y Clarín," *Boletín del Instituto de Estudios Asturianos* 41 (1987): 433–61.

2. All textual references to *Marta y María* in this chapter are to the first edition (Barcelona: Biblioteca "Arte y Letras," 1883). For the success of the novel and Palacio Valdés's difficulties in recovering his rights to republish the novel from the editors (the Casa Domenech of Barcelona), see Antón del Olmet and Torres Bernal, *Palacio Valdés*, 73–4.

3. Luis Bonafoux claims, albeit only in passing, that Leopoldo Alas's *La regenta* (1884) was inspired by *Marta y María*; see his *Yo y el plagiario Clarín* (Madrid: 1888), 66. The connection, if such exists, would be in the portrayals of María and Ana de Ozores, both discontented and basing their lives on literature. Beth Wietelmann Bauer argues that Marta is a case of *bovarysme* and is in Palacio Valdés's representation a false, literary character condemned for her challenge to patriarchal cultural codes; see Bauer, "*Marta y María*: misticismo y romanticismo en Palacio Valdés," *Estudios sobre Armando Palacio Valdés*, 24–35. On the other hand, María Martínez Sierra, recalling her youthful read-

ing of *Marta y María*, notes the daring nature of Palacio Valdés's portrayal of Marta: Marta's taking of the initiative in love, the description of the onset of puberty, Marta's attempted suicide, the hint of incest; see "Armando Palacio Valdés, novelista para mujeres," *Palacio Valdés. Homenaje en el primer centenario de su nacimiento* (Buenos Aires: Ateneo Jovellanos, 1953), 29–34.

4. Cf. the similar failure to achieve martyrdom in late nineteenth-century Spain of the eponymous hero of Galdós's *Nazarín* (1895).

5. For example, see the narrator's interjection in praise of Marta's humility and honesty (348).

6. See Brian J. Dendle, "Eroticismo y anticlericalismo en la primera edición de *Marta y María*, de Armando Palacio Valdés," *Boletín de la Biblioteca Menéndez Pelayo* 65 (1989): 305–16.

7. Palacio Valdés's hostility to the devotion to the Sacred Heart was probably inspired by its novelty in Spain (Marie Alacoque was beatified only in 1864) and its foreign origin. Cf. the complaint voiced by the priest Don Juan in Galdós's *Angel Guerra* (1891): "This invasion by foreign sodalities is a humiliation for our nation. I'm getting fed up with all this Sacred Heart and Marie Alacoque, Bernadette and I know not what" (Benito Pérez Galdós, *Obras completas* [Madrid: Aguilar, 1942], 5: 1512). Cf. the similar hostility expressed in *La hermana San Sulpicio* to the French order of nuns which exploits Sister San Sulpicio.

8. Palacio Valdés resisted recognition of the significance of his own creation. He thus dismissed the beach scene in a letter to Leopoldo Alas: "What seems certain to me is that I falsified Marta's character in the beach scene; you must realize, however, that she was drunk" (Letter of 29 August 1883, in Adolfo Alas, *Epistolario a Clarín* [Madrid: Ediciones Escorial, 1951], 120).

9. See Dendle, "Eroticismo y anticlericalismo," 306–7.

10. Much later, in 1911, Palacio Valdés again expressed his disapproval of young ladies who abandon their parents to care for the parents of others; see "El viaje de la monja," *Papeles del doctor Angélico*, 275.

11. See, for example, 258–9, a passage suppressed in later editions, in which Palacio Valdés posits a connection between sensuality and religious practices.

12. Leopoldo Alas, who had objected to the excessive length of *Marta y María*, complained that *El idilio de un enfermo* lacked spontaneity and, in its brevity, was merely the outline of a novel (*Sermón perdido* [Madrid: Fernando Fe, 1885], 235–48). Andrés González Blanco merely repeats Clarín's negative criticism (*Historia de la novela en España desde el romanticismo hasta nuestros días* [Madrid: Sáenz de Jubera, 1909], 517–9). The suggestion that Clarín's sentimental tale ¡*Adiós Cordera!* was inspired by an incident in *El idilio de un enfermo* (Barja, *Libros y autores*, 376) to my mind lacks foundation.

13. Palacio Valdés served on the editorial board of *Arte y Letras*, which was published by Editorial Domenech (the publishers of *Marta y María*), edited by José Yxart, and distributed without charge to subscribers to the collection "Biblioteca Arte y Letras." See David Torres, "Indice de la revista ilustrada, *Arte y Letras* (Barcelona, 1882–1883)," *Hispania* 66 (1983): 345–7.

14. Thus: "The heart-rending lamentations of the unhappy wives and of the children calling for their fathers still sound in my ears" 262). A similar procedure—that of narratorial intervention with a switching to the present tense—occurs in *La aldea perdida* (1903).

15. For example, see Andrés González Blanco, *Historia de la novela*, 520. Because of its maritime setting, most critics compare *José* to Pereda's *Sotileza* (1885). Despite its brevity, the most useful account of the novel is given by

Pedro Penzol, "José en Inglaterra," *Boletín del Instituto de Estudios Asturianos* 7 (1953): 422–5. Penzol identifies three strands of the plot: the love of José and Elisa, the scheming of Isabel to prevent the wedding, and the protection offered by Meira. Penzol compares *José* with English pantomimes in its characters (the model young lovers, the repulsive, domineering, and miserly mother of the groom), in the appearances of the geniuses of good and evil, and in its happy ending. In this novel of the North ("almost an English novel") the hero struggles physically against the sea and morally against the envy of his neighbors. The success of the novel with its readers is due to its strong moral elements. Penzol recalls Ramón Pérez de Ayala's claim that the Asturian landscape "tiene tinieblas en las cumbres" (is dark on its mountain tops) (425).

16. José María de Pereda's *Pedro Sánchez* (1883) is, so far as I can recall, the only other nineteenth-century Spanish bildungsroman. The first two series of *episodios nacionales* of Benito Pérez Galdós cannot be included in this category, for Galdós's concern is more with historical events than with the moral growth of the protagonists, Gabriel Araceli and Salvador Monsalud.

17. Cf. Palacio Valdés's second wife's comment to the journalist Matilde Muñoz that in earlier years Palacio Valdés "had a somewhat violent character" (Matilde Muñoz, "Como vive el patriarca de las letras españolas," *Estampa*, 3 January 1928).

18. Palacio Valdés, then aged thirty, had married his sixteen-year-old bride on 4 October 1883. Years later, in *Páginas escogidas* (1917), he denied the autobiographical nature of the two novels, but confessed that the character of Maximina was based on that of his wife.

19. Thus: "He fell on his knees at her feet begging forgiveness, embracing and kissing them while trembling with terror and sensual delight" (1: 125). Cf. a similar theme of enslavement to passion in *Los majos de Cádiz*.

20. Clarín, in his review of the novel, objected to the inclusion of anecdotes and episodes not related to the development of the plot; see Leopoldo Alas, "Riverita," *Nueva Campaña (1885–1886)* (Madrid: Fernando Fe, 1887), 243–5.

21. Miguel de Unamuno, for example, presented the novel to his bride, doubtless for her to find inspiration in the submissive Maximina (Unamuno, "Por Armando Palacio Valdés," *Obras completas* [Madrid: Afrodisio Aguado, 1958] 5: 317–8). W. D. Howells found that, save for "a Latin frankness here and there," *Maximina* was "a flawless praise of marriage and wifehood, and one of the most exquisitely touching and consoling books ever written" (*Harpers* 76 [January 1888], 316–20). More recently, Gómez-Ferrer has found that "Maximina's type corresponds perfectly with the feminine ideal of a domestically-oriented middle class" (*Palacio Valdés y el mundo social de la Restauración*, 105).

22. Rivera's commonsense advice to Utrilla is treated as follows: "Such was, with slight variations, the advice which in the early ages of Greece Minerva, the bright-eyed goddess, gave to the divine Achilles in his famous quarrel with Agamemnon, the son of Atreus" (1: 100). Similar ironical references to the gods occur throughout *La aldea perdida*.

23. Solís identifies the romería with that of La Luz (Avilés); see Jesús-Andrés Solís, *La Asturias de Palacio Valdés* (Avilés: Gráf. Careaga, 1973), 113.

24. His abdication of responsibility and flight into literature is exemplified by the stoicism with which he receives the news of Venturita's flight from the convent: "Indeed, what was the significance of that purely individual pain which afflicted him in comparison with universal suffering, with the slow, certain advance of humanity toward its destiny? At that time he had just read

a famous pamphlet by a French author, entitled *The World Advances*, and his brains were muddled and dazzled by its great historical syntheses, which helped him not a little to bear the blow" (2: 328). Palacio Valdés's irony in this passage is Cervantine.

25. Palacio Valdés related that the theme of the novel had been suggested by the spectacle of the divisions and animosities aroused in a provincial town with the founding of a newspaper that leveled vicious personal attacks on local citizens ("*El cuarto poder,*" *ABC*, 11 February 1932). Palacio Valdés had already briefly treated a similar theme when describing the two provincial newspapers *La Crónica* and *El Occidente* (*Maximina*, 2: 175–6).

26. A similar defense of fidelity to one's promised word is expressed in Ricardo's refusal to betray his oath of military loyalty in *Marta y María*.

27. "I did it for him, not for you!" Cecilia exclaims melodramatically (2: 263). William Dean Howells denounced the episode for its falsity and "efectismo." For Palacio Valdés's comments on Howell's remarks, see the prologue to *La hermana San Sulpicio* (Madrid: Tipografía de Manuel G. Hernández, 1889), lxxv.

28. Cf. the portrayal of brawling, self-centered clergymen and the implication that, in his recruitment of future nuns, the priest Don Benigno employs the tactics of a seducer (1: 279–80).

29. Cf. the similar portrayal of a perverted enslavement to passion in *Los majos de Cádiz;* in the later novel, however, Manolo Velázquez is able to exercise free will and renounce Soledad. Note also that in *El cuarto poder* Flores's love of Cecilia increases with rejection.

30. For brief accounts of the circumstances of composition, see Cruz Rueda, *Armando Palacio Valdés* (2d ed.), 105–7, 116–8, and Pitollet, "Recuerdos," 88–90.

31. The point is made by Daniel Henri Pageaux, "Eléments pour une lecture de *La hermana San Sulpicio* de Armando Palacio Valdés," *Iberoromania* 16 (1982): 106.

32. Father Francisco Blanco García, objecting to Palacio Valdés's treatment of religious persons and authority, doubted the success of the marriage of Gloria Bermúdez and Ceferino Sanjurjo: "If *La hermana San Sulpicio* had a second part, the author himself would probably have indicated the unpleasant consequences of the marriage of Gloria Bermúdez and her worshiper" (*La literatura española en el siglo XIX*, 2: 535).

33. The satirical rendering of Llagostera's inability to speak Castilian correctly is purely for comic, *costumbrista* effect, in the manner of Mesonero Romanos's "La posada o España en Madrid." Palacio Valdés offers a favorable portrayal of a Catalan, without regional prejudice, in "Cómo se casó Taulet" (*Tiempos felices*).

34. Daniel Henri Pageaux, 103. Interestingly, in 1898 Pierre Louÿs, who had visited Sevilla in 1895 and 1896, offered a powerful portrayal of the pathological degradation wrought by sexual passion in the highly successful novel *La Femme et le pantin; roman espagnol*, written in the first person and set in the same stereotypical Sevilla as that depicted by Palacio Valdés. However, it is unlikely—given his rudimentary knowledge of Spanish—that Louÿs was acquainted with *La hermana San Sulpicio*.

35. Stephen M. Hart, without considering the influence of the *folletín*, examines Palacio Valdés's debt to romanticism. Palacio Valdés establishes in *La hermana San Sulpicio* "an ambiguous dialogue with the discourse of romanticism." Sanjurjo is a self-confident representative ot national culture; his strong

sense of self differentiates him from the romantic hero: "Unlike the ill-defined beings who populate romantic literature, Sanjurjo has a fixed understanding of his own identity; in other words, he is a phallic being without doubts as to his self-worth." See Stephen M. Hart, "Deshilando el nudo romántico en *La hermana San Sulpicio,*" *Estudios sobre Armando Palacio Valdés,* 36–46. Treatment of Sanjurjo's self-conscious irony (not mentioned by Hart) would reinforce Hart's argument of Sanjurjo's sense of superiority and self-worth.

CHAPTER 4. THE NOVELS OF THE 1890S

1. The contemporary critic Ramón Perés y Perés correctly termed *La espuma* a "work of combat," "somewhat revolutionary, but revolutionary in a right and honorable way" (*A dos vientos* [Barcelona: Librería "L'Avenç," 1892], 57). Maurice Hemingway confirms that for Palacio Valdés "the future belongs to the doctor, to the university professor, that is, to the *bourgeoisie,* and by preference to the liberal *bourgeoisie;* the aristocracy, on the other hand, is a pernicious anachronism." For Hemingway, Palacio Valdés is overtimid in not lending stronger support to the socialist doctor's program; see Maurice Hemingway, "Palacio Valdés y la novela aristocrática," *Estudios sobre Armando Palacio Valdés,* 47–61. Guadalupe Gómez-Ferrer usefully compares Luis Coloma's *Pequeñeces* and *La espuma* and indicates Palacio Valdés's reformism and sympathy with Utopian socialism ("La clase dirigente madrileña en dos novelas de 1890," in *Madrid en la sociedad del siglo XIX* [Madrid: Revista ALFOZ/Facultad de Geografía e Historia Universidad Complutense/Comunidad de Madrid Consejería de Cultura, 1986], 1: 533–6).

2. Arturo Berenguer Carisomo observes: "it is one of his weakest and worse constructed novels . . . all the figures who appear in it are specters, fabrications of the novelist and not authentic human beings"; see "Armando Palacio Valdés (Esbozo de su novelística)," in *Palacio Valdés. Homenaje en el primer centenario de su nacimiento,* 58.

3. The 1909 edition of *La fe* contains a "Declaración del autor" in which Palacio Valdés quotes Saint François de Sales and Saint Jeronimus to justify his portrayal of a priest beset by doubt (a step on the path to faith and salvation) and his satire of unworthy clergymen; Palacio Valdés ends his "Declaración" with a declaration of faith in "the doctrines of the Catholic Church to which I take pride in living subject." The *Oxford Companion to Spanish Literature* claims, erroneously, that *La fe* could not be published in Spain during the Franco period. However, the 1945 Aguilar edition of the *Obras completas* includes the text of *La fe.* Although this is not the place to discuss the haphazard workings of the Franco censorship. it should be noted that chapter 12 of *La fe,* that detailing Padre Gil's flight with Obdulia, is reproduced in Rafael Narbona, *Palacio Valdés o La armonía* (1941); Narbona emphasizes Padre Gil's religious faith and sense of Christian mission (137). Wilfred A. Beardsley also claims that the novel portrays the "sincerity of religious experience" ("Certain Considerations Inviting Reappraisal of *La fe,* by Armando Palacio Valdés," *Hispania* 17 [1934]: 138).

4. Leopoldo Alas, in his review of *La fe,* stressed the novelty in Spanish literature of Palacio Valdés's portrayal of a priest's religious doubt; see Alas, "*La fe,*" in his *Ensayos y revistas 1888–1892* (Madrid: Manuel Fernández y Lasanta, 1892), 371–7.

5. Palacio Valdés acknowledged the justice of this reproach in the "Decla-

ración del Autor" that precedes the 1909 edition (viii). A similar failure to convey mystical experience is evident in Somerset Maugham's popular novel *The Razor's Edge*.

6. Jesús Fernández Alvarez, "Un probably eco de Henry Fielding en *La fe* de Armando Palacio Valdés," *Filología Moderna* Nos. 33–4 (October 1969): 101–8.

7. For a full discussion of Pérez Galdós's debt in *Nazarín* to *La fe*, see Peter A. Bly, "*La fe* y Galdós," *Estudios sobre Armando Palacio Valdés*, 62–73.

8. "The novel begins like a serial novel ['feuilleton'] by Ponson du Terrail" (H. Peseux-Richard, "Armando Palacio Valdés," *Revue Hispanique* 42 [1918]: 409).

9. The reference to Medea was first made by L. Bordes, "Armando Palacio Valdés," *Bulletin Hispanique* 1 (1899): 63.

10. Thus, the narrator justifies her superstitious fear that some ill will follow her excessive mirth: "Women, without doubt, are more in touch than men with the magnetic forces which operate secretly in Nature's bosom" (*El origen del pensamiento* [Madrid: Los Hijos de M. G. Hernández, 1893], 413).

11. Armando Palacio Valdés, *Páginas escogidas* (Madrid: Casa Editorial Calleja, 1917), 179–80; Pitollet paraphrases Palacio Valdés's declaration ("Recuerdos"). Two years previously, however, Palacio Valdés had told José María Carretero ("El Caballero Audaz") that the novel in which he had invested his soul was *Tristán o el pesimismo* and that his most original work was *La aldea perdida* (Carretero, *Lo que sé por mí* [Madrid: Sanz Calleja, 1915], 147–8). On another occasion, Palacio Valdés claimed that his favorite work was *Maximina* and that his best work from the literary point of view was *Marta y María* (Pitollet, "Don Armando Palacio Valdés," *Bulletin Hispanique* 40 [1938]: 205).

12. The prologue has not been reprinted in Spanish, although an English version exists: "The Decadence of Modern Literature," in *The Book of Literature*, edited by Richard Garnett, Leon Vallée, and Alois Brandl, vols. 23–4 (New York: The Grolier Society, 1899): xiii–xxxviii.

13. In the first edition, *Los majos de Cádiz* is presented as a "novel of customs." In the edition published by *Revista Literaria*, it is termed a "historical novel" (Serie "Novelas y cuentos," No. 209, 5 October 1935).

14. For earlier examples of moments of magic and mystery in Palacio Valdés's novels, cf. the romería in *El señorito Octavio*, the boat excursion in *Marta y María*, and the lovers' flight in *El idilio de un enfermo*.

15. Examples of classical references are: the allusion to Cicero (24); the comparison of Soledad's feet with "those of Hebe, the immortal cupbearer of the gods," (107); the comparison of Cádiz with Venus (the city is "encircled, like the Cypriot goddess, by a soft girdle of foam," 137); the reference to the moon as "the white goddess" (157) and the description of Soledad as "calm as a goddess" (162). A typical example of Andalusian speech would be Uceda's greeting of Soledad in the first chapter: "¡Para mí, criatura, eres y serás la Virgen del Carmen y la Santísima Trinidad y el copón y la hostia . . . !" (For me, lass, you are and will be the Virgin of the Carmen and the most holy Trinity and the ciborium and the host . . . !) (10). The melodramatic presentation, in terms of the *folletín*, of certain characters confirms the impression of a popular, violent, and sentimental Andalusianism; thus, Uceda's jealousy: "El alma del viajero quedó negra como la noche" (The soul of the traveler turned as black as night) (11).

16. Cf. Palacio Valdés's declaration many years later that we are not necessarily controlled by our temperaments: "We are not fatally bound by our tempera-

ment. Certainly we are born with good or evil tendencies, but our moral sense can be developed just as our intelligence" ("Opiniones imparciales," *Album de un viejo*, 65).

17. For a further example of repentance that leads to the triumph of love, see the final chapter of the tale "Como se casó el marqués de Guadaira" in *Tiempos felices* (1933).

18. "¡Pero si eso es un folletín! . . . Ya que usted me desahucia y me obliga a abandonar la partida por lo menos no me convierta en un seductor de novela por entregas de los que excitan la cólera de las modistas" (But this is a veritable *feuilleton!* . . . Since you're kicking me out and forcing me to give up, at least don't make me into a seducer from one of those serial novels that stir the emotions of dressmakers) (220).

19. Vézinet claimed that the novel portrays a conflict between the morality of Nietzsche and that of Christ; see F. Vézinet, *Les maîtres du roman espagnol contemporain* (Paris: Hachette, 1907), 199. Rafael Altamira considered *La alegría del capitán Ribot* to be Palacio Valdés's most balanced and perfect work, its moral conflict one of touching nobility and elevation; see Rafael Altamira, "Palacio Valdés," in his *Arte y realidad* (Barcelona: Editorial Cervantes, 1921), 112. For Gilbert Paolini, the novel illustrates the Ciceronian concept of friendship; Palacio Valdés advocates, through Ribot, national regeneration through moral progress; see Paolini, "Resonancia armónica del mundo mágico del porvenir en *La alegría del capitán Ribot*," in Juan Fernández Jiménez, José J. Labrador, and L. Teresa Valdivieso, editors, *Estudios en Homenaje a Enrique Ruiz Fornells* (Erie, Penn.: ALDEEU, 1990), 479–85.

CHAPTER 5. *THE LATER WORKS*

1. Many years later, Palacio Valdés drew attention to the contrast between the sordid customs and abject thoughts of the peasants of the mountains of Asturias and their melodious and poetic songs ("Divagando," *Album de un viejo*, 180).

2. Many critics have failed to appreciate the irony of Palacio Valdés's portrayal of a patriarchal Arcadia. Thus, in his two studies of *La aldea perdida*, Francisco Caudet claims that Palacio Valdés vindicates a reactionary, traditional society, is unwilling to accept industrial progress, and is blind to social ills; see Francisco Caudet, "Armando Palacio Valdés : alcance ideológico de *La aldea perdida*," *Diálogos Hispánicos de Amsterdam* 4 (1984): 109–23; and "*La aldea perdida* (1903), novela de tesis," *Estudios sobre Armando Palacio Valdés*, 85–97. Ciriaco Morón Arroyo, on the other hand, in a brilliant and sensitive treatment of the novel, defends Palacio Valdés against charges of superficiality and reaction. Morón Arroyo stresses the complexity or "polyphony" of the text: the dual viewpoint of the narrator who is both a child (who nostalgically recalls the past in epic terms and is incapable of seeing the defects of his society) and an adult realist. Morón Arroyo explores the wealth of classical allusions, which reinforce the dual structure of the novel: child/adult, classical world/contemporary history. For Morón Arroyo, the narrator is ambiguous toward his theme; the ambiguity lies not so much in the text as in life itself: "Palacio Valdés neither praises nor condemns but dramatizes the ambiguity of progress." (See Ciriaco Morón Arroyo, "*La aldea perdida* entre el pasado y el presente," *Estudios sobre Armando Palacio Valdés*, 98–110.) Guadalupe Gómez-Ferrer Morant has indicated the contradictory nature and ambiguity of Palacio Valdés's ideo-

logical posture in *La aldea perdida* ("Apoliticismo y fisiocracia entre las clases medias españolas de comienzos del siglo XIX," *Cuadernos de historia moderna y contemporánea* 1 [1980]: 200).

3. For a useful discussion of Tristán's pessimism—which Baquero believes reflects Palacio Valdés's own pessimism—see the "Estudio crítico" by Mariano Baquero Goyanes that precedes his edition of *Tristán o el pesimismo* (Madrid: Narcea, 1971), 59–62. Antonio Vallejo Nágera's description of Tristán's paranoia, on the other hand, is brief and shallow (*Literatura y psiquiatría* [Barcelona: Barna, 1950], 145–9).

4. Tristán parrots certain Buddhist truths ("birth is suffering," etc., 337). However, his behavior (selfish, violent, slanderous) is totally contrary to the teaching of Buddha. In his later essay "Intermedio del editor," Palacio Valdés confuses Buddhists ("who lie in front of the chariot of the gods in order to be crushed") (*Papeles del doctor Angélico*, 137) with the worshipers of Juggernaut. The Augustinian friar Father Graciano Martínez identifies Tristán in his pessimism and neurasthenia with Nietzsche; see his *De paso por las Bellas Letras* (Madrid: Ediciones Hispano-americanas, n. d.), 1: 270–1.

5. Certain of the essays may be of earlier composition. Thus, in "El gobierno de las mujeres," María Cristina is treated as the reigning regent.

6. "When we have made ourselves happy, we shall be able to make others happy. And even then our action on others must not be violent and overeager" ("Experiencias y efusiones," *Papeles del doctor Angélico* [Madrid: Imprenta de Bernardo Rodríguez, 1911], 323). The emphasis on gentleness recalls the Buddhist "middle way."

7. The others were Vicente Blasco Ibáñez and the poets Ramón Perés y Perés and Juan Ramón Jiménez. See Brian J. Dendle, "Les écrivains espagnols et King Albert's Book, 1914," *Les Lettres Romanes* 42 (1988): 211–7.

8. Among other writers and intellectuals to sign were: Gabriel Alomar, Manuel Azaña, "Azorín," Américo Castro, Manuel B. Cossío, Antonio Machado, Ramiro de Maeztu, Gregorio Marañón, Gregorio Martínez Sierra, Ramón Menéndez Pidal, José Ortega Gasset, Benito Pérez Galdós, Ramón Pérez de Ayala, Miguel de Unamuno, and Ramón del Valle-Inclán.

9. A French translation of this work—*La guerre injuste, lettres d'un Espagnol* (Paris: Bloud et Gay, 1917); translation by Albert Glorget—was published in the war propaganda series "Pages Actuelles (1914–1917)." For a more detailed description of *La guerra injusta* and the attitude of Spanish intellectuals during the First World War, see Brian J. Dendle, "Spanish Intellectuals and World War I," in Alain Toumayan, ed., *Literary Generations: A Festschrift in Honor of Edward D. Sullivan by His Friends, Colleagues, and Former Students* (Lexington: French Forum, 1992), 66–8.

10. See Pitollet, "Recuerdos," 80.

11. Enrique Díez-Canedo, "La hija de Natalia," *Revista de Occidente* 3 (1924): 381.

12. The irony is already present in the part 2. The *marquesita* Cristobalina, who "converts" Rogelia, admires the devotion of her father, the Duke of Monterraigoso, who, his daughter believes, spends his nights away from home to fulfill political duties and to hear early mass; she also believes that the duke flagellates himself as a penitent "in memory of the passion of Our Lord" (179). In reality, the duke is whipped by his mistresses and is one more example of the sexual perverts portrayed by Palacio Valdés.

13. For Galdós's irony in *Nazarín*, see Brian J. Dendle, "Point of View in *Nazarín*: An Appendix to Goldman," *Anales Galdosianos* 9 (1974): 113–21.

Cf. also the ironic description of the false mysticism of María, who tries to imitate Saint Elizabeth of Hungary in *Marta y María*.

14. Félix García, "Palacio Valdés (Con motivo de *Los cármenes de Granada*)," *Al través de almas y libros* (Barcelona: Editorial Araluce, 1935), 86–7.

15. Alberto Guillén, *La linterna de Diógenes* (Madrid: Editorial América, n. d.), 35–6.

16. Donald L. Shaw, *A Literary History of Spain. The Nineteenth Century* (London: Ernest Benn, 1972), 130. Arturo Berenguer Carisomo, "Armando Palacio Valdés (Esbozo de su novelística)," *Palacio Valdés . Homenaje en el primer centenario de su nacimiento* (Buenos Aires: Ateneo Jovellanos, 1953), 54.

17. See Edwin H. Cady, "Armando Palacio Valdés Writes to William Dean Howells," *Symposium* 2 (1948): 28.

18. Palacio Valdés notes in the first edition of *Tiempos felices* that "Cómo se casó Taulet" had been published some years previously by *Prensa Gráfica* with the title "El Salvador."

19. For a full discussion of Palacio Valdés's contribution to *ABC*, see Brian J. Dendle, "Los artículos de Armando Palacio Valdés en *ABC*, 1932–1936," *Boletín del Instituto de Estudios Asturianos* 44 (1990): 233–79.

CHAPTER 6. CONCLUSIONS

1. The cautious literary scholar will, of course, avoid attributing too great a precision to the term *realism*. For a general introduction to Spanish realism, see Jeremy T. Medina, *Spanish Realism: The Theory and Practice of a Concept in the Nineteenth Century* (Madrid: José Porrúa Turanzas, 1979), 7–97. Medina finds in Palacio Valdés a mixture of "realistic" and "idealistic" tendencies (221–36). Edwin H. Cady, in a most useful discussion, indicates the many elements in Palacio Valdés's work that do not fit conventional definitions of "realism." Rather, Cady indicates, Palacio Valdés revealed in his literary doctrines "devotion to German transcendental esthetics, and the worship of the classics" ("Armando Palacio Valdés Writes to William Dean Howells," 32–3).

2. The physical deformities of characters in *La hermana San Sulpicio*, on the other hand, are portrayed for comic effect.

3. A further deformation is the aping of foreign ways, by Belinchón in *El cuarto poder* and by the aristocracy in *La espuma*.

4. In his discussion of Palacio Valdés, José María Roca Franquesa has pertinently indicated the prevalence of "neo-romantic" values in Spain in the period 1870 to 1885 (*Clases sociales y tipos representativos en la novelística de Armando Palacio Valdés* [Oviedo: Instituto de Estudios Asturianos, 1980], 31).

5. Palacio Valdés's debt to the popular novel has been properly recognized by the French critics H. Peseux-Richard, Camille Pitollet, and Daniel Henri Pageaux. A similar debt by Galdós to the popular novel has been indicated by Jacques Beyrie, *Galdós et son mythe* (Paris: Librairie Honoré Champion, 1980), 2: 123–49; and by myself, "El audaz: historia de un radical de antaño," in A. H. Clarke and E. J. Rodgers, eds., *Galdós' House of Fiction* (Llangranog: Dolphin, 1991), 41–53.

6. Examples are the fatuous Octavio of *El señorito Octavio*, the weak-willed Heredia of *El idilio de un enfermo* and Gonzalo of *El cuarto poder*, and Palacio

Valdés's well-meaning but somewhat ineffective alter egos Miguel Rivera and Angel Jiménez.

7. Exceptions worthy of mention are the emotionally healthy Marta (*Marta y María*) and Rosa (*El idilio de un enfermo*) and the loving and high-spirited Julia (*Riverita, Maximina*) and Natalia (*Papeles del doctor Angélico*).

Bibliography

ABBREVIATIONS

APV   Armando Palacio Valdés

BBMP   *Boletín de la Biblioteca Menéndez Pelayo*

BIEA   *Boletín del Real Instituto de Estudios Asturianos* (Formerly *Boletín del Instituto de Estudios Asturianos*)

EAPV   *Estudios sobre Armando Palacio Valdés*, edited by Brian J. Dendle and Stephen Miller. (Ottawa Hispanic Studies 14) Ottawa: Dovehouse Editions, Canada, 1993.

Harpers *Harper's New Monthly Magazine*

WORKS BY ARMANDO PALACIO VALDÉS

Books

A cara o cruz. Madrid: Editorial Pueyo, 1929.

Aguas fuertes. Madrid: Ricardo Fe, 1884. This first edition lacks "El crimen de la calle de la Perseguida," "El potro del señor cura," and "Polifemo."

Aguas fuertes. Madrid: Librería de Victoriano Suárez, 1921. Vol. 10 of the *Obras completas.*

Album de un viejo. Madrid: Librería General de Victoriano Suárez, 1940.

La aldea perdida. Madrid: Los Hijos de M. G. Hernández, 1903.

La alegría del capitán Ribot. Madrid: Imprenta de los Hijos de M. G. Hernández, 1899.

Años de juventud del doctor Angélico. Madrid: Librería General de Victoriano Suárez, 1918.

Los cármenes de Granada. Madrid: Librería General de Victoriano Suárez, 1927.

Crotalus horridus. Madrid: Casa Editorial de Medina, n d. (1879?). In same volume: Félix de Aramburu y Zuloaga, *Lola Lee;* Eduardo Hano Busillo, *Troncos y ramas.*

El cuarto poder. 2 vols. Madrid: Tipografía de Manuel Ginés Hernández, 1888.

Cuentos escogidos. Madrid: Rivadeneyra, n. d. Contains *Crotalus horridus,* "¡Solo!," "Seducción," and selections from *Aguas fuertes, Papeles del doctor Angélico, La novela de un novelista.*

La espuma. 2 vols. Barcelona: Imprenta de Heinrich y Compañía, 1890.

La fe. Madrid: Manuel Ginés Hernández, 1892.

———. Madrid: Librería General de Victoriano Suárez, 1909. Preceded by a "Declaración del autor," v–ix.

El gobierno de las mujeres. Madrid: Librería de Victoriano Suárez, 1931. Contains as appendix "Una opinión" (the essay "El gobierno de las mujeres" from *Papeles del doctor Angélico*).

La guerra injusta. Barcelona/Paris: Bloud & Gay, 1917.

La hermana San Sulpicio. 2 vols. Madrid: Tipografía de Manuel G. Hernández, 1889. Preceded by "Prólogo" by APV.

La hija de Natalia. Madrid: Librería de Victoriano Suárez, 1924.

El idilio de un enfermo. Madrid: Ricardo Fe, 1884.

———. Madrid: Librería de Victoriano Suárez, 1894. Vol. 1 of the *Obras completas*; edition preceded by a thirteen-page "Dedicatoria."

José. Madrid: Imprenta de Manuel G. Hernández, 1885.

(With Leopoldo Alas) *La literatura en 1881.* Madrid: Alfredo de Carlos Hierro, 1882.

El maestrante. Madrid: Los Hijos de M. G. Hernández, 1893.

Los majos de Cádiz. Madrid: Tipografía de los Hijos de M. G. Hernández, 1896. Edition preceded by a "Prólogo" by APV, "Observaciones acerca de la composición de la novela."

Marta y María. Barcelona: Biblioteca "Arte y Letras," 1883.

———. Madrid: Librería de Victoriano Suárez, 1895. Revised edition; Vol. 2 of the *Obras completas*.

———. Madrid: Librería de Victoriano Suárez, 1906. Edition preceded by an "Aclaración" by APV.

Maximina. 2 vols. Madrid: Tipografía de Manuel G. Hernández, 1887.

La novela de un novelista. Madrid: Librería de Victoriano Suárez, 1921.

Los novelistas españoles. Semblanzas literarias. Madrid: Casa Editorial de Medina, n. d. Preceded by "Al Lector," by APV, v–xi.

Nuevo viaje al Parnaso. Poetas contemporáneos. Madrid: Imprenta Plaza de la Armería, 1879.

Obras completas. Prologue by Luis Astrana Marín. 2 vols. Madrid: M. Aguilar, 1945.

Los oradores del Ateneo. Madrid: Casa Editorial de Medina, n. d.

El origen del pensamiento. Madrid: Los Hijos de M. G. Hernández, 1893.

Páginas escogidas. Madrid: Casa Editorial Calleja, 1917. Preceded by "Confidencia Preliminar" by APV.

Papeles del doctor Angélico. Madrid: Imprenta de Bernardo Rodríguez, 1911.

Riverita. 2 vols. Madrid: Tipografía de Manuel G. Hernández, 1886. Vol. 2 contains advertising for the Librería de Victoriano Suárez.

Santa Rogelia. Madrid: Imprenta Helénica, 1926.

Semblanzas literarias. Madrid: Librería General de Victoriano Suárez, 1908. Vol. 11 of the *Obras completas*. Abridged version, with new preface, of *Los oradores del Ateneo, Los novelistas españoles,* and *Nuevo viaje al Parnaso*.

El señorito Octavio. Madrid: Fernando Fe, 1881.

———. Madrid: Librería de Victoriano Suárez, 1896. Revised edition; Vol. 3 of the *Obras completas*.

Sinfonía pastoral. Madrid: Librería de Victoriano Suárez, 1931.

¡Solo! Madrid: Biblioteca Mignon, n. d. Illustrations by R. París; also contains *El pájaro en la nieve.*

Testamento literario. Madrid: Librería de Victoriano Suárez, 1929.

Tiempos felices. Escenas de la época esponsalicia. Madrid: Librería de Victoriano Suárez, 1933.

Tristán o el pesimismo. Madrid: Librería General de Victoriano Suárez, 1906.

Short Stories

"Los amores de Clotilde." *Arte y Letras* 9 (May 1883): 66–7, 70–1. Also published in *Aguas fuertes.*

"Crotalus horridus." *Revista Europea* 12 (1878): 554–61, 586–92.

"El drama de las bambalinas." *Arte y Letras* 15 (Dec. 1883): 115, 118. Also published in *Aguas fuertes.*

"Los puritanos (novela)." *Arte y Letras* 7 (March 1883): 49–51, 54. Also published in *Aguas fuertes.*

"Seducción. (Agua Fuerte)." *España Moderna* No. 6 (June 1889): 5–17.

"La tela de araña." *La Esfera* No. 2 (10 January 1914). Reprinted in *EAPV*, 124–6.

Articles and Speeches

"Acerca de *Las vengadoras*." *La Epoca* 7 April 1884.

"Ateneo de Madrid." *La Libertad*, 10 February 1924. Speech as President of the Ateneo. Reprinted in Pitollet, "Recuerdos," 81–5.

"Carta a la Comisión Organizadora del Homenaje, Oviedo, 1906." Reprinted in Luis Fernández Castañón, "Los homenajes." *BIEA* 7 (1953): 366–71; and in Jesús-Andrés Solís, *Homenajes a Palacio Valdés en Asturias*, 23–9. Candás: Imprenta el Faro, 1976.

"La catedral y la fábrica." *Blanco y negro*, 15 May 1932.

"Correo de Madrid." *Revista de Asturias* No. 13 (15 March 1878): 122–3; No. 15 (25 March 1878): 139–40; No. 17 (15 April 1878): 167–70; No 19 (5 May 1878): 202–3; No. 21 (25 May 1878): 237–8.

"Correspondencia de Madrid." *Ecos del Nalón* 2 (8 January 1878): 57–8.

"Covadonga, tres etapas." *La Esfera* No. 239 (27 July 1918). Reprinted in Brian J. Dendle, "Covadonga, tres etapas." *BIEA* 42 (1988): 831–5.

"Cualidades de la crítica." *Revista de Asturias* 4, No. 17 (15 September 1880): 266–8.

"The Decadence of Modern Literature." In Richard Garnett, Léon Vallée, and Alois Brandl, eds. *The Book of Literature*, 23: xiii–xxxviii. New York: The Grolier Society, 1922.

"Después de la paz." *España*, 5 March 1915. Reprinted in Brian J. Dendle and Frederick de Rosset. "Cinco artículos no recogidos de Armando Palacio Valdés, 1915–1932." *EAPV*, 113–6.

"Discurso leído en el homenaje, Avilés, 1918." Reprinted in Luis Fernández Castañón, "Los homenajes." *BIEA* 7 (1953): 374–6; and in Jesús-Andrés Solís,

Homenajes a Palacio Valdés en Asturias, 38–41. Candás: Imprenta el Faro, 1976.

"Discurso leído en el homenaje, Avilés, 1920." Jesús-Andrés Solís, *Homenajes a Palacio Valdés en Asturias*, 53–7. Candás: Imprenta el Faro, 1976.

"Discurso leído en el homenaje, Oviedo, 1926." Jesús-Andrés Solís, *Homenajes a Palacio Valdés en Asturias*, 72–6. Candás: Imprenta el Faro, 1976.

"Estética del carácter." *España Moderna*. No. 21 (Sept. 1890): 123–45. Novelistic theory.

"Un estudiante de Canarias." *Arte y Letras* 13 (October 1883): 97–98. Reprinted in Brian J. Dendle. "Palacio Valdés' 'Un estudiante de Canarias': A Forgotten Article of 1883." *Anales Galdosianos* 24 (1989): 97–101. On Pérez Galdós.

"Iconoclastas." *El Debate*, 15 October 1932. Reprinted in Brian J. Dendle and Frederick de Rosset. "Cinco artículos no recogidos de Armando Palacio Valdés, 1915–1932." *EAPV*, 121–3.

"El lenguaje académico," *La Ilustración Gallega y Asturiana*, No. 27 (28 September 1881): 320–1.

"La leyenda del rey Alberto." In *King Albert's Book*, edited by Hall Caine, 179. London: Hodder and Stoughton, 1914. Reprinted in Brian J. Dendle, "Les écrivains espagnols et *King Albert's Book*, 1914," *Les Lettres Romanes* 42 (1988): 211–7.

"Niñerías." *España Moderna* No. 9 (September 1889): 57–67. Review of work by Manuel Tolosa Latour.

"La novela en América." *Revista de la Unión Ibero-Americana* 20, 1 March 1906, 26–7.

"Una opinión (Para el Ateneo Obrero de Gijón)." In Luis Antón del Olmet and José de Torres Bernal, *Palacio Valdés*, 285–92. Madrid: Imprenta de Juan Pueyo, 1919.

"Los oradores del Ateneo. Don José Moreno Nieto." *La Política*. 15 June 1875.

"Oradores políticos." *España Moderna* No. 18 (June 1890): 55–61. Review of work by Miguel Moya.

"Pereda." *BBMP* 15 (1933): 5–7.

"Raquel Meller." In *Raquel Meller*, edited by Enrique Gómez Carrillo, 14–5. Madrid: Sociedad Española de Librería, n. d.

"El tema del teatro." *El Imparcial*, 2 June 1879.

"El último bohemio." *Arte y Letras* 8 (April 1883): 57–9. Also published in *Aguas fuertes*.

"Valencia." Reprinted in Luis Fernández Castañón, "Los homenajes," *BIEA* 7 (1953): 379–83.

Articles in the Revista Europea

"Apuntes críticos." *Revista Europea* 8 (1876): 601–3. Opening of the Institución Libre de Enseñanza.

"Apuntes críticos." *Revista Europea* 8 (1876): 633–5. Moreno Nieto's opening address in the Ateneo.

"Apuntes críticos." *Revista Europea* 9 (1877): 115–7. Reviews works by Azcárate, Huelín, Olivier, and Zorrilla.

"Don Antonio F. Grilo." *Revista Europea* 13 (1879): 760–4.

"Don Benito Pérez Galdós." *Revista Europea* 11 (1878): 335–9, 400–5. Reprinted in Noël M. Valis. "Una opinión olvidada de Palacio Valdés sobre Benito Pérez Galdós." *BIEA* 82 (1982): 691–714.

"Don Carlos María Perier." *Revista Europea* 9 (1877): 304–5.

"Don Emilio Castelar." *Revista Europea* 11 (1878): 12–25, 154–8.

"Don Enrique Pérez Escrich." *Revista Europea* 12 (1878): 453–8.

"Don Francisco de P. Canalejas." *Revista Europea* 10 (1877): 725–7.

"Don Francisco Javier Galvete." *Revista Europea* 10 (1877): 796–8.

"Don Francisco Navarro Villoslada." *Revista Europea* 11 (1878): 712–4.

"Don Gabriel Rodríguez." *Revista Europea* 11 (1878): 20–2.

"Don Gumersindo de Azcárate." *Revista Europea* 9 (1877): 765–7.

"Don José Carvajal." *Revista Europea* 9 (1877): 631–2.

"Don José de Castro y Serrano." *Revista Europea* 12 (1878): 629–33.

"Don José Echegaray." *Revista Europea* 13 (1879): 20–5.

"Don José Moreno Nieto." *Revista Europea* 9 (1877): 601–2.

"Don José Selgas." *Revista Europea* 12 (1878): 657–62.

"Don José Zorrilla." *Revista Europea* 13 (1879): 206–11.

"Don Juan Valera." *Revista Europea* 9 (1877): 470–2. Series "Los oradores del Ateneo."

"Don Juan Valera." *Revista Europea* 11 (1878): 519–23, 593–7. Series "Los novelistas españoles."

"Don Laureano Figuerola." *Revista Europea* 9 (1877): 408–10.

"Don Luis Vidart." *Revista Europea* 9 (1877): 702–4.

"Don Manuel de la Revilla." *Revista Europea* 10 (1877): 766–8.

"Don Manuel Fernández y González." *Revista Europea* 11 (1878): 659–63.

"Don Manuel Pedregal." *Revista Europea* 9 (1877): 792–4.

"Don Miguel Sánchez." *Revista Europea* 9 (1877): 248–50.

"Don Pedro Antonio de Alarcón." *Revista Europea* 11 (1878): 465–69.

"Don Ramón de Campoamor." *Revista Europea* 13 (1879): 465–8, 568–72.

"Don Segismundo Moret y Prendergast." *Revista Europea* 9 (1877): 281–3.

"La economía política cristiana." *Revista Europea* 11 (1878): 293–8.

"Fernán Caballero." *Revista Europea* 11 (1878): 241–6.

"La moda. Apuntes económicos." *Revista Europea* 11 (1878): 418–21.

"El problema religioso." *Revista Europea* 4 (1875): 466–71. Reviews work by Francisco de Paula Canalejas.

Articles in El Día

"Los buenos y los sabios" (Campoamor). *El Día*, 27 March 1881.

"El código del honor" (D. José Echegaray). *El Día*, 26 January 1881. Also published in *La literatura en 1881*.

"Discursos académicos." *El Día*, 22 March 1881. Also published in *La literatura en 1881*.

"Esbozos y rasguños" (D. José Pereda). *El Día*, 24 April 1881.

"El espejo" (D. Mariano Pina Domínguez). *El Día*, 12 January 1881. Also published in *La literatura en 1881*.

"El frío del teatro español." *El Día*, 16 March 1881. Also published in *La literatura en 1881*.

"El Gran Galeoto" (D. José Echegaray). *El Día*, 26 March 1881. Also published in *La literatura en 1881*.

"El grano de arena" (D. Antonio García Gutiérrez). *El Día*, 17 December 1880. Also published in *La literatura en 1881*.

"Hard Times." *El Día*, 24 December 1880.

"La muerte en los labios" (D. José Echegaray). *El Día*, 11 December 1880.

"Poesías leídas en el Ateneo científico, literario y artístico de Madrid, por D. Francisco Abarzuza." *El Día*, 16 April 1881. Also published in *La literatura en 1881*.

"Poesías *líricas* de D. Ventura Ruiz Aguilera." *El Día*, 9 January 1881. Also published in *La literatura en 1881*.

"Puntos de vista" (Miguel Moya). *El Día*, 31 December 1880.

"El sainete." *El Día*, 13 March 1881.

"El sainete. Al Sr. D. Ricardo de la Vega." *El Día*, 6 April 1881.

"El teatro francés en España." *El Día*, 30 April 1881.

"Los teatros menudos." *El Día*, 21 January 1881. Also published in *La literatura en 1881*.

Articles in ABC

"Antes y ahora." *ABC*, 11 May 1933. Reprinted in Brian J. Dendle. "Los artículos de Armando Palacio Valdés en *ABC*, 1932–1936." *BIEA* 44 (1990): 255–6.

"Blasco Ibáñez." *ABC*, 29 January 1928. Reprinted in Brian J. Dendle and Frederick de Rosset. "Cinco artículos no recogidos de Armando Palacio Valdés, 1915–1932." *EAPV*, 116–8.

"¿Cómo debería organizarse el futuro régimen?" *ABC*, 9 February 1928. Reprinted in Brian J. Dendle and Frederick de Rosset. "Cinco artículos no recogidos de Armando Palacio Valdés, 1915–1932." *EAPV*, 118–9.

"El cuarto poder." *ABC*, 11 February 1932. Reprinted in Brian J. Dendle. "Los artículos de Armando Palacio Valdés en *ABC*, 1932–1936." *BIEA* 44 (1990): 241–2.

"El despido." *ABC*, 28 May 1932. Reprinted in Brian J. Dendle. "Los artículos de Armando Palacio Valdés en *ABC*, 1932–1936." *BIEA* 44 (1990): 249–51.

"El estatuto de Villagata." 29 June 1932. Reprinted in Brian J. Dendle. "Los artículos de Armando Palacio Valdés en *ABC*, 1932–1936." *BIEA* 44 (1990): 251–3.

"Extremismos." *ABC*, 19 January 1935. Reprinted in Brian J. Dendle. "Los artículos de Armando Palacio Valdés en *ABC*, 1932–1936." *BIEA* 44 (1990): 263–5.

"Grilletes." *ABC*, 14 March 1936. Reprinted in Brian J. Dendle. "Los artículos de Armando Palacio Valdés en *ABC*, 1932–1936." *BIEA* 44 (1990): 277–9.

"Hada maléfica." *ABC*, 20 April 1935. Reprinted in Brian J. Dendle. "Los artículos de Armando Palacio Valdés en *ABC*, 1932–1936." *BIEA* 44 (1990): 267–9.

"La Iluminación." *ABC*, 6 June 1936. Also published in *Album de un viejo*.

"La importancia artística del cinematógrafo." *ABC*, 16 January 1929. Reprinted in Brian J. Dendle and Frederick de Rosset. "Cinco artículos no recogidos de Armando Palacio Valdés, 1915–1932." *EAPV*, 120–1.

"Intelectuales y obreros (I)." *ABC*, 2 April 1932. Reprinted in Brian J. Dendle. "Los artículos de Armando Palacio Valdés en *ABC*, 1932–1936." *BIEA* 44 (1990): 242–4.

"Intelectuales y obreros (II)." *ABC*, 3 April 1932. Reprinted in Brian J. Dendle. "Los artículos de Armando Palacio Valdés en *ABC*, 1932–1936." *BIEA* 44 (1990): 244–5.

"Los libros." *ABC*, 28 June 1936. Also published in *Album de un viejo*.

"El milagro." *ABC*, 28 March 1936. Also published in *Album de un viejo*.

"Morfina." *ABC*, 23 June 1936. Also published in *Album de un viejo*.

"La ola negra." *ABC*, 6 August 1932. Reprinted in Brian J. Dendle. "Los artículos de Armando Palacio Valdés en *ABC*, 1932–1936." *BIEA* 44 (1990): 253–55.

"Opiniones femeninas. La belleza." *ABC*, 18 June 1936. Published also in *Album de un viejo*.

"Opiniones femeninas. El estudio de la historia." *ABC*, 14 December 1935. Reprinted in Brian J. Dendle. "Los artículos de Armando Palacio Valdés en *ABC*, 1932–1936." *BIEA* 44 (1990): 275–77.

"La oración de Pachín." *ABC*, 19 February 1936. Published also in *Album de un viejo*.

"Perspectivas." *ABC*, 6 May 1936. Published also in *Album de un viejo*.

"El problema económico." *ABC*, 19 April 1935. Reprinted in Brian J. Dendle. "Los artículos de Armando Palacio Valdés en *ABC*, 1932–1936." *BIEA* 44 (1990): 265–7.

"Profesión de fe del vicario vascongado." *ABC*, 14 July 1934. Reprinted in Brian J. Dendle. "Los artículos de Armando Palacio Valdés en *ABC*, 1932–1936." *BIEA* 44 (1990): 257–9.

"El romanticismo." *ABC*, 15 June 1935. Reprinted in Brian J. Dendle. "Los artículos de Armando Palacio Valdés en *ABC*, 1932–1936." *BIEA* 44 (1990): 271–3.

"Los salvadores." *ABC*, 11 May 1935. Reprinted in Brian J. Dendle. "Los artículos de Armando Palacio Valdés en *ABC*, 1932–1936." *BIEA* 44 (1990): 269–71.

"El santo comunismo." *ABC*, 28 April 1932. Reprinted in Brian J. Dendle. "Los artículos de Armando Palacio Valdés en *ABC*, 1932–1936." *BIEA* 44 (1990): 246–9.

"Sensualidad." *ABC*, 12 July 1936. Also published in *Album de un viejo*.

"El siglo XVIII." *ABC*, 7 December 1935. Reprinted in Brian J. Dendle. "Los artículos de Armando Palacio Valdés en *ABC*, 1932–1936." *BIEA* 44 (1990): 273–5.

"Tiempos borrascosos." *ABC*, 24 November 1934. Reprinted in Brian J. Dendle. "Los artículos de Armando Palacio Valdés en *ABC*, 1932–1936." *BIEA* 44 (1990): 259–61.

"El valor del socialismo." *ABC*, 13 December 1934. Reprinted in Brian J. Dendle. "Los artículos de Armando Palacio Valdés en *ABC*, 1932–1936." *BIEA* 44 (1990): 261–3.

"La vejez." *ABC*, 24 December 1935. Also published in *Album de un viejo*.

Letters

Adolfo Alas, ed. *Epistolario a Clarín*, 113–62. Madrid: Ediciones Escorial, 1951.

Cady, Edwin H. "Armando Palacio Valdés Writes to William Dean Howells." *Symposium* 2 (1948): 19–37.

Cienfuegos, Casimiro. "Del epistolario de Palacio Valdés." *BIEA* 7 (1953): 340–59.

Cruz Rueda, Angel. Extracts from APV's letters to Cruz Rueda are included in *Palacio Valdés*, 131–40. See section on "Studies of APV."

Dendle, Brian J. "Diez cartas inéditas de Armando Palacio Valdés a Edmund Gosse y a William Heinemann," *BIEA* 47 (1993): 303–13.

Fernández Rodríguez-Avello, Manuel. *Vida y obra literaria de Juan Ochoa Betancourt*, 157–71. Oviedo: Instituto de Estudios Asturianos, 1955. 15 letters by APV, 1893–1899.

Gómez-Ferrer, Guadalupe. "Palacio Valdés en los años noventa: la quiebra del positivismo." See section on "Studies of APV." Contains important letter of 11 November 1899 concerning APV's conversion and marriage.

Howells, Mildred, ed. *Life in Letters of William Dean Howells*, 1: 405–6; 2: 49–50, 302, 311–2. Garden City, N.Y.: Doubleday, Doran, 1928. Howells's letters to APV; English translations of APV's letters to Howells. See also Cady.

Nuez, Sebastián de la, and José Schraibman. *Cartas del archivo de Pérez Galdós*, 103–24, Madrid: Taurus, 1967. 16 letters by APV, 1878–1906.

Palacio Valdés, Armando. "Carta-prólogo" to José Benigno García ("Marcos del Torniello"), *Orbayos de la Quintana*. 1924. Rptd. in Solís, *La Asturias de Palacio Valdés*, 49–50. See section on "Studies of APV."

———. "Una carta de Palacio Valdés." *El Liberal de Murcia*, 30 August 1920. The death of Miguel Moya.

———. *El Eco de Avilés*, 1869. Reprinted in Solís, *La Asturias de Palacio Valdés*, 38. See section on "Studies of APV." In defense of Don José Alonso Buján, translator of Ovid's *Pyramus and Thisbe*.

Pereda, José María de. "Cartas de Pereda a Palacio Valdés." *BBMP* 33 (1957): 121–30.

Torres, David. "Del archivo epistolar de Palacio Valdés." *Revista de Literatura* 43 No. 86 (1981): 263–78; also published in *BBMP* 58 (1982): 263–85. Letters to Yxart.

English translations of Palacio Valdés's works, listed in order of first Spanish publication

Marta y María (1883). Translated by Nathan Haskell. *The Marquis of Peñalta*. New York: Thomas Y. Crowell, 1886.

José (1885). Translated by Minna Caroline Smith. New York: Brentano's, 1901.

[Republished 1931] Also translated by Harriet de Onís. Woodbury, N.Y.: Barron's Educational Books, 1961.

Maximina (1887). Translated by Nathan Haskell Dole. *Maximina.* New York: T. Y. Crowell, 1888.

El cuarto poder (1888). Translated by Rachel Challice. *The Fourth Estate.* 2 vols. London: Grant Richards, 1901. New York: P. V. Collier & Son, 1901; New York: Brentano, 1901 and 1904.

La hermana San Sulpicio (1889). Translated by Nathan Haskell Dole. *Sister Saint-Sulpice.* New York: T. Y. Crowell, 1890.

La espuma (1890). Translated by Clara Bell; introduction by Edmund Gosse, v–xii. *Froth.* London: Heinemann, 1891. American edition: *Scum.* New York: United States Book Co., 1890.

La fe (1892). Translated by Isabel F. Hapgood. *Faith.* New York: Cassell, 1892.

El maestrante (1893). Translated by Rachel Challice; introduction by Edmund Gosse. *The Grandee.* London: Heinemann, 1894; New York: G. G. Peck, 1895.

El origen del pensamiento (1893). Translated by I. F. Hapgood. *The Origin of Thought. The Cosmopolitan Magazine* (New York) 16 (November 1893-April 1894): 436–58, 542–57, 706–26; 17 (May 1894-October 1894): 87–101, 185–202, 335–51, 485–94.

La alegría del capitán Ribot (1899). Translated by Minna Caroline Smith. *The Joys of Captain Ribot.* New York: Brentano's, 1900.

Tristán o el pesimismo (1906). Translated by Jane B. Reid. *Tristan.* Boston: The Four Seas Co., 1925.

"Alone" and Other Stories. Translated by Robert M. Fedorchek. Lewisburg: Bucknell University Press, 1993. Translations of "¡Solo!," "Seducción," and stories from *Aguas fuertes* and *Papeles del doctor Angélico.*

French Translations of Palacio Valdés's works, listed in order of first Spanish publication

Marta y María (1883). Translated by Mme. Devismes de Saint-Maurice. Published in *Le Monde Moderne.* Also translated by Mme. Tissier de Mallerais. *Marthe et Marie.* Paris: Sorlot, 1944.

El idilio de un enfermo (1884). Translated by Albert Savine. Published in *Les Heures du Salon et de l'Atelier.*

Aguas fuertes (1884). Certain of the stories from this collection were published in *L'Indépendance Belge* and *Le Journal de Genève.* "El potro del señor cura" and "Polifemo" were translated by Mme. Camille Du Val Asselin. *Nouvelles: Un colon des Douaires; le Poulain du curé; Poliphème.* Le Puy: R. Marchessou, 1903.

José (1885). Translated by Mlle. Sara Oquendo. Published in the *Revue de la Mode.*

Riverita (1886). Translated by Julien Lugol. Published in the *Revue Internationale.*

El cuarto poder (1888). Translated by B. d'Etroyat. Published in *Le Temps.*

La hermana San Sulpicio (1889). Translated by Mme. Th. Huc (Max Deleyne). *Soeur Saint-Sulpice.* (Préface d'Emile Faguet, ix-xi.) Paris: Paul Ollendorff, 1903. Also translated by Mme. Tissier de Mallerais. *La Soeur Saint-Sulpice.*

(Préface de Louis Bertrand) Paris: Marpon, 1929. Later editions: Paris: F. Sorlot, 1944; Paris: Le Club Français du Livre, 1952. According to Pitollet, "Nécrologie," 205, the Tissier de Mallerais translation was published as the *feuilleton* in *Le Temps*, 27-XI-1928 to 17-I-1929.

a fe (1892). Translation and Preface by Jules Laborde. *La Foi*. Paris: Librairie des "Annales politiques et littéraires," 1910.

l maestrante (1893). Translated by J. Gaure, with a preliminary study by M. Bordes.

l origen del pensamiento (1893). Translated by Dax Delime. Published in the *Revue Britannique*.

os majos de Cádiz (1896). Translated by Albert Glorget. Published in the *Journal des Débats*. Also translated by Mme. Tissier de Mallerais. *Sous le ciel de Cadix*. Paris: Sorlot, 1942.

a alegría del capitán Ribot (1899). Translated by Mme. Camille Du Val Asselin. *La joie du capitaine Ribot*. Paris: Librairie des "Annales politiques et littéraires," 1909.

ristán o el pesimismo (1906). Translated by Mme. Berthe Bridé. *Tristan, roman de moeurs*. Paris: Les Presses Universitaires de France, 1927.

a guerra injusta (1917). Translated as *La guerre injuste*. Paris: Bloud et Gay, 1917.

a novela de un novelista (1921). Translated by Mme. Tissier de Mallerais. *Le roman d'un romancier, scènes d'enfance et d'adolescence*. Paris: Gallimard, 1927. Pittollet ("Nécrologie," p. 206) claims that the novel was published as the *feuilleton* in *L'Action Française* in 1927.

a hija de Natalia (1924). Translated by Mme. Tissier de Mallerais. *Lalita*. Paris: Librairie Plon, 1929.

anta Rogelia (1926). Translated by Mme. Philine Burnet. *Sainte Rogélie (de la Légende dorée)*. Paris: Plon, 1930.

os cármenes de Granada (1927). Translated by Mme. Tissier de Mallerais. *Les jardins de Grenade*. Paris: F. Sorlot, 1944.

American textbook editions of Palacio Valdés's works (to indicate the popularity of these texts, later editions are also noted by year of publication)

cara o cruz. Edited by Glen Barr. New York: Macmillan, 1932, 1951.

a alegría del capitán Ribot. Edited by Frederic W. Morrison and Philip H. Churchman. Boston: D. C. Heath, 1906, 1907, 1909.

a hermana San Sulpicio. Edited by J. G. Gill. New York: Henry Holt, 1912, 1922, 1923, 1927, 1928, 1938, 1949.

——. Edited by John M. Pittaro. Boston/New York: Ginn, 1925.

——. Edited by John M. Hill. Boston/New York: Heath, 1925.

——. Edited by Pierre T. De Roche. New York: Translation Publication Co., 1930.

osé. Edited by F. J. A. Davidson and Alice P. F. Hubbard. Boston: D. C. Heath, 1900, 1903, 1906, 1909.

——. Edited by Guy Everett Suavely and Robert Calvin Ward. Boston and New York: Allyn and Bacon, 1920.

―――. Edited by Juan Cano and Edith Cameron. New York: Doubled Doran, 1932.

―――. Edited by Joseph W. Barlow. New York: Prentice-Hall, 1932. Also, Ne York: F. S. Crofts, 1943, 1947.

Marta y María. Edited by H. M. Martin. New York/Boston: Ginn, 1926.

―――. Edited by Willis Knapp Jones and H. H. Arnold. Boston: D. C. Heat 1929.

―――. Edited by Edith B. Sublette. New York: The Odyssey Press, 196 Abridged text.

La novela de un novelista. Edited by William S. Hendrix. Boston/New Yo Ginn, 1931.

―――. Edited by H. Alpern and J. Martel; introduction by Federico de On Boston: D. C. Heath, 1931. Abridged text.

Los puritanos y otros cuentos. Edited by W. F. Faulkner. New York: W. R. Je kins, 1904.

Riverita. Edited by Joseph E. A. Alexis. Lincoln, Nebr.: Midwest Book Co., 192 1945. Abridged version.

Santa Rogelia. Edited by Howard L. Schug and Francis M. Kercheville. N York: F. S. Crofts, 1941.

Selections from Armando Palacio Valdés. Edited by Glenn Barr and Har James Russell. New York: American Book Co., 1935. From *Aguas fuertes.*

Short Stories from Palacio Valdés. Edited by Albert Shapiro and Frederick Hurley. New York: Henry Holt, 1926, 1928. Abbreviated texts of "Perico Bueno," El crimen de la calle de la Perseguida," "El profesor León," "Po femo," "¡Solo!" "El potro del señor cura," "El pájaro en la nieve," "La abeje

Sinfonía Pastoral. Edited by Joseph W. Barlow. New York: American Book C 1933. Abridged version. Illustrated by Fernando Marco.

Films

José. 1925. Starring Javier de Rivero and Enriqueta Soler.

La hermana San Sulpicio. (Silent version) 1928. Directed by Florián Rey; st ring Imperio Argentina and Ricardo Núñez. (Sound version) 1935; starri Imperio Argentina and Miguel Ligero. (Remake) 1952; starring Carmen S illa and Jorge Mistral.

REVIEWS OF PALACIO VALDÉS'S WORKS

Aicardo, J. M. *De literatura contemporónea (1901–1905),* 240–1. Madrid: Suc ores de Rivadeneyra, 1905. Review of *La aldea perdida.*

―――. "El realismo ideal de Palacio Valdés." *España Moderna* No. 11 (Nove ber 1889): 204–6. Review of *Maximina;* translation of "Valdés's Ideal Re ism," published in *The Critic.*

Alas, Leopoldo. "Aguas fuertes," and "Riverita." *Nueva campaña (1885–188* 187–92, 239–46. Madrid: Fernando Fe, 1887.

―――. "La fe." *Ensayos y revistas 1888–1892,* 371–7. Madrid: Manuel Fern dez y Lasanta, 1892.

———. "*La hermana San Sulpicio.*" *Madrid Cómico*, 11 May 1889. Reprinted in José Martínez Cachero, "'Clarín,' crítico de su amigo Palacio Valdés," *BIEA* 7 (1953): 411.

———. "*Marta y María,*" and "*El idilio de un enfermo.*" In *Sermón perdido,* 121–30, 235–48. Madrid: Fernando Fe, 1885.

———. "*Maximina.*" In *Mezclilla,* 207–13. Madrid: Fernando Fe, 1889.

———. "*El señorito Octavio.*" *El Mundo Moderno,* 19 March 1881, 20 March 1881, 25 March 1881.

Anon. "Faith." *Harpers* 85 (October 1892): 802–3. Brief review of *La Fe.*

———. "*La guerra injusta.*" *España* No. 105 (25 January 1917).

Blas, Ruy. "*El señorito Octavio.*" *El Progreso,* No. 369 (7 May 1882).

Burnet, Philine. "Nos amis d'Espagne." *L'Express du Midi,* 22 April 1924. Review of *La hija de Natalia.*

———. "*La Novela de un Novelista.*" *L'Express du Midi,* 3 April 1922.

Casares, Julio. "*Años de juventud del doctor Angélico.*" In *Crítica efímera,* 2: 69–74. Madrid: Editorial "Saturnino Calleja," n. d. Preceded by brief letter from APV to Casares, 15–6.

Díez-Canedo, Enrique. "*La hija de Natalia.*" *Revista de Occidente* 3 (1924): 378–82.

Gómez de Baquero, E. "*La espuma.*" *La Epoca,* 9 January 1891.

González Blanco, Pedro. "*La aldea perdida.*" *Nuestro Tiempo* 3 (April 1903): 63–72.

González Serrano, U. "*La hermana San Sulpicio*" and "*La espuma.*" In *Estudios críticos,* 99–112, 114–20. Madrid: Escuela Tipografía del Hospicio, 1892.

Howells, William Dean. "*El cuarto poder.*" *Harpers* 77 (October 1888): 802–3.

———. "*Marta y María.*" *Harpers* 72 (April 1886): 811–2.

———. "*Marta y María*" and "Scum." *Criticism and Fiction and Other Essays,* 125–8, 128–9. Westport, Conn.: Greenwood Press, 1977. Reprints of reviews originally published in *Harpers.*

———. "*Maximina.*" *Harpers* 76 (January 1888): 316–20.

———. "The Papers of Dr. Angélico." *Harpers* 123 (November 1911): 958–61; 124 (1912): 471–4.

———. "Riverita and *José.*" *Harpers* 73 (1886): 964.

———. "The Sister of San Sulpizio." *Harpers* 79 (November 1889): 963–7.

López Prudencio, J. "*Tiempos felices.*" *ABC,* 19 March 1933.

M. C. "*Album de un viejo.*" *Revista de Filología Española* 25 (1941): 124–5.

Maeztu, Ramiro de. "Palacio Valdés: la *Sinfonía pastoral* y el *Testamento literario.*" *La Prensa* (Buenos Aires), 30 August 1931. Reprinted in Maeztu, *Las letras y la vida en la España de entreguerras,* 190–9. Madrid: Editora Nacional, 1958.

Mathiex, Paul. "Souvenirs d'Enfance." *L'Express du Midi,* 6 February 1924. Review of French translation of *La novela de un novelista.*

Pardo Bazán, Emilia. "*La fe,* novela de Armando Palacio." *Nuevo Teatro Crítico* No. 13 (January 1892). Reprinted in Pardo Bazán, *Obras completas* (Madrid: Aguilar, 1973), 3: 1034–7.

———. "Juicios cortos: *La espuma.* Un crítico neoclásico. Hispanofilia." *Nuevo Teatro Crítico* No. 2 (February 1891): 68–6.

———. "El maestrante." Nuevo Teatro Crítico No. 26 (February 1893). Reprinted in Emilia Pardo Bazán, Obras completas, 3: 1138–41. Madrid: Aguilar, 1973.

Peres, R. D. "Tristán o el pesimismo." Cultura Española No. 2 (May 1906): 424–8.

Santa María, Francisco. "El origen del pensamiento." España Moderna No. 69 (September 1894): 126–7.

Sevilla, Alberto. "Tristán o el pesimismo." El Liberal de Murcia, 23 February 1906.

Tuero, Tomás. "El señorito Octavio." La Iberia, 28 March 1881.

Valdivia, Aniceto. "El señorito Octavio." Madrid Cómico, 27 March 1881, 3 April 1881, 24 April 1881.

Villegas, Francisco F. "La Fe." España Moderna No. 36 (December 1891): 175–8.

———. "El maestrante." España Moderna No. 52 (April 1893): 206–7.

Yxart, J. "La hermana San Sulpicio." España Moderna No. 6 (June 1889): 161–71. Discussion of APV's Prologue.

Zeda. "La alegría del capitán Ribot." La Epoca, 4 March 1899.

———. "La Fe." La Epoca, 14 December 1891.

STUDIES OF ARMANDO PALACIO VALDÉS

Abad, Carlos María. "Novelistas católicos. II. Armando Palacio Valdés." Razón y Fe 68 (1924): 45–63.

Aicardo, J. M. "El homenaje a Palacio Valdés." La Esfera No. 346, 21 August 1920.

———. "La novela y las candilejas." ABC (Sevilla), 6 February 1938. Palacio Valdés and the theater.

Albornoz, Alvaro de. "Discurso." (Homenaje a Palacio Valdés, Oviedo, 1906). Reprinted in Luis Fernández Castañón, "Los homenajes," BIEA 7 (1953): 386–8.

Alcalá Galiano, Alvaro. "El paisaje en los libros." In his Conferencias y ensayos, 254–5. Madrid: Imprenta Helénica, 1919.

Alonso Cabeza, María Dolores. Introduction to APV. La aldea perdida, 1–36. Barcelona: PPU, 1989.

Alpern, Hymen. "Don Armando, the Patriarch." Modern Language Journal 16 (1931): 22–5.

Altamira y Crevea, Rafael. "Palacio Valdés." In his Arte y realidad, 107–14. Barcelona: Editorial Cervantes, 1921.

Altolaguirre, Manuel. "Don Armando Palacio Valdés." Hora de España 14 (February 1938): 90.

Alvarez-Gendín, Sabino. "Palacio Valdés y Asturias." BIEA 7(1953): 479–82.

Alvarez Sánchez, Manuel. "Calle de Armando Palacio Valdés," "Teatro Palacio Valdés," and "Publicaciones periodísticas que hubo en Avilés." Avilés, 308–9, 380–4, 393–8. Madrid: Imprenta de G. Hernández y Galo Sáez, 1927. Work preceded by brief congratulatory letter by APV.

Antón del Olmet, Luis, and José de Torres Bernal. Palacio Valdés. Madrid: Imprenta de Juan Pueyo, 1919.

Armas Ayala, Alfonso. "Armando Palacio Valdés." In his *Galdós: Lectura de una vida*, 242–51. Santa Cruz de Tenerife: Servicio de Publicaciones de la Caja General de Ahorros de Canarias, 1989.

Astrana Marín, Luis. "Prólogo" to APV. *Obras completas*. 1: 11–23. Madrid: M. Aguilar, 1945.

Astur Fernández, Nestor. "Evocación de don Armando." In *Palacio Valdés. Homenaje en el primer centenario de su nacimiento*, 7–15. Buenos Aires: Ateneo Jovellanos, 1953.

Balseiro, José A. "Armando Palacio Valdés." In his *Novelistas españoles modernos*, 388–449. New York: Las Américas, 1963.

Baquero Goyanes, Mariano. "Estudio crítico" to APV. *Tristán o el pesimismo*, 11–77. Madrid: Narcea, 1971.

Barbieri, Marie E. "La visión de Armando Palacio Valdés: Unas notas sobre sus escritos teóricos." *Romance Quarterly* 39 (1992): 81–6.

Barcia Trelles, Augusto. "Palacio Valdés en el centenario de su nacimiento." In *Palacio Valdés. Homenaje en el primer centenario de su nacimiento*, 17–21. Buenos Aires: Ateneo Jovellanos, 1953.

Barja, César. "Armando Palacio Valdés." In his *Libros y autores modernos*, 376–90. Los Angeles, Campbell's Book Store, 1933.

Baroja, Pío. *Desde la última vuelta del camino. Obras completas* 7: 762–3, 784, 806. Madrid: Biblioteca Nueva, 1949.

Bauer, Beth Wietelmann. "Innovación y apertura: La novela realista del siglo XIX ante el problema del desenlace." *Hispanic Review* 59 (1991): 187–203.

———. "*Marta y María*: Misticismo y romanticismo en Palacio Valdés." *EAPV*, 24–35.

Baxter, Sylvester. "A Great Modern Spaniard." *Atlantic Monthly* 85(1900): 546–9.

Beardsley, Wilfred A. "Certain Considerations Inviting Reappraisal of *La fe*, by Armando Palacio Valdés." *Hispania* 17(1934): 127–38.

———. "Priesthood and Religion in the Novels of Armando Palacio Valdés." In *Todd Memorial Volumes Philological Studies*, edited by John D. Fitz-Gerald and Pauline Taylor. 1: 59–69. New York: Columbia University Press, 1930.

Bell, Aubrey F. G. *Contemporary Spanish Literature*, 69–75. New York: Knopf, 1933.

Berenguer Carisono, Arturo. "Armando Palacio Valdés (Esbozo de su novelística)." In *Palacio Valdés. Homenaje en el primer centenario de su nacimiento*, 45–73. Buenos Aires: Ateneo Jovellanos, 1953.

Bishop, William Henry, "A Day's Life in Literary Madrid,"*Scribner's Magazine* 7 (January-June 1890): 186–201. Reprinted in William Henry Bishop, *A House-Hunter in Europe*, 144–5, 162, 66. New York: Harper & Brother, 1893.

Blanco Aguinaga, Carlos, Julio Rodríguez Puértolas, and Iris M. Zavala. *Historia social de la literatura española*. 2: 151–2. Madrid: Castalia, 1978.

Blanco García, Padre Francisco. *La literatura española en el siglo XIX*. 2: 532–6, 604–5. Madrid: Sáenz de Jubera, 1910.

Bly, Peter A. "*La fe*: Palacio Valdés Looks Back to Alas and Forward to Unamuno." *Romance Quarterly* 35 (1988): 339–46.

———. "*La fe* y Galdós." *EAPV*, 62–73.

Bonafoux, Luis. *Yo y el plagiario Clarín*, 66. Madrid: [no publisher given], 1888.

Bordes, L. "Armando Palacio Valdés." *Bulletin Hispanique* 1(1899): 45–76.

Botrel, Jean-François. "Paysages et industrialisation: Les visions d'Armando Palacio Valdés dans *La aldea perdida*." In *L'Homme et l'espace dans la littérature, les arts et l'histoire en Espagne et en Amérique Latine au XIXe. siècle*, edited by Claude Dumas, 157–69. Lille: Université de Lille III, 1985.

Brenan, Gerald. *The Literature of the Spanish People*, 410–1. Cambridge: Cambridge University Press, 1953.

Bueno, Manuel. "El modernismo español." *El Liberal de Murcia*, 30 April 1906. Includes discussion of APV.

C. C. [C. Cienfuegos] "De cómo se escribe una novela." *BIEA* 7(1953): 459–65.

Cabal, Constantino. "Esta vez era un hombre de Laviana. . . ." *BIEA* 7 (1953): 162–278.

Cabezas, Juan Antonio. "El paisaje asturiano en Palacio Valdés."*BIEA* 7 (1953): 413–21.

Campos, Jorge. Introduction to APV. *José*, 11–53. Madrid: Cátedra,1980.

Capellán Gonzalo, Angel. "William Dean Howells and Armando Palacio Valdés: A Literary Friendship." *Revista de Estudios Hispánicos* 10 (1976): 451–71.

Caravaglios, Beatrice Palumbo. *Armando Palacio Valdés*. Aquila: Officine Tipografiche Aquilane, 1938.

Carretero, José María ["El Caballero Audaz"]. "Palacio Valdés." In his *Lo que sé por mí*, 145–54. Madrid: Sanz Calleja, 1915. Article accompanied by a letter from APV. First published in *La Esfera*, No. 2 (10 January 1914); the *La Esfera* version is followed by APV's tale "La tela de araña."

Castilla, Juan de. "Palacio Valdés en la intimidad." *ABC* (Sevilla), 10 February 1938.

Castro, Cristóbal de. "La evolución de la novela y los novelistas españoles." *La Esfera* No. 647 (2 May 1926).

———. "Palacio Valdés y los obreros." *La Esfera* No. 288 (5 June 1919).

Caudet, Francisco. "*La aldea perdida* (1903), novela de tesis."*EAPV*, 85–97.

———. "Armando Palacio Valdés: alcance ideológico de *La aldea perdida*." *Diálogos Hispánicos de Amsterdam* 4 (1984): 109–23.

Cejador y Frauca, Julio. "Armando Palacio Valdés." In his *Historia de la lengua y literatura castellana*. 9: 56–9. Madrid: "Revista de Archivos, Bibliotecas y Museos," 1918.

Childers, J. Wesley. "Sources of Palacio Valdés' 'Las Burbujas.'"*Hispania* 41 (1958): 181–5.

Cimorra, Clemente. "Don Fernando de Meira, enterizo y quijotesco." In *Palacio Valdés. Homenaje en el primer centenario de su nacimiento*, 41–4. Buenos Aires: Ateneo Jovellanos, 1953.

Cruz Rueda, Angel. *Armando Palacio Valdés*. Paris/Madrid/Lisbon: Agence Mondiale de Librairie, 1925. Rev. 2d ed. Madrid: SAETA, 1949.

———. *Palacio Valdés*. Granada: Editorial y Librería Prieto,1938.

Cuenca, José Manuel, and Soledad Miranda García. "La Andalucía de Palacio Valdés." *BIEA* 46 (1993): 163–77.

Dendle, Brian J. "Armando Palacio Valdés, the *Revista Europea*, and the Krausist Movement." *Letras Peninsulares* 4 (1991): 25–33.

———. "Armando Palacio Valdés y Francia." *Estudios de Investigación Franco-española* 4 (1991): 79–90.

———. "Los artículos de Armando Palacio Valdés en *ABC*, 1932–1936." *BIEA* 44 (1990): 233–79.

———. "'Covadonga, tres etapas': Un artículo no recogido de Armando Palacio Valdés." *BIEA* 42 (1988): 831–5.

———. "The Early Writings of Armando Palacio Valdés." In *Proceedings of the Pennsylvania Foreign Language Conference*, edited by Gregorio C. Martín, 55–61. Pittsburgh: Duquesne University, Department of Modern Languages, 1988.

———. "Les écrivains espagnols et *King Albert's Book*, 1914," *Les Lettres Romanes* 42 (1988): 211–7. Includes text of APV, "La leyenda del rey Alberto."

———. "Erotismo y anticlericalismo en la primera edición de *Marta y María*, de Armando Palacio Valdés." *BBMP* 65 (1989): 305–16.

———. "Palacio Valdés' 'Un estudiante de Canarias': A Forgotten Article of 1883." *Anales Galdosianos* 24 (1989): 97–101. Contains text of APV, "Un estudiante de Canarias."

———. "*Riverita-Maximina*: Palacio Valdés's Flawed *Bildungsroman*?" In *Selected Proceedings of the Pennsylvania Foreign Language Conference*, edited by Gregorio C. Martín, 120–7. Pittsburgh: Duquesne University, Department of Modern Languages, 1993.

———. "Spanish Intellectuals and World War I." In *Literary Generations: A Festschrift in Honor of Edward D.Sullivan by His Friends, Colleagues, and Former Students*, edited by Alain Toumayan, 66–78. Lexington: French Forum, 1992.

———. *The Spanish Novel of Religious Thesis, 1876–1936*. Madrid: Castalia, 1968.

———. "Tres 'novelas morales' de Armando Palacio Valdés: *Los majos de Cádiz, Tristán o el pesimismo, y Santa Rogelia*." *EAPV*, 74–84.

———. "Las variantes textuales de *El señorito Octavio*, de Armando Palacio Valdés." *BIEA* 41 (1987): 463–74.

———, and Frederick de Rosset. "Cinco artículos no recogidos de Armando Palacio Valdés, 1915–1932." *EAPV*, 111–23.

DeWinter, Urbain J. "Pérez de Ayala and the Subversion of the Poetic Novel of Spanish Life." *Hispanic Review* 56 (1988): 209–29. On *La aldea perdida*.

Entrambasaguas, Joaquín de. "Estudio" of *Tristán y el pesimismo*. In *Las mejores novelas contemporáneas. III. (1905–1909)*, 3–79. Barcelona: Editorial Planeta, 1967. Contains bibliography.

F. F. "La casa del escritor será un museo este mismo año." *La Voz de Asturias* (28 January 1988): 21.

Fernández, Félix. "La entrañable unión entre Palacio Valdés y el concejo que le vio nacer." *La Voz de Asturias* (28 January 1988): 20.

Fernández, James D. *Apology to Apostrophe*, 120–7. Durham, N.C.: Duke University Press, 1992. On *La novela de un novelista*.

Fernández Almuzara, E. "Palacio Valdés (1853–1938)." *Razón y Fe* 113 (1938): 422–34.

Fernández Alvarez, Jesús. "Un probable eco de Henry Fielding en *La fe de*

Armando Palacio Valdés." *Filología Moderna* Nos. 33–34 (October 1969): 101–8.

Fernández Castañón, Luis. "Los homenajes." *BIEA* 7 (1953): 364–88.

Fernández González, Angel R. "A. Palacio Valdés y 'Clarín' opinan sobre la literatura en 1881." In *Clarín y "La Regenta" en su tiempo*, 1037–51. Oviedo: Universidad de Oviedo, 1987.

Ferreras, J. Ignacio. "La prosa en el siglo XIX." In J. M. Díez Borque, coordinator. *Historia de la literatura española*. Vol. 3 ("Siglos XIX y XX"), 120–2. Madrid: Guadiana, 1974.

Fitzmaurice-Kelly, James. *A New History of Spanish Literature*, 474–5. Oxford: Oxford University Press, 1926.

Fontanillas, M. "El Avilés de Palacio Valdés." *BIEA* 7 (1953): 301–10.

García, Padre Félix. "Palacio Valdés (Con motivo de *Los cármenes de Granada*)." In his *Al través de almas y libros*, 75–94. Barcelona: Editorial Araluce, 1935.

García Blanco, Manuel. "El novelista asturiano Palacio Valdés y Unamuno." *Archivum* 8 (1958): 5–13.

Giles, Mary E. "Descriptive Conventions in Pereda, Pardo Bazán, and Palacio Valdés." *Hispania* 50 (1967): 285–91.

Glascock, C. C. "Aesthetic Elements in the Art of Fiction as Advocated by Juan Valera, Pardo Bazán, and Palacio Valdés." *Hispania* 10 (1927): 409–18.

———. "Two Modern Spanish Novelists: Emilia Pardo Bazán and Armando Palacio Valdés." *University of Texas Bulletin* No. 2625 (1 July 1926): 5–87.

Gómez Carrillo, Enrique. *Treinta años de mi vida*. Vol. 3 (*La miseria de Madrid*), 173–4. Madrid: Sociedad Española de Librería, 1921.

Gómez de Baquero, Eduardo. *El renacimiento de la novela española en el siglo XIX*, 81–7. Madrid: Editorial Mundo Latino, 1924.

Gómez-Ferrer Morant, Guadalupe. "Apoliticismo y fisiocracia entre las clases medias españolas de comienzos del siglo XIX."*Cuadernos de historia moderna y contemporánea* 1 (1980): 187–209.

———. "Armando Palacio Valdés en la transición del XIX al XX." *Revista de la Universidad Complutense* 28 No. 116 (1979): 231–60.

———. "La clase dirigente madrileña en dos novelas de 1890." In *Madrid en la sociedad del siglo XIX*, 1: 535–56. Madrid: Revista ALFOZ/Facultad de Geografía e Historia Universidad Complutense/Comunidad de Madrid Consejería de Cultura, 1986. On Coloma's *Pequeñeces* and APV, *La espuma*.

———. "La imagen de la mujer en la novela de la Restauración: Ocio social y trabajo doméstico I." In *Mujer y sociedad en España 1700–1975*, 2nd ed., edited by Rosa María Capel Martínez, 147–73. Madrid: Ministerio de Cultura, Instituto de la Mujer, 1986.

———. "Introducción" to APV, *La espuma*. Madrid: Castalia, 1990.

———. "Literatura y sociedad: reflejos y actitudes sociales en el mundo de la Restauración." In *Homenaje a José Antonio Maravall*. 2: 199–213. Madrid: Centro de Investigaciones Sociológicas, 1985.

———. "Palacio Valdés en los años noventa: la quiebra del positivismo." In *Clarín y "La Regenta" en su tiempo*, 1055–66. Oviedo: Universidad de Oviedo, 1987.

————. *Palacio Valdés y el mundo social de la Restauración*. Oviedo: Instituto de Estudios Asturianos, 1983.

González Blanco, Andrés. "Armando Palacio Valdés." In his *Historia de la novela en España desde el romanticismo a nuestros días*, 511–35. Madrid: Sáenz de Jubera, 1909.

————. "Don Armando Palacio Valdes." *Nuestro Tiempo* 24, No.307 (July 1924): 149–65.

González Blanco, Edmundo. "El P. Luis Coloma." *La Esfera* No. 78 (26 June 1915). Discusses *La espuma.*

González Blanco, Pedro. "Armando Palacio Valdés." *La Lectura* 6, No. 1 (1906): 271–9.

González Fernández, José. "Aspectos regionales en Jovellanos, Palacio Valdés y Clarín." *BIEA* 41 (1987): 433–61.

González Serrano, U. "Palacio Valdés." In his *Siluetas*, 53–7. Madrid: R. Rodríguez Serra, 1899.

Guillén, Alberto. "Armando Palacio Valdés." In his *La linterna de Diógenes*, 33–40. Madrid: Editorial América, n. d. Interview.

Hart, Stephen M. "Deshilando el nudo romántico en *La hermana San Sulpicio.*" *EAPV*, 36–46.

Hemingway, Maurice. "Palacio Valdés y la novela aristocrítica."*EAPV*, 47–61.

Hurtado y J. de la Serna, Juan, and Angel González Palencia, *Historia de la literatura española*, 961–5. Madrid: Tipografía de Archivos, 1932.

L. "La paysanne dans les romans de Palacio Valdés." *Bulletin Hispanique* 24 (1922): 131–48.

López Prudencio, J. "La obra de Palacio Valdés." *ABC*, 18 February 1938.

Maeztu, Ramiro de. "Don Armando o la voluntad." *Ahora*, 30 January 1931. Reprinted in Ramiro de Maeztu, *Las letras y la vida en la España de entre-guerras*, 185–9. Madrid: Editora Nacional,1958.

————. "Palacio Valdés." *Acción*, 8 July 1916. Reprinted in *ABC*, 21 June 1936, and in Ramiro de Maeztu, *Las letras y la vida en la España de entreguerras*, 180–4. Madrid: Editora Nacional, 1958.

"Manifiesto de adhesión a las naciones aliadas." *España* 1 (9 July 1915)*.* Manifesto signed by APV.

Mariscal de Gante, Jaime. "La vida y las obras de Don Armando Palacio Valdés contada por el glorioso escritor." *ABC*, 3 April 1927. Interview.

Martínez, Emilio. "La Laviana de Palacio Valdés." *BIEA* 7 (1953): 279–300.

Martínez, Padre Gracián. "Armando Palacio Valdés y *Tristán o el pesimismo.*" In his *De paso por las Bellas Letras*, 1: 252–77. Madrid: Ediciones Hispano-Americanas, n. d.

Martínez Cachero, José María. "'Clarín,' crítico de su amigo Armando Palacio Valdés." *BIEA* 7 (1953): 401–12.

————. "40 Fichas para una bibliografía 'sobre' Armando Palacio Valdés." *BIEA* 19 (1953): 467–78.

Martínez de la Riva, Ramón. "La novela españolista." *Blanco y Negro*, 9 February 1919. Interview.

Martínez Olmedilla, Augusto. "Armando Palacio Valdés." *Nuestro Tiempo* 4 (October 1904): 17–34.

————. "Proemio" to APV. *La hermana San Sulpicio*. Barcelona: Ramón Sopena, n. d.

Martínez Sierra, G. "Palacio Valdés." *La Lectura* 3, No. 1 (1903): 401–3.

Martínez Sierra, María. "Armando Palacio Valdés, novelista para mujeres." In *Palacio Valdés. Homenaje en el primer centenario de su nacimiento*, 29–34. Buenos Aires: Ateneo Jovellanos, 1953.

Medina, Jeremy T. "Armando Palacio Valdés." In his *Spanish Realism: The Theory and Practice of a Concept in the Nineteenth Century*, 221–36. Madrid: José Porrúa Turanzas, 1979.

Mérimée, Ernest, and S. Griswold Morley. *A History of Spanish Literature*, 554–5. New York: Henry Holt, 1930.

Miller, Stephen. "La crítica y teoría socio-literarias de Palacio Valdés en su evolución creadora entre 1878 y 1882." *EAPV*, 11–23.

Montañés, Ceferino. "Martínez Cachero: 'La obra de Palacio Valdés es en muchos casos superficial.'" *La Nueva España*, 31 January 1988.

Morón Arroyo, Ciriaco. "*La aldea perdida* entre el pasado y el presente." *EAPV*, 98–110.

Muñoz, Matilde. "Como vive el patriarca de las letras españolas."*Estampa*, 3 January 1928.

Narbona, Rafael. *Palacio Valdés o la Armonía*. Madrid: Librería General de Victoriano Suárez, 1941.

Northup, George Tyler. *An Introduction to Spanish Literature*, 382–3. Rev. 3d ed. Chicago: University of Chicago Press, 1962.

O'Connor, D. J. "Filiation, the Eucharist and the Grotesque in Palacio Valdés' *La fe* (1892)." *Letras Peninsulares* 1 (1988): 51–69.

————. "Mrs. Humphrey Ward's *Robert Elsmere* (1888) and Palacio Valdés's *La fe* (1892)." *Romance Quarterly* 37 (1990): 331–6.

————. "Parallel Plots and Fates in Palacio Valdés' *El origen del pensamiento* (1894)." *España Contemporánea* 3 (1990): 105–15.

Ortega Munilla, J. "Palacio Valdés." *La Esfera* No. 346 (21 August 1920).

Pagano, José León. "Armando Palacio Valdés." In his *Al través de la España literaria*, 129–40. Barcelona: Casa Editorial Maucci, n. d. [1904]. Interview.

Pageaux, Daniel Henri. "Eléments pour une lecture de *La hermana San Sulpicio* de Armando Palacio Valdés." *Iberoromania* 16 (1982): 95–109.

Paolini, Gilbert. "La Psicopatología en la Literatura Italo-española: D'Annunzio y Palacio Valdés." In *The Two Hesperias. Literary Studies in Honor of Joseph G. Fucilla*, edited by Americo Bugliani, 275–89. Madrid: Porrúa Turanzas, 1978.

————. "Resonancia armónica del mundo mágico creadora del porvenir en *La alegría del Capitán Ribot*." In *Estudios en Homenaje a Enrique Ruiz Fornells*, edited by Juan Fernández Jiménez, José J. Labrador Herraiz, and L. Teresa Valdivieso, 479–85. Erie, Penn.: ALDEEU, 1990.

Pascual Rodríguez, Manuel. *Armando Palacio Valdés. Teoría y práctica novelística*. Madrid: Sociedad General Española de Librería, 1976.

Pedro, Valentín de. "Don Armando Palacio Valdés en mi recuerdo."In *Palacio Valdés. Homenaje en el primer centenario de su nacimiento*, 35–9. Buenos Aires: Ateneo Jovellanos, 1953.

Peñalosa, Joaquín Antonio. Introduction to APV. *La hermana San Sulpicio,* ix–xxvi. Mexico: Editorial Porrúa, 1972.

Penzol, Pedro. "José en Inglaterra." *BIEA* 7 (1953): 422–5.

Perés y Perés, Ramón D. "Armando Palacio Valdés y sus tres últimas novelas." *A dos vientos,* 25–65. Barcelona: Librería"L'Avenç," 1892. Reviews of *El cuarto poder, La hermana San Sulpicio,* and *La espuma,* originally published in *La Vanguardia.*

Pérez de Ayala, Ramón. "La aldea lejana. Con motivo de *La aldea perdida.*" *Obras completas* 1: 1088–95. Madrid: Aguilar, 1964.

Peseux-Richard, H. "Armando Palacio Valdés." *Revue Hispanique* 42(1918): 305–480.

Pitollet, Camille. "Don Armando Palacio Valdés." *Bulletin Hispanique* 40 (1938): 201–8.

———. "Don Armando Palacio Valdés à Capbreton." *L'Indépendant des Basses Pyrénées,* 20 August 1925.

———. "Recuerdos de don Armando Palacio Valdés." *BBMP* 33(1957): 72–120.

Posada, Adolfo. "Los 'peripatéticos' de Vetusta." *La Esfera* No.871 (13 September 1930). APV's friendship with Alas, Tuero, and Pío Rubín.

"Pumarín." "Enjundia astur de Palacio Valdés." In *Palacio Valdés. Homenaje en el primer centenario de su nacimiento,* 23–8. Buenos Aires: Ateneo Jovellanos, 1953.

Ríos Ríos, Max. *Armando Palacio Valdés. Novela, Siglo XIX.* New York University, 1947. Abridgment of doctoral dissertation.

Roca Franquesa, José María. *Clases sociales y tipos representativos en la novelística de Armando Palacio Valdés.* Oviedo: Instituto de Estudios Asturianos, 1980.

———. "La novela de Palacio Valdés: clasificación y análisis." *BIEA* 7 (1953): 426–58.

———. *Palacio Valdés, técnica novelística y credo estético.* Oviedo: Instituto de Estudios Asturianos, 1951.

Romano Colangeli, Maria. *A. Palacio Valdés Romanziere.* Lecce: Libreria Editrice Milella, n. d.

Rubín, Pío G. "Tres páginas de recuerdos." *BIEA* 7 (1953): 360–3. Reprinted from *El Correo de Asturias,* 8 April 1906.

Sáinz de Robles, Federico Carlos. "Armando Palacio Valdés." In his *La novela española en el siglo XX,* 49–52. Madrid: Pegaso,1957.

Sánchez-Roca, Mariano. "Palacio Valdés en Asturias." *La Esfera* No. 664 (25 September 1926).

Sánchez Rojas, José. "Armando Palacio Valdés." *El Hogar* (Buenos Aires), 19, No. 712 (8 June 1923): 9.

Sarrailh, Jean. "Palacio Valdés." In his *Prosateurs espagnols contemporains,* 77–92. Paris: Librairie Delagrave, 1927.

Señas Encinas, Fernando. "El Oviedo de Palacio Valdés." *BIEA* 7(1953): 311–9.

Sevilla, Alberto. "Una vacante." *El Liberal de Murcia,* 21 March 1906. Also published in Alberto Sevilla, *Gazapos literarios,* 131–5. Murcia: Imprenta de Nougués, 1909. Proposes that Palacio Valdés occupy Pereda's seat in the Real Academia Española.

Shaw, Donald L. *A Literary History of Spain. The Nineteenth Century*, 122–30. London: Ernest Benn Ltd., 1972.

Showerman, Grant. "A Spanish Novelist." *The Sewanee Review* 22 (1914): 385–404.

Solís, Jesús-Andrés. *La Asturias de Palacio Valdés*. Avilés: Gráf. Careaga, 1973.

———. *Homenajes a Palacio Valdés en Asturias*. Candás: Imprenta el Faro, 1976.

Torres, David. "Indice de la revista ilustrada, *Arte y Letras* (Barcelona, 1882–1883)." *Hispania* 66 (1983): 345–47.

Trinidad, Francisco. *Palacio Valdés y Laviana*. Laviana: Excmo. Ayuntamiento, 1983.

Ullman, Pierre L. "José as a Male Cinderella." *Romance Quarterly* 35 (1988): 331–7.

Unamuno, Miguel de. "Por Armando Palacio Valdés." *Obras completas* 5: 317–8. Madrid: Afrodisio Aguado, 1958.

Valbuena Prat, Angel. *Historia de la literatura española*, 3: 426–9. Barcelona: Editorial Gustavo Gili, 1968.

Valdés Solís, Martín Andreu. "Contribución a su centenario y reservas al mismo." *BIEA* 7 (1953): 389–400.

Valis, Noël M. "Una opinión olvidada de Palacio Valdés sobre Benito Pérez Galdós." *BIEA* 82 (1982): 691–714.

———. "Palacio Valdés' First Novel." *Romance Notes* 20 (1980): 317–21.

Vallejo Nágera, Antonio. *Literatura y psiquiatría*, 145–9. Barcelona: Barna, 1950. Brief remarks on *Tristán o el pesimismo*.

Varela Jácome, Benito. "En el centenario de Palacio Valdés. Los ambientes de sus novelas." *ABC*, 9 October 1953.

Vézinet, F. "A. Palacio Valdés." In his *Les maîtres du roman espagnol contemporain*, 167–202. Paris: Hachette, 1907.

Villacicencio, Laura N. de. "El estilo de época y la expresión personal en las descripciones de Pereda, Pardo Bazán y Palacio Valdés." *Hispanófila* 60 (1977): 21–44.

Wagenheim, Leah R. "A Chat with Armando Palacio Valdés on Feminism." *Hispania* 12 (1929): 439–6.

Ward, Philip, ed. *Oxford Companion to Spanish Literature*, 438. Oxford: Clarendon Press, 1978.

Williams, Stanley T. *The Spanish Background of American Literature*. 2: 248–53, 260–5, 365. New Haven: Yale University Press, 1955. Relations with Howells.

Wood, Jennifer J. "Armando Palacio Valdés's *La Fe*: Providential Novel." *Hispanic Journal* 7 (1985): 51–7.

Zapico, Marta. "Avilés y Laviana recordaron a Palacio Valdés." *La Nueva España*, 30 January 1988.

OTHER WORKS CONSULTED

Alas, Leopoldo. "*Juan Ruiz*" (Periódico humorístico). Transcribed by Sofía Martín Gamero. Madrid: Espasa-Calpe, 1985.

Aldaraca, Bridget. "El ángel del hogar: The Cult of Domesticity in Nineteenth-Century Spain." In *Theory and Practice of Feminist Literary Criticism*, edited by Gabriela Mora and Karen S. Van Hooft, 62–87. Ypsilanti, Mich.: Bilingual Press, 1982.

Atkinson, Nora. *Eugène Sue et le roman-feuilleton*. Paris: Nizet et Bastard, 1929.

Balzac, Honoré de. *La comédie humaine*. 7 vols. Paris: Gallimard, 1976.

Baquero Goyanes, Mariano. *El cuento español en el siglo XIX*. Madrid: CSIC, 1949.

Baroja, Pío. "Bohemia madrileña." *La Esfera*, No. 53 (2 January 1915).

———. *Obras completas*. 8 vols. Madrid: Biblioteca Nueva, 1946–1951.

———. "Prólogo casi doctrinal sobre la novela." *La nave de los locos*, 63–95. Madrid: Caro Raggio/Cátedra, 1987.

Beuchat, Charles. *Histoire du naturalisme français*. 2 vols. Paris: Editions Corréa, 1949.

Beyrie, Jacques. *Galdós et son mythe*. 3 vols. Paris: Librairie Honoré Champion, 1980.

Bobadilla, Emilio. *Capirotazos*. Madrid: Fernando Fe, 1890.

Bory, Jean-Louis. *Eugène Sue*. Paris: Hachette, 1962.

Botrel, Jean-François. *La Diffusion du livre en Espagne (1868–1914)*. Madrid: Casa de Velázquez, 1988.

A Catalogue of the Gosse Correspondence in the Brotherton Collection. Leeds: University of Leeds, 1950.

Cazottes, Gisèle. "Feuilletonistes à la mode et cosmopolitisme dans les quotidiens madrilènes sous Alphonse XII. Catalogue."*Iris* No. 2 (1989): 1–58.

———. *La Presse périodique madrilène entre 1871 et 1885*. Montpellier: Université Paul Valéry, 1982.

Delgado Gómez, Ignacio. *La "Revista Europea" (1874–1879) y su significado filosófico*. Salamanca: Ediciones de la Universidad, 1983.

Dendle, Brian J. "*El audaz: historia de un radical de antaño*." In *Galdós' House of Fiction*, edited by A. H. Clarke and E. J. Rodgers, 41–53. Llangranog (Wales): Dolphin Book Co., 1991.

———. *Galdós: The Early Historical Novels*. Columbia: University of Missouri Press, 1986.

———. *Galdós: The Mature Thought*. Lexington: University Press of Kentucky, 1980.

———. "Point of View in *Nazarín*; An Appendix to Goldman."*Anales Galdosianos* 9 (1974): 113–21.

———. "The Second Republic, the Spanish Civil War, and the *episodios nacionales*." *Crítica Hispánica* 13 (1991): 141–55.

Etreros, Mercedes. "El naturalismo español en la década de 1881–1891." In Mercedes Etreros, María Isabel Montesinos, and Leonardo Romero, 49–131. *Estudios sobre la novela española del siglo XIX*. Madrid: CSIC, 1977.

Ezama Gil, Angeles. "Adiciones a la bibliografía de Juan Ochoa Betancourt." *BIEA* 42 (1988): 103–13.

Fernández Cifuentes, Luis. *Teoría y mercado de la novela en España: Del 98 a la república*. Madrid: Gredos, 1982.

Fernández Rodríguez Avelló, Manuel. *Tomás Tuero (La leyenda de un periodista)*. Oviedo: Instituto de Estudios Asturianos, 1958.

Flaubert, Gustave. *L'Education sentimentale*. Paris: Garnier, 1964.

Fournier, Alain. *Le Grand Meaulnes*. Paris: Editions G. P.: 1959.

France, Anatole, *Le Crime de Sylvestre Bonnard, membre de l'Institut, Oeuvres*. Vol. 1. Paris: Gallimard, 1984.

———. *Le Livre de mon ami*. Paris: Calmann-Lévy, n. d.

García Barrón, Carlos. *Vida, obra y pensamiento de Manuel de la Revilla*. Madrid: Ediciones José Porrúa Turanzas, 1987.

Gómez Aparicio, Pedro. *Historia del periodismo español*. Madrid: Editora Nacional, 1971.

Gómez-Santos, Mariano. *Leopoldo Alas "Clarín." Ensayo bio-bibliográfico*. Oviedo: Instituto de Estudios Asturianos, 1952.

González Herrán, José Manuel. *La obra de Pereda ante la crítica literaria de su tiempo*. Santander: Delegación de Cultura del Excmo. Ayuntamiento de Santander y Ediciones de Librería Estudio, 1983.

Granjel, Luis S. "La novela corta en España (1907–1936)." *Cuadernos Hispanoamericanos* No. 222 (June 1968): 477–508.

Gullón, Germán, *El narrador en la novela del siglo XIX*. Madrid: Taurus, 1976.

Hemingway, Maurice. *Emilia Pardo Bazán: The Making of a Novelist*. Cambridge: Cambridge University Press, 1983.

Jagoe, Catherine. "Krausism and the Pygmalion Motif in Galdós's *La familia de León Roch*." *Romance Quarterly* 39 (1992): 41–52.

López Jiménez, Luis. *El naturalismo y España. Valera frente a Zola*. Madrid: Alhambra, 1977.

Louÿs, Pierre. *La Femme et le pantin; roman espagnol*. Paris: Société du Mercure de France, 1898.

Mainer, José-Carlos. *La Edad de Plata (1902–1939)*. Madrid: Ediciones Cátedra, 1981.

Maugham, William Somerset. *The Razor's Edge*. Garden City, N.Y.: Doubleday, Doran, 1944.

Mesonero Romanos, Ramón de. "La posada de España en Madrid." *Escenas matritenses*. Madrid: Imprenta y Librería de Gaspar y Roig, 1851.

Miralles, Enrique. *La novela española de la Restauración (1875-1885): Sus formas y enunciados narrativos*. Barcelona: Puvill, 1979.

Montesinos, José F. *Pereda o la novela idilio*. Madrid: Castalia, 1969.

Moufflet, André. "Le style du roman-feuilleton." *Mercure de France* 225 (1 February 1931): 513–54.

Muñoz Molina, Antonio. "Sospecha de una trampa." *El País* (26 May 1991): 11.

Ossorio y Bernard, Manuel. *Ensayo de un catálogo de periodistas españoles del siglo XIX*. Madrid: J. Palacios, 1903 [1904].

Percival, Anthony. *Galdós and his Critics*. Toronto: University of Toronto Press, 1985.

Pérez Bautista, Florencio L. *El tema de la enfermedad en la novela realista española*. Salamanca: Universidad de Salamanca, 1972.

———. *Sociedad y medicina en la novela realista española*, 36–42. Salamanca: Universidad de Salamanca, 1974.

Pérez de Ayala, Ramón. *Artículos y ensayos en los semanarios "España," "Nuevo Mundo," y "La Esfera."* Oviedo: Universidad de Oviedo, 1986.

Pérez Galdós, Benito. *Obras completas.* 6 vols. Madrid: Aguilar, 1942.

Praz, Mario. *The Romantic Agony.* Cleveland: The World Publishing Co., 1967.

Roche, Alphonse V. *Alphonse Daudet.* Boston: Twayne, 1976.

Rubio Cremades, Enrique. *Juan Valera.* Madrid: Taurus, 1990.

Sánchez, Federico. "Cudillero. Por tierras de Asturias." *Hispania* 11 (1928): 500–2.

Schwartz, Kessel. "A Fascist View of Nineteenth-Century Spanish Literature (1936–1939)." *Romance Notes* 7 (1965): 117–22.

Segura Covarsi, E. *Indice de la "Revista de Occidente."* Madrid: CSIC, 1952.

Segut, Marie-Françoise. *Les mémoires manuscrits de Camille Pitollet à la Bibliothèque Municipale de Dijon.* Dijon: Université de Dijon, Faculté de Langues et Civilisation Etrangères, 1979–1980. Mémoire pour la maîtrise d'espagnol.

Seminario de Bibliografía Hispánica. *Veinticuatro diarios, Madrid, 1850–1900.* Vol. 3. Madrid: CSIC, 1972.

Tintoré, María José. *"La Regenta" de Clarín y la crítica de su tiempo.* Barcelona: Editorial Lumen, 1987.

Torrente Ballester, Gonzalo. *Literatura española contemporánea (1898–1936).* Madrid: Afrodisio Aguado, n. d.

Valis, Noël M. *Leopoldo Alas (Clarín). An Annotated Bibliography.* London: Grant and Cutler, 1986.

———. *Jacinto Octavio Picón, novelista.* Barcelona: Editorial Anthropos, 1991.

Yndurain, Francisco. *Galdós entre la novela y el folletín.* Madrid: Taurus, 1970.

Zola, Emile. *L'Assommmoir. Oeuvres complètes.* Vol. 3. Paris: Fasquelle, 1967.

Index